# because we are human

SUNY series in Queer Politics and Cultures
——————————
Cynthia Burack and Jyl J. Josephson, editors

# because
## we are
# human

Contesting US Support for Gender and
Sexuality Human Rights Abroad

cynthia burack

**SUNY**
PRESS

Published by State University of New York Press, Albany

For information, contact State University of New York Press, Albany, NY
www.sunypress.edu

### Library of Congress Cataloging-in-Publication Data

Names: Burack, Cynthia, 1958– author.
Title: Because we are human : contesting US support for gender and sexuality
   human rights abroad / Cynthia Burack.
Description: Albany : State University of New York Press, Albany, [2018] |
   Series: SUNY series in queer politics and cultures | Includes bibliographical
   references and index.
Identifiers: LCCN 2017033591 | ISBN 9781438470139 (hardcover) |
   ISBN 9781438470146 (pbk.) | ISBN 9781438470153 (ebook) Subjects: LCSH:
Gay rights. | United States—Foreign relations.
Classification: LCC HQ76.5 .B87 2018 | DDC 323.3/264—dc23
LC record available at https://lccn.loc.gov/2017033591

10  9  8  7  6  5  4  3  2  1

*For the members of the LGBT Caucus of the*
*American Political Science Association, past and present.*
*Their scholarship on politics has made my work,*
*and this book, possible.*

# Contents

# Acknowledgments

As always, I am thankful to many friends and colleagues. Those who have read a portion of the manuscript and given me their unvarnished views and suggestions are a real blessing. So, to Michelle Abate, Phillip Ayoub, Elizabeth Bloodgood, Amy Bonomi, Felon Evans, Suzanne Franks, Charles Gossett, Dan Lewis, Laree Martin, Bonnie Morris, Linda Nicholson, Franke Wilmer, and Diana Zoelle: thank you! I'm also grateful to Brooke Ackerly, Michael Goodhart, and Karen Zivi for patiently answering my questions. Huge thanks to Jeff Mann for squiring me to Saints and Sinners, giving me the vampire makeover, and conducting the very best Big Queer Convocations.

I'm grateful to SUNY Press and the editor of the Queer Politics and Cultures book series when this book went to press, Beth Bouloukos. Jyl Josephson is an excellent colleague and coeditor, and I'm glad we started down this road together. Because I am closer to the end of my career as an academic than I am to its beginning, I look back with gratitude to my professors, especially Fred Alford, Steve Elkin, Jim Glass, Karol Soltan, and Ron Terchek (Steve: I'm sorry I was so slow to pick up that thing about the importance of institutions).

In the Department of Women's, Gender and Sexuality Studies at Ohio State, I am grateful to Katelyn Hancock for research assistance with this book when it was in its early stages and to Cara Clark for assistance at the end of the process. Thanks are also due to the small but hardy band of grad students who read with me on the subject of "LGBTQ Human Rights" in spring 2015: Jon Branfman, Rorie Dean, Lee Evans, and Courtney Hammond. The Women's, Gender and Sexuality Department provided funds for a 2015 research trip that was crucial to completing this book, and the Department and College supported publication by way of a subvention grant.

A big thank you to Diana Zoelle for sharing her human rights library and inviting me to talk about the project at Bloomsburg University, and to Marie Griffith and Rebecca Wanzo for inviting me to talk at the Danforth Center on Religion and Politics at Washington University in St. Louis (WUSTL). I deeply appreciate the engagement of so many WUSTL faculty and grad students in the political theory seminar where I presented some of this project, particularly Elizabeth Borgwardt and Frank Lovett. I am indebted to the government officials and LGBTQ people who spoke with me in the course of my research and writing. Finally, I was thrilled to have this book project selected as a recipient of Eastern Michigan University's Equality Knowledge Project Research Award for 2016–2018.

Excerpts from this book first appeared as two chapters in edited volumes: Christine (Cricket) Keating and Cynthia Burack, "Sexual Orientation, Gender Identity, and Human Rights," in *Human Rights: Politics and Practice*, 3rd edition, edited by Michael Goodhart (Oxford: Oxford University Press, 2016), 182–97; reprinted by permission of Oxford University Press; and Cynthia Burack, "Top Down, Bottom Up, or Meeting in the Middle? A SOGI Human Rights Case Study," in *LGBTQ Politics: A Critical Reader*, edited by Marla Brettschneider, Susan Burgess, and Cricket Keating (New York: NYU Press, 2017), 477–92.

A personal note: one of the most important lessons my mother taught me when I was growing up was the opposite of what she intended, but I give her credit for the lesson nonetheless. No doubt hoping I would fit in and keep a low profile, my mother often told me: "Cindy, everyone can't be wrong." What a great relief it turned out to be when I realized that many people, at least, *can* be wrong. What wonderful freedom it is not to obey God, Christian conservatives, community standards, political leaders, radical academic colleagues, or the students who correct me when they discover I haven't appropriately internalized the political beliefs and values they associate with my office. I'll keep reminding myself to be deeply grateful for the opportunity I've had to speak, write, and teach my mind.

# Introduction

## *Putting the SOGI in Human Rights*

### From Human Rights to SOGI Human Rights

Since the turn of the millennium, agents and agencies of the US government have been engaging in programs and projects with the stated purpose of protecting the human rights of lesbians, gay men, bisexuals, transgender women and men, men who have sex with men (MSM), women who have sex with women (WSW), and same-sex-loving adults outside the United States.[1] As I have learned more about these programs and projects and discussed them with academic colleagues and other well-educated citizens, I discovered that the existence of such initiatives has not been well known. More fascinating is the variety of responses I received to describing this project since I began working on it in early 2013.

These responses came in two basic types: some interlocutors stated their conviction that no such initiatives existed and that I would look for them in vain. Had these colleagues been correct, this would have been a short project indeed. Others conceded that if such initiatives existed, I might be able to discover their true purpose, which surely would be a covert geopolitical or economic interest of US elites and not a commitment—however fruitful or misguided—to aiding lesbian, gay, bisexual, transgender, or queer (LGBTQ) people outside the United States in their struggles against discrimination and violence. Even though I believe it's possible for policies and projects to serve multiple purposes at once, as well as fail to serve any or all of the purposes for which they were designed, I don't think these colleagues are correct, either. On these disagreements, the reader ultimately can judge for herself.

At the outset, it is important to clarify what this book is and what it is not. My first goal is to construct an empirical account of US government programs, policies, and interventions outside the United States on behalf of the human rights of LGBTQ people, those who engage in sexual relations with same-sex partners, and those whose gender identity or expression puts them at odds with—or in danger from—people, including government authorities, in their own countries. Another way of pointing to this same object of research is to use the term "sexual orientation and gender identity" (SOGI) human rights, a phrase that isolates and directs attention to forms of discrimination and human rights jeopardy aimed at people of minority sexuality and/or gender identity.

The SOGI human rights programs and projects with which I concern myself here have been designed by a variety of government actors and have taken a variety of forms. US government officials have created programs to advance gender and sexual minority human rights abroad; funded individuals and groups engaged in social, legal, or political advocacy on behalf of LGBTQ people abroad; worked closely with local and regional activists and groups to provide support and resources to LGBTQ people; provided resources to protect individuals who are targeted for their minority sexual identity or behavior, or for their minority gender identity or presentation; brokered relationships among human rights actors that include governments, civil society organizations (CSOs), faith communities and faith-based groups, and corporations; and advocated for SOGI human rights in regional, national, and international forums. "Capacity building"—empowering people and organizations in contexts that present SOGI human rights challenges—is consistently cited as a goal by US government officials whose work is focused on human rights and in venues dedicated to SOGI human rights.[2] In his study of a prominent Western transnational LGBTQ rights organization, Ryan R. Thoreson explains that human rights advocates participate in constructing, promoting, and institutionalizing LGBT human rights, and this characterization broadly applies to SOGI efforts of US government officials.[3]

The first goal of this book is to construct an empirical account of these US government interventions on behalf of SOGI human rights. My second goal is to enunciate and examine key arguments against these programs, policies, and interventions that originate on both the conservative right and the progressive academic—especially critical humanist—left. Hence, this book is not a comprehensive account of the activism by and on behalf of LGBTQ actors and groups, CSOs, nation-states, or supranational

bodies and institutions. It is rather an attempt to document US government interventions in recent years concerning LGBTQ people around the
world and then place those interventions into their unavoidable context
of intra-US political and intellectual discourse and critique.

Opposition within the United States to the federal government designing and executing programmatic and rhetorical interventions that link
SOGI rights and human rights proper comes in two ideological packages
crafted by distinct sets of moral entrepreneurs.[4] One of these packages hails
from the political right. In May 2013, *The Economist* published an article
titled "The War on Gays: Strange Bedfellows," that featured the subhead
"American Christian zealots are fighting back against gay rights—abroad."[5]
Indeed, the belief system and activism of these very Christians constitutes
the main form of opposition from the political right to US government
investments in human rights protections for LGBTQ people and the
projection of those protections abroad in US spheres of influence. For
social conservatives who oppose characterizing SOGI rights as civil and
human rights, the inclusion of LGBTQ people in categories populated by
members of racial, ethnic, religious, and other groups of what they regard
as genuine victims of oppression is an insult to the dignity of these groups
and a cynical redefinition of immorality as abjection. US Christian right
leaders have been implicated in anti-LGBTQ funding, lobbying, political
activism, and cultural projects around the world.[6]

By contrast, opposition from a critical humanist academic left is not
motivated by animus toward LGBTQ people and the belief that same-sex
sexuality and gender nonconformity should be stigmatized and punished.
However, many humanist scholars who focus their research on US domestic and/or foreign policy are skeptical about government participation in
human rights abroad, particularly US government intervention in parts
of the world where human rights are most precarious. Left-progressive
skepticism about—if not outright opposition to—discourse such as Secretary of State Hillary Clinton's 2011 equation of gay rights and human
rights underpins an explicit critique of the camouflaging of US national
and neoliberal business interests as disinterested virtues exercised on behalf
of disempowered groups. It also repudiates, often on cultural grounds, the
notion that there can be a set of human rights or values that does not reflect
a Western, universalizing—and therefore culturally imperialistic—ideal.[7]

There is no single intellectual source for the skepticism about human
rights discourse and interventions that originate on the academic left. Often
overlapping with each other, versions of this human rights skepticism

proliferate, especially in humanities disciplines and in the humanist subfields of some traditional social science disciplines. Intellectual sources include anarchism, feminism, some forms of critical theory, and the many kinds of thought that have been heavily influenced by poststructuralist theory, including postcolonial, anti-imperialist, and queer theories and discourses. Although it isn't possible to survey all formulations from these various traditions of academic progressive thought that bear on human rights, it is possible to abstract from them a set of claims that constitute a case not only against US human rights interventions but also against human rights discourse when it is associated with agents and institutions of the US government. Informed by legal, historical, and political accounts of US national hypocrisy, foreign policy cynicism, cultural and economic imperialism, and realpolitik, scholarship on politics in these fields often demonstrates "coherence as a political project."[8]

There is no readily available and agreed-on term to denote academic critics of US government intervention in SOGI human rights. Terms that scholars might use to characterize their work include "critical," "radical," and "progressive," in addition to whatever words are appropriate to denote the particular kinds of theory being practiced. For my purposes, I'm concerned with scholarship that is critical/radical/progressive humanist scholarship on government, domestic policy, and/or foreign policy. I'm neither concerned with nor critical of humanist scholarship on other topics besides government, politics, and policy. For the purposes of this project, I refer to this scholarship as critical humanism and those who produce it as critical humanists.

A final caveat about the category of scholarship I evaluate for its cogency in rejecting a US government role in SOGI human rights: social science scholars in the field of human rights explore, debate, and disagree intellectually about many foundational questions, including what rights are fundamental human rights? Where do human rights come from—or, is there a source of human rights to which everyone can and should subscribe? What kinds of responsibilities do states have to protect the human rights of their own citizens—or the citizens of other nations? Are human rights universal? How should human rights be implemented and enforced at national and multinational levels? What can and should be done about the problem of powerful states exempting themselves from human rights standards and conventions?[9] These key questions in the theory and practice of human rights are common themes in human rights scholarship and may never be completely settled. Although there may be some overlap, these questions aren't the same as the concerns endemic in the critical humanist literature I take up later in this book.

Whatever their orientation toward LGBTQ identities, desire, or behavior, most Americans would not be surprised to learn that the most vehement opposition to the promotion of SOGI civil and human rights comes from the conservative right, especially from the Christian right movement. What probably would surprise many people is the opposition to certain facets of the movement for SOGI human rights that originates on the humanist left from critics of political and philosophical liberalism. This feature of SOGI human rights—contested not only from the US political right but also from an intellectual redoubt on the political left—distinguishes this configuration of identity-based human rights from those that came before it. To be more specific, SOGI human rights advocacy offers a rare example of disapproval of the US government in human rights assistance mounted by those who belong to, identify with, or are well disposed toward the targeted communities.

In this introduction I lay the foundation for a consideration and analysis of SOGI US government policies and acts by briefly surveying certain key discourses and institutions. These include debates over human rights and the Universal Declaration of Human Rights (UDHR); the appearance of international LGBTQ organizations that use human rights principles and discourse; the adoption of nonnormative sexuality and gender identity as human rights issues by mainstream human rights organizations; the groundbreaking promulgation of the Yogyakarta Principles; United Nations engagement with SOGI human rights; and finally, an outline that focuses on the chronology of US government LGBTQ/SOGI human rights discourse and intervention as well as the political-intellectual context for such advocacy in the United States.

## Human Rights: What Are They Good For?

The idea (to say nothing of the reality) of SOGI human rights is a very recent invention. In many cases, anti-SOGI attitudes and public policies in the postcolonial world are a product of the domination exercised by Western colonial powers over colonized peoples. This is particularly true of sodomy laws imposed throughout the British Empire in Africa and Asia and the consequences of those laws.[10] Contemporary situations of vulnerability to discrimination and violence in which LGBTQ people find themselves are a result of complex histories of colonial rule and of the unique cultural and political circumstances of individual nations and regions. Twenty-first-century transnational SOGI human rights discourse takes place in a complicated context of Western culpability, religious worldviews, convictions with regard to cultural authenticity, and elite political interests.

In honor of International Human Rights Day, December 6, 2011, Secretary Hillary Clinton delivered a speech in a European capital pledging US commitment to the human rights of LGBTQ the world over: "Remarks in Recognition of International Human Rights Day." Clinton premised her case for universal human rights that include gender and sexual minorities on the UDHR. Like Clinton, I begin with that key text of our contemporary human rights regime. Submitted to the United Nations in 1948 and ratified by the General Assembly in 1949, the UDHR is a cornerstone of the post–World War II international order. The declaration was drafted by the UN Human Rights Commission, whose chair, Eleanor Roosevelt, was the first US representative to the international body and a longtime human rights advocate.

The UDHR consists of a brief preamble and thirty articles that set forth general principles, specific rights in different domains of life (civic, political, social, cultural, and economic), remedies for violations of human rights, and responsibilities of individuals, groups, and nations to the principles and protection of human rights. Focusing on individuals, the UDHR affirms "the dignity and worth of the human person" and a commitment to "the equal and inalienable rights of all members of the human family." At a more collective level of analysis, the UDHR links "barbarous acts" that display a "disregard and contempt for human rights" to the aspiration of "friendly relations between nations," even though the exact nature of the connection between human rights violations against individuals or members of particular groups and foreign relations remains unstated. In the decades since its ratification, the UDHR has been supplemented with a variety of international conventions, covenants, and treaties, and has provided widely cited definitions of human rights. It has also provided a template for national constitutions and international treaties, as well as being widely considered a foundational document of customary international law.

Because of its status as a venerable, widely circulated international statement of human rights, the UDHR has been analyzed extensively by legal and political theorists who produce critiques and interpretations of political texts. Soon after ratification, the UDHR began to be criticized by legal experts as not having binding significance in international law.[11]

Some political theorists trenchantly criticize "culturally specific concepts" and "family" metaphors of the sort that appear in the declaration and unpack the forms of domination and subordination implicit in conceptions of "the individual" that circulate in Western liberal democracies.[12] Others question the meaning and political implications of concepts such as "dignity." Although many human rights proponents regard respect for and protection of human dignity to be a foundational concept, inquiries into the concept have demonstrated that there are a variety of accounts of human dignity and of the intersection of dignity with human rights. As Franke Wilmer puts it, "globalization . . . highlights philosophical differences in the ways that various cultural traditions conceive of human dignity."[13] Particularly relevant to the case of SOGI human rights is Karen Zivi's concern that dignity can function as a normative standard against which LGBTQ people are measured. Under these circumstances, LGBTQ people may be understood as failing to embody and comport themselves with a dignity that would justify human rights protections. Zivi also argues that even though dignity-based arguments have costs, these costs don't negate the value of dignity as a central concept for SOGI human rights.[14]

Critics have assailed the UDHR and other human rights discourses as embodying an individualistic and culturally Western perspective on people on whose behalf human rights claims are made. Two prominent strands of criticism have included the charge of Western cultural bias and an emphasis on political over economic rights. It is not unusual for critiques of the UDHR to include both grievances: first, "the Western conception of human rights" is "meaningless" and "inapplicable" to people in developing areas owing to deep cultural differences that may be elided by "human rights." Second, human rights regimes too often focus on the legal and political standing of individuals rather than the economic development and satisfaction of basic economic needs that are more important to people in many poor nations.[15] Of these two charges, the first is more likely to be invoked to dispute and delegitimize the application of the UDHR or other statements of universal human rights to LGBTQ people, MSM, and WSW. With regard to the second charge, as many researchers and activists understand, it's possible to apply intersectional approaches to SOGI human rights, including those that integrate links between poverty, insecurity, and discrimination against outgroups.

Today the aspiration for universal human rights continues to be a matter of academic debate, but it's a matter of political debate as well. For Christian conservatives, the UDHR's recognition in Article 16 of "the family" as "the natural and fundamental group unit of society [that] is entitled to protection by society and the State" provides support for opposition to LGBTQ human rights.[16] Even as virtually all nations recognize dimensions of human rights as they are codified in such conventions as the declaration, national representatives and opinion leaders from cultures and regimes that seek to exclude LGBTQ people from human rights protections decry universalizing human rights discourses in ways that recall scholarly arguments against universal human rights. Claims for "Asian values" or "Islamic values" that are different from the values of the West, the United States, Europe, or the global North, are often central to these debates over SOGI human rights and measures intended to protect gender and sexual minorities. Such multicultural objections to universal human rights stimulate a variety of rejoinders, among which are: (1) arguing that human rights values have arisen at different times and places and been championed by people outside the West; (2) acknowledging that principles of individual human rights arose in the West but discounting the significance of this history for human rights concerns in the present; (3) observing that the kinds of values enshrined in various international declarations and treaties can usefully be understood as dividing global sectors, continents, and nation-states against themselves instead of only dividing East from West (or global North from South); and (4) reframing the history of human rights ideas and discourse as a product of modernity rather than a product of Western thought and imposition.

Taking these criticisms in turn, first, it has been common for arguments that cleanly distinguish between Western and non-Western values to go relatively uncontested among scholars for whom such a distinction is a fundamental assumption.[17] However, this doesn't mean that such arguments are uncontested. Amartya Sen has been a proponent of the position that the values underlying respect for human rights can be found in a variety of cultural sources. In his lecture "Human Rights and Asian Values," Sen challenges the perspective that the values associated with human rights are only found in Western traditions. He traces some dimensions of the "diversity of Asian values" and delineates one basis of misunderstandings of the human rights legacies of East and West:

> The question has to be asked whether these constitutive components can be found in Asian writings in the way they can be found in Western thought. The presence of these components must not be confused with the absence of the opposite, that is, with the presence of ideas and doctrines that clearly do not

emphasize freedom and tolerance.

Here, Sen calls attention to the attribution of "nonfreedom" values of order, discipline, loyalty, and obedience to the East as though these are the only Asian values and as though such values also have been unknown in the West. He explains that it's not coincidental that "Asian values" have been championed by authoritarian regimes, which appeal to indigenous values and traditions to evade human rights scrutiny.[18]

Second, some scholars of human rights acknowledge a Western provenance to human rights discourse, especially discourse that advocates for inalienable individual rights. Abdullahi An-Na'im points out the Western provenance of foundational principles of individual human rights such as those found in the UDHR. However, he qualifies this confirmation by arguing that human rights are not inherently reconcilable with any political system or faith tradition, including Islam, Christianity, and Judaism. Thus, respect for human rights cannot be taken for granted in particular global contexts or among particular groups and is an achievement wherever it occurs. A common feature of this process is that citizens "encourage" and "motivate" states to commit to and protect human rights.[19]

Third, some scholars reframe the critique of imposition of Western values outside the ambit of the West in ways that call attention to the differences that reside within cultures, nations, and transnational regions. The Pew Research Center's 2013 report, "The Global Divide on Homosexuality: Greater Acceptance in More Secular and Affluent Countries," surveys transnational attitudes toward same-sex sexuality in thirty-nine countries and finds "broad acceptance of homosexuality in North America, the European Union, and much of Latin America, but equally widespread rejection in predominantly Muslim nations and in Africa, as well as in parts of Asia and in Russia."[20] This broad picture of acceptance and rejection provides important information about the well-being and prospects of LGBTQ people around the world, but the big picture conceals regional and individual variations and recent and ongoing attitude shifts. For example, as chapter 4 shows, the values codified in international covenants cannot be understood as Western in the sense that they are uncontested in the United States. Writing of sex education, Jonathan Zimmerman makes an argument that is relevant to the case of SOGI human rights:

> certain parts of the world are [not] "conservative" or "traditional" on the topic. Instead, conservatives around the globe have united across borders to block or inhibit sex education. On

issues of sex and reproduction, it's not East vs. West anymore. It's liberals vs. conservatives, each of which often have more in common with their ideological soulmates in other parts of the world than they do with people next door.[21]

Finally, Jack Donnelly takes a position that locates human rights principles neither in many world cultures nor in the West, pointing out instead that human rights discourse and ideals did not come into existence in any traditional societies, East or West. Instead, he argues, human rights are a product of modernity that properly belongs to all people.[22] Some SOGI human rights–respecting developments might be adduced to support multiple perspectives on the provenance or diffusion of human rights, including human rights as an achievement anywhere in the world, contested even in the global North, and a product of modernity. One example of such a development is a 2009 Issue Paper produced by the Council of Europe Commissioner for Human Rights, "Human Rights and Gender Identity." The booklet explains gender and transgender identity, discrimination against transgender women and men, and the applicability of international human rights law to transgender people. The production of this paper and its translation into several languages suggests that in 2009 European citizens needed to be informed about the "ignored and neglected" "human rights situation of transgender persons."[23]

Having studied the US Christian right for many years, I can attest to that movement's ongoing opposition to all forms of LGBTQ rights and recognition, here and abroad. On the other hand, in early 2014, I attended the wedding in Washington, DC, of two women who fled Iran after being warned that they would face prosecution for their sexuality. Throughout the wedding, I kept an iPad camera trained on the couple so the mother of one of the partners could participate in the ceremony from her home in Tehran. For that mother watching the marriage of her daughter to another woman, the Pew findings, though accurate, did not reflect her attitude toward same-sex sexuality and LGBTQ equality under the law. She was proud and happy that her daughter was marrying the woman she loved at the same time that US Christian conservatives were intensifying their own anti–same-sex marriage rhetoric in the face of the adverse Supreme Court decisions of 2013. Of course, similar intranational divisions prevail outside and inside the United States.[24]

Even though it is well over fifty years old, the UDHR and other statements and conventions continue to be subject to debate, among nations and among social, political, and intellectual communities. On one hand, governments and human rights advocates and organizations acknowledge and use the principles enshrined in the declaration to advance human rights and try to hold states accountable for human rights violations.[25] An example of the incorporation of the declaration into the LGBT advocacy of a government entity is the Swedish International Development Cooperation Agency (Sida). Sida is a government agency whose broad mission is "to ensure that people living in poverty and under oppression have the ability to improve their living conditions."[26] Sida works on many issues and with many constituencies, and among these groups is LGBTQ people around the world whose human rights are in jeopardy. The text of an English-language Sida brochure on "Human Rights of Lesbian, Gay, Bisexual and Transgender Persons: Conducting a Dialogue" begins:

> The Universal Declaration of Human Rights includes the right of every person to life, privacy, health and equality before the law, as well as the right to freedom of expression and freedom from discrimination and violence, including torture. Lesbian, gay, bisexual and transgender (LGBT) persons are constantly at risk of persecution and gross violations of their fundamental human rights in a number of countries. Many LGBT persons fear or face imprisonment, torture, abuse and even murder, solely because they live in a context that does not tolerate their sexual orientation, gender identity or gender expression.[27]

Thus, Sida prefaces its literature on LGBT human rights with direct appeals to the legitimacy of the UDHR and its applicability to sexuality, sexual orientation, and gender identity and expression.

An additional consideration is relevant to the question of women's and SOGI human rights, even though it should not be a determining factor in cultural or national decisions about whether to discriminate against groups because the question of whether to apply human rights principles is not an issue best decided by macroeconomic analysis. However, it turns out that, like discrimination against women, widespread discrimination against LGBTQ people is economically wasteful and harms national economies. However, it is useful to understand how exclusion and discrimination cost the societies that practice group-based stigma and oppression. In 2014, a forum at the World Bank headquarters in Washington, DC, highlighted ongoing research on "The Economic Cost of Homophobia: How LGBT

Exclusion Impacts Development." The forum brought together economists, World Bank and UN officials, and human rights professionals to address how LGBT exclusion affects economic development. Although transnational economic impact research is in its early stages, it is clear that discriminatory policies and social practices are costly in a variety of ways, including to the health of individuals affected by these policies and practices and to national measures of productivity and fiscal sustainability.[28] Thus, research that surveys the economic costs of large-scale inequalities based on sex, race, and sexuality/gender identity, among other categories, can be understood implicitly to uphold a cross-cultural set of human rights norms.[29]

Even as critics debate these issues, a broad coalition of advocates find in human rights principles and their codification in instruments such as the UDHR indispensable resources for supporting the "dignity and worth of the [LGBTQ] person." As critics of LGBTQ human rights on the political right point out, SOGI human rights did not exist as a category for human rights advocates in the early decades after the UDHR. When same-sex sexual behavior, identity, and orientation began to be integrated deliberately into the discourse of human rights, those who led these efforts understood the threats faced by gender and sexual minorities firsthand. These activists created a path for other human rights advocates to take up the banner of SOGI human rights.

## International LGBT Organizations

Historians of LGBTQ rights generally agree that a movement for SOGI rights began in Germany at the turn of the twentieth century with Dr. Magnus Hirschfeld's founding of the Scientific Humanitarian Committee (Wissenschaftlich-humanitäres Komitee), later the Institute for Sexual Research. All traces of Hirschfeld's institute were decimated by the Nazis.[30] In the post–World War II period, organizations formed in Nordic and Western European states; 1950 saw the launch of two gay organizations: in the United States, the Mattachine Society and in Sweden, the Federation for Sexual Equality (Riksförbundet för Sexuellt Likaberättigande).[31] Other gay and lesbian organizations formed in the United States throughout the 1950s and 1960s, embracing a "homophile" label that soon became synonymous with self-abasement.

The decade after the Stonewall riots occurred in New York City was a politically fertile period in the United States. Many gay advocacy and media organizations were founded in the 1970s, especially in Europe, the United Kingdom, and the United States. Some US organizations founded in the immediate aftermath of the riots do not survive, including the Redstockings (1969–70), the Gay Liberation Front (1969–72), the Gay Activists Alliance (1969–74), and the Lavender Menace (later Radicalesbians, 1970–72). Others established in this period are still viable: the National Gay and Lesbian Task Force (1973–present), the National Center for Lesbian Rights (1977–present), Gay and Lesbian Advocates and Defenders (1978–present), and the Human Rights Campaign (1980–present). The Human Rights Campaign Fund—since 1995, the Human Rights Campaign—was founded in the wake of the October 1979 National March on Washington for Lesbian and Gay Rights, the first LGBTQ civil rights march in the United States.

Today, many scholars of sexuality distinguish between LGBT and queer organizations, marking the former (most often the Human Rights Campaign) pejoratively as "assimilationist" and the latter (for example, ACT UP and Queer Nation) approvingly as "liberationist." Nevertheless, other perspectives problematize this distinction between assimilationist and liberationist groups and political agendas. For example, what constitutes liberationism in style or agenda may be contested, as Julie Mertus contests the liberationism of Queer Nation and places it in the category of "liberal, self-worth promoting"—presumably assimilationist—organizations of its advocacy moment.[32] Craig Rimmerman takes a different approach in his study of "the lesbian and gay movements," examining them through a lens of assimilationist or liberationist goals and methods, and the "intersection between . . . assimilationist and liberationist strategies over time." Surveying LGBTQ movements in the United States from the Stonewall riots to the present, Rimmerman persuasively demonstrates that rather than the assimilation and liberation marking a divide between groups and movements, the divide of assimilation versus liberation has run *through* LGBTQ movements, groups, and issue formations since the 1950s. For example, he analyzes the goals, practices, and strategies of the AIDS Coalition to Unleash Power (ACT UP), usually invoked as an exemplar of liberationism, and concludes that "what makes ACT UP such an interesting organization to study is the fact that it has embraced both liberationist and assimilationist approaches to political, social, and cultural change."[33]

One feature of LGBTQ rights and justice claims and activism in the United States that has distinguished domestic US activism from global advocacy, including advocacy outside the country by US activists, has been the use of civil and constitutional—rather than human—rights claims. Julie Mertus explains that in spite of the "strategic importance" of "linking human rights and LGBT issues," in the United States, "policy-makers, the general public, and even many social change advocates still view human rights as something that applies not at home, but in some distant land."[34] Mertus outlines three reasons domestic US LGBT activists generally haven't used human rights frames in their advocacy. The explanation she seems to favor is that identitarian human rights frames are antithetical to conceptions of "gender and sexuality [as] socially constructed and fluid" that have been embraced by many LGBTQ political activists since the 1970s.

I'm more persuaded by other reasons she gives: first, that, for Americans, human rights invokes connotations of "gross human rights violations committed against faraway victims"; and second, that US political institutions and elites have been "unreceptive" to human rights discourse and even, as we shall see in chapter 4, vigorously opposed to international law.[35] Implicit in Mertus's analysis but not spelled out explicitly, a final reason for US LGBTQ activists' decision not to use human rights frames might well be that until recently there was no basis in international law or in human rights discourse for recognition of discrimination and abuse based on nonnormative sexuality or gender expression or identity. US activists in the 1970s, 1980s, 1990s, and 2000s would have been hard-pressed to look to human rights principles or discourse for vindication before a plurality of the global human rights community stood firmly behind their claims.

The oldest of the gay, queer, or LGBT-oriented international human rights organizations is the Astraea Lesbian Foundation for Justice (Astraea), founded in the United States in 1977 as ASTRAEA, National Lesbian Action Foundation. Astraea bills itself as "the only philanthropic organization working exclusively to advance LGBTQI human rights around the globe, with a focus on reinforcing the political leadership of lesbians, women, transgender people and people of color."[36] Astraea pursues its own LGBTQI (the *I* stands for intersex) human rights projects and grantmaking, especially with activists and organizations in rural areas, and organizations led by lesbians, transgender people, and/or people of color.[37] In addition, today Astraea plays a key role as a mediating organization between LGBTQ/SOGI donors and indigenous activists throughout the world.

Shortly after the founding of Astraea, in 1978, the International Lesbian, Gay, Bisexual, Trans, and Intersex Association (ILGA) was formed in the United Kingdom as the International Gay Association. ILGA is a global umbrella federation of over 1,000 LGBTQ advocacy organizations worldwide and functions as "an international platform to collectively campaign against the discrimination, and at times persecution, faced by LGBTI people around the world."[38] ILGA representatives have participated in meetings of multilateral organizations since the 1980s, lobbying the Conference on Security and Cooperation in Europe and the Inter-American Commission of Human Rights, among others.

In 1993, ILGA was the first LGBTQ organization to achieve consultative status as a recognized nongovernmental organization at the United Nations; however, this achievement required that the UN Economic and Social Council suspend its usual consensus method for so designating organizations. Initially supportive, the United States soon challenged consultative status for ILGA over the membership of the North American Man/Boy Love Association (NAMBLA), a group formed in 1978 "to end the extreme oppression of men and boys in mutually consensual relationships."[39] Under pressure from proponents of NAMBLA and a liberationist ethos and from conservative critics, ILGA was embroiled in controversy throughout the mid-1990s.[40] ILGA sponsors regional and world conferences that provide forums for elections, agenda-setting, and other movement activities.

In 1990, activist Julie Dorf founded the International Gay and Lesbian Human Rights Commission (IGLHRC), which for some time employed the motto "Human Rights for Everyone. Everywhere."[41] In 2015, IGLHRC changed its name to OutRight Action International. In a video, Executive Director Jessica Stern explains the two reasons that drove the decision to rename the organization: because the old name (and abbreviation) was "something of a mouthful to pronounce" and "more importantly," because "we decided it was long past time to make it clear that we support everyone in our community," including those whose bisexual, transgender, and intersex identities weren't explicitly denoted in the original name.[42] OutRight concentrates its work at multiple levels: "improving the lives" of people harmed because of their sexuality or gender identity or expression, "strengthening the capacity" of the global LGBT human rights movement, and "engaging in human rights advocacy" with a broad set of partners that includes the United Nations, governments, and CSOs around the world.[43] Today, OutRight operates under the leadership of Stern, an international staff, and a board. The organization documents its activist work in a variety of ways, including through videos such as "In Their Own Words: Documenting Violence and Discrimination against Lesbians, Bisexual Women, and Transgender People in Asia" and country reports such as "Exposing Persecution of LGBT Individuals in Iraq."[44] Since 2011, OutRight has held consultative status with the UN Economic and Social Council.[45]

Finally, there is the Council for Global Equality (CGE), a single-issue nonprofit organization with the goal of "advancing an American foreign policy inclusive of sexual orientation and gender identity." Founded during the 2008 presidential election campaign and led by Council Chair Mark Bromley, the CGE is a new group among US and Western human rights organizations. It is an umbrella group with organizational members, many (but not all) of which are LGBT rights organizations: American Jewish World Service, Amnesty International, Anti-Defamation League, Center for American Progress, Freedom House, Gay and Lesbian Institute, Global Rights, Heartland Alliance, Human Rights Campaign, Human Rights First, Human Rights Watch, Immigration Equality, International Gay and Lesbian Human Rights Commission, Metropolitan Community Churches, National Center for Lesbian Rights, National Center for Transgender Equality, National Gay and Lesbian Chamber of Commerce, National Gay and Lesbian Task Force, ORAM (Organization for Refuge, Asylum and Migration) Institute, Out and Equal Workplace Advocates, and the Robert F. Kennedy Center for Justice and Human Rights.[46] The CGE operates under the fiscal sponsorship of San Francisco–based Community Initiatives and is one of many LGBTQ and mainstream human rights groups that partners and coordinates with the US government for SOGI human rights initiatives.

In the global history of the juxtaposition of human rights with same-sex sexuality, homosexual—later gay, and still later, LGBT+—individuals, media, and organizations first led the organized resistance against antigay and antitransgender bias, discrimination, and violence. However, a key development occurred when mainstream human rights "gatekeeper" organizations formally incorporated discrimination and human rights violations based on sexuality, sexual orientation, and gender identity into their missions, often in response to lobbying from LGBT people within their ranks.[47] Thus, in briefly documenting the turn of mainstream human rights organizations toward advocating on behalf of LGBT human rights, I emphasize US-based human rights groups. These organizations and activists associated with them have pushed the US government to affirm support for SOGI human rights and partnered with the government to accomplish ends associated with SOGI.[48]

## The Mainstreaming of LGBT Human Rights

The first mainstream human rights organization to commit to supporting
LGBTQ human rights was Amnesty International, founded in the United
Kingdom in the early 1960s. Amnesty is a mass-membership human rights
organization that bills itself as "the world's largest grassroots human rights
organization," a "global movement of people fighting injustice and promoting human rights." Although it engages in many activities, Amnesty is best
known for its targeted mobilizing of publicity and support for individuals
who suffer human rights deprivations around the world. Today there are
Amnesty chapters in more than 150 countries, and the largest of these is
the US chapter, with approximately 250,000 members.[49]

In 1991, Amnesty took a position on judicial detainment or imprisonment based on same-sex sexual behavior, calling these acts of governments "a grave violation of human rights."[50] This development was not
uncontested; in addition to predictable disapproval from constituencies
in the United States that disagreed that people of nonnormative sexual
orientation and those who engaged in same-sex sexuality were proper
candidates for human rights protections, disapproval arose from within
the organization itself. Amnesty's decision to include persecution based
on same-sex sexuality and gender identity as violations of human rights
upon which the organization would act was opposed by some chapters
in Asia, Africa, and Latin America. The controversy within Amnesty was
a case of an organization whose leaders and members generally agree on
the universality of human rights disputing the application of that principle
in the case of same-sex sexuality. In the end, the internal argument over
whether to include persecution based on same-sex sexuality in the group's
portfolio was concluded by political means when Amnesty's International
Executive Committee, on which northern and western national chapters
enjoyed stronger representation, settled the matter in favor of the North
American and European chapters.[51] Another milestone was the publication
by Amnesty International UK of the global report, *Breaking the Silence:
Human Rights Violations Based on Sexual Orientation*.[52] Today, Amnesty
calls for the decriminalization of same-sex sexual relations, civil marriage
equality, judicial recourse for human rights violations based on same-sex
sexual identity and gender identity and expression, equality for LGBT
people in the administration of justice, and protections for those who
defend the human rights of LGBT people.

A second international human rights organization to embrace the human rights of LGBT people is Human Rights Watch (HRW), which came into existence in the United States in 1978 as Helsinki Watch and extended its network of "watch committees" throughout the world in the 1980s. HRW engages in investigation, monitoring, documentation, analysis, and reporting of human rights violations worldwide, and it presses governments to address and resolve categories of the human rights violation it identifies. HRW targets a wide range of categories of human rights abuses and campaigns that include rape as a war crime, women's human rights, landmine abolition, workers' human rights, human trafficking, and use of child soldiers. The organization declared its commitment to report on human rights violations against gay men and lesbians in 1996. After partnering extensively with IGLHRC, HRW integrated these concerns into its operations in the form of an LGBT Human Rights Program:

> Human Rights Watch works for lesbian, gay, bisexual, and transgender people's rights, with activists representing a multiplicity of identities and issues.
>
> We document and expose abuses based on sexual orientation and gender identity worldwide—including torture, killing and executions, arrests under unjust laws, unequal treatment, censorship, medical abuses, discrimination in health and jobs and housing, domestic violence, abuses against children, and denial of family rights and recognition.
>
> We advocate for laws and policies that will protect everyone's dignity. We work for a world where all people can enjoy their rights fully.[53]

A smaller Western human rights nongovernmental organization is Human Rights First (HRF), established in New York in 1978 as the Lawyers Committee for International Human Rights and renamed in 2003. The motto of HRF is "American ideals, Universal values," a slogan that acknowledges the US roots of the organization while attesting to a belief in the universality of human rights principles. The United States looms large in the mission of HRF, which emphasizes encouraging and leveraging US leadership to redress human rights violations—"harnessing American influence to secure core freedoms"—and pressuring the US government and corporations to support human rights in their spheres of influence around the world.[54] HRF incorporated support for LGBTI human rights into its principles and operations after 2000 and included hate crimes based on SOGI into its 2005 report, *Everyday Fears: A Survey of Violent Hate Crimes in Europe and North America* under the category, "Bias Crimes Based on Discrimination Other Than Racism."[55] Among its concerns for other populations, HRF is committed to supporting "fundamental human rights protections for LGBTI persons," and the organization has taken a particular interest in the difficulties of LGBTI refugees, who frequently are confronted with "discrimination, marginalization, and bias-motivated violence" in ways that exacerbate their vulnerability as refugees. HRF works with the United Nations Refugee Agency and the US government to advocate for the needs of this vulnerable population in conflict zones and in places throughout the world in which people are displaced.[56]

As is clear from this brief history of LGBTQ and mainstream human rights advocacy on behalf of LGBTQ people and issues of minority gender and sexuality, LGBTQ groups pioneered this advocacy, although mainstream multifocus human rights groups increasingly have become champions of these causes. Through the 1990s and into the early decades of the new millennium, human rights defenders and organizations throughout the world at local, regional, and international levels have been working, and sometimes cooperating on, problems related to gender and sexuality. Key events in this transnational organizing and advocacy occurred in 2006: first, when the Declaration of Montreal was presented at an International Conference on LGBT Human Rights in Canada,[57] and second, when human rights professionals, activists, scholars, and leaders from around the world came together for a conference at Gadjah Mada University on Java, Indonesia. The representatives who met in Yogyakarta set out to articulate a set of human rights principles and state obligations with regard to violations based on sexuality, sexual orientation, and gender identity. The resulting Yogyakarta Principles have not been uncontroversial. But they continue to be influential in debates and advocacy regarding those who may suffer ill consequences because of gender or sexuality.

## The Yogyakarta Principles

The November 2006 conference of human rights leaders—including members of the International Commission of Jurists and the International Service for Human Rights—held in Yogyakarta produced "The Yogyakarta Principles on the Application of International Human Rights Law in Relation to Sexual Orientation and Gender Identity." The Yogyakarta Principles website introduces the document delivered by the conference as follows:

> In 2006, in response to well-documented patterns of abuse, a distinguished group of international human rights experts met in Yogyakarta, Indonesia to outline a set of international principles relating to sexual orientation and gender identity. The result was the Yogyakarta Principles: a universal guide to human rights which affirm binding international legal standards with which all States must comply. They promise a different future where all people born free and equal in dignity and rights can fulfil that precious birthright.[58]

The twenty-nine principles that follow are divided into eight broad categories: rights to universal enjoyment of human rights, nondiscrimination, and recognition before the law; rights to human and personal security; economic, social, and cultural rights; rights to expression, opinion, and association; freedom of movement and asylum; rights of participation in cultural and family life; rights of human rights defenders; and rights of redress and accountability.[59]

The principles are explicitly universalizing but also multinational and multicultural, at least in two respects. First, signatories to the principles constitute a who's who of human rights service and advocacy from around the world. Perhaps the most well-known signatory in the West is former President of Ireland (and former UN High Commissioner for Human Rights) Mary Robinson; however, only one signatory is from the United States, and just nine of twenty-four are from North America, Australia, and Western Europe. Second, those who met to develop and finalize the principles intended them to serve as a normative set of standards that *should* guide states and national communities regardless of the differences that might prevail between them. On the website constructed to disseminate the final document, the Yogyakarta Principles are translated into the six official languages of the United Nations: English, Spanish, French, Russian, Arabic, and Chinese.

Since its publication, the Yogyakarta Principles have been subjected to a range of responses, from praise to various forms of criticism through disapproval and rejection. Some criticisms, especially by experts in law and human rights, were relatively modest, including qualifications regarding the scope of individual principles, their provenance in international instruments, their likely impact on international "soft law," and their availability and usefulness to grassroots activists throughout the world.[60] Another important critique of the principles is acknowledged by Michael O'Flaherty, who served as rapporteur for the conference that produced the principles, and coauthor John Fisher in the "first published critical commentary on the Principles." They point out that the "achievement" of principles that are gender-neutral

> came at the price of the invisibility in the text of any reference to the particular situation of women. It may be considered that this omission detracts from the capacity of the document to forcefully address the problems confronting lesbians in numerous countries.[61]

O'Flaherty and Fisher note that the Institute for Democracy in South Africa reports that lesbians there are twice as likely to be victims of rape than are heterosexual women, and many perpetrators target lesbians for rape because of their sexual orientation in assaults that have come to be known as "corrective rapes."[62] However, the principles aren't the only site of lesbian erasure in LGBTQ human rights. For example, Bronwyn Winter calls attention to the relative invisibility of the struggles of lesbian asylum seekers in a male-dominated "global LGBTI human rights model."[63]

In addition to critiques at the margins by commentators well disposed to SOGI human rights, the Yogyakarta Principles have been disparaged and rejected by officials from "states [that] do not acknowledge that HR violations based on SOGI constitute legitimate areas of HR concern."[64] A common motif of such repudiations of SOGI human rights—whatever their source—is cultural difference, usually paired with a critique of the West for inappropriately imposing or seeking to impose its cultural values on nations that do not subscribe to SOGI human rights.

In the decade since their promulgation, the Yogyakarta Principles have been taken up transnationally by SOGI human rights advocates. One evidence of the fruitfulness for SOGI/LGBTQ human rights organizing and activism is the Courage Unfolds Campaign and the thirty-minute video of the same name produced by IGLHRC and the Philippines-based Lesbian Activism Project (LeAP!).[65] *Courage Unfolds* features Asian LGBTQ people, activists, and activist organizations and relates the narratives of and social conditions for LGBTQ people in many Asian nations directly to human rights and the Yogyakarta Principles. The film informs viewers about the development of the principles and how they work to connect LGBTQ human rights to preexisting discourses and practices of human rights law and practice. Echoing the interpretive framework set out by O'Flaherty and Fisher, OutRight (formerly IGLHRC) Asia Pacific Program Coordinator Grace Poore notes that "the Yogyakarta Principles is premised on existing human rights laws that already outline and speak to the rights of LGBT people."

The video employs a pedagogical device that links each personal narrative of harm to an individual principle being violated in that case. After LGBTQ activists and individuals speak (some have their identity obscured to protect their anonymity), the screen displays the number and description of the specific principle that bears on or is violated by the kind of harms narrated by the speakers. For example, King Oey of Arus Pelangi (an Indonesian LGBTQ advocacy organization) describes a 2000 attack in Yogyakarta on a gathering of LGBTQ people—"gays" and "warias[,] transgender people"—by fundamentalist "Muslim radicals." As the camera tracks scenes of the attack's aftermath, phrases appear: first, "Violation of Principle 5: the right to security of the person," and then "Violation of Principle 20: the right to freedom of peaceful assembly and association." In an interview segment, Vitit Muntarbhorn, professor of law at Thailand's Chulalongkorn University and a signatory of the principles, calmly reduces the complexity of the principles to three central tenets: "no discrimination, please"; "no violence, please"; and "no criminalization, please."[66]

Having detailed some legal "inaccuracies" in the Yogyakarta Principles, David Brown concludes that "on balance the Principles have been very successful in becoming a standard-setting document and the inspiration for a variety of efforts to combat sexual orientation and gender identity discrimination in international law, government policy, and domestic courts." For Brown, "the Principles' overreaching nature" is in part responsible for the document's "inspirational" quality and impact on SOGI human rights activism. Indeed, the principles have had a profound effect on international human rights discourse, perhaps especially with regard to gender identity human rights.[67] And they have provided guidelines for SOGI human rights claiming in international forums. In 2017, another group of human rights experts met, this time in Geneva, to update the Principles, promulgating the Yogyakarta Principles + 10 (YP + 10). YP + 10 adds nine new principles and 112 additional state obligations related to SOGI.

Throughout the 1990s and into the first years of the new century, efforts were made in international forums to support—and undermine—SOGI human rights. An example of commitments to claiming and disclaiming SOGI is the 1995 Fourth World Conference on Women in Beijing, organized by the UN Commission on the Status of Women. In spite of lesbian visibility, activism, and organizing at the conference, references to sexual orientation were not included in the final Platform for Action.[68] It was not until 2008 that the first statement of support for sexual orientation and gender identity human rights was introduced in the UN General Assembly. The statement was supported by sixty-six nations, including six countries on the African continent, but it was not supported by the United States. The statement was opposed by some individual states and by an alternative statement sponsored by the Organization of the Islamic Conference.[69] Although this germinal statement did not become a UN resolution, it became the first move within the United Nations to ratify SOGI human rights *as* human rights, and to call on member states to recognize these rights in international forums and protect them at home.

## The UN and Member States Support SOGI Human Rights

Besides continuing opposition to recognizing SOGI human rights in many parts of the world, two specific obstacles have complicated the process of fully incorporating sexual orientation and gender identity into the discourse, legal framework, and practices of the United Nations. First is the fact that these categories of identity and human rights jeopardy were not included in foundational documents such as the UDHR. Hence, countries that disapprove of incorporating these human rights can appeal to cultural objections as well as the criticism that such rights are newly minted and different in kind than other categories of human rights. As we will see in chapter 4, these objections overlap with objections to SOGI human rights and help Christian conservatives in the United States make common cause with those who resist SOGI human rights worldwide. In addition to rhetorical common cause, a second obstacle to incorporating SOGI human rights into the United Nations has been the institutional efforts of conservative faith communities from the world's major religions to advocate for the "natural family" and block efforts to instantiate women's, children's and SOGI human rights.[70]

After the controversial 2008 General Assembly Statement on SOGI human rights was introduced, UN Secretary-General Ban Ki-moon celebrated the 2010 International Human Rights Day by delivering a speech in New York on SOGI human rights. In it, the secretary-general spoke exclusively to SOGI human rights, proclaiming that "where there is tension between cultural attitudes and universal human rights, universal human rights must carry the day." He ended with a plea and an invitation:

> The watchwords of civilization have always been tolerance, understanding and mutual respect.
> That is why we are here today.
> And that is why we ask the nations and the peoples of the world to join us.
> To join us in common cause in the name of justice and a better life for all.[71]

As he promised, Ban Ki-moon has continued to support LGBTQ equality and SOGI human rights, making a number of public statements on the issue in different venues.[72]

In 2011, the UN Human Rights Council more formally placed the imprimatur of the United Nations on the pursuit of the human rights of those persecuted or prosecuted on the basis of sexuality, sexual identity, or gender identity. For members of the international human rights community, Resolution 17/19 "was a watershed moment because it was the first UN resolution to bring specific focus on human rights violations based on sexual orientation and gender identity."[73] Passage of the resolution was widely praised by organizations and advocates in the global human rights community, and seventeen human rights organizations issued a joint statement recognizing the "groundbreaking achievement" and its "signal of support to human rights defenders." The joint statement recorded the votes of representatives in four categories: states voting in support of the resolution, states voting against the resolution, abstentions, and states cosponsoring the resolution. This voting roll reflects majoritarian or elite differences in attitudes regarding same-sex sexuality and nonnormative gender identity.[74]

Note that because of a change in administrations between 2008 and 2011, the United States—which did not support the SOGI human rights General Assembly statement in 2008—did back the 2011 SOGI human rights resolution. In the 2011 resolution, the Human Rights Council called for a study to document and analyze the conditions for LGBTQ people around the world. Published in 2012, this study was "Discriminatory Laws and Practices and Acts of Violence against Individuals Based on Their Sexual Orientation and Gender Identity." Another report, "Born Free and Equal: Sexual Orientation and Gender Identity in International Human Rights Law," appeared at the same time as "Discriminatory Laws and Practices" and complements it. With a foreword written by High Commissioner for Human Rights Navi Pillay, "Born Free and Equal" gives "the purpose of th[e] booklet . . . [as] set[ting] out the core obligations that States have towards LGBT persons, and describ[ing] how United Nations mechanisms have applied international law in this context."[75]

In the aftermath of the passage of Resolution 17/19, a conference was convened under the imprimatur of the United Nations to address the challenges of SOGI human rights. Held in April 2013 in Oslo, the International Conference on Human Rights, Sexual Orientation and Gender Identity was sponsored by the Republic of South Africa and the Norwegian Ministry of Foreign Affairs.[76] In September 2014, the UN Human Rights Council passed a statement on SOGI human rights and the plight of LGBTQ people. Applying the same set of "core legal obligations" with regard to SOGI human rights that it has propounded with regard to other vulnerable groups, the UN states that:

> protecting the human rights of LGBT people include obligations [of states] to
>
> - *Protect* individuals from homophobic and transphobic violence.
>
> - *Prevent* torture and cruel, inhuman and degrading treatment.
>
> - *Repeal* laws criminalizing homosexuality and transgender people.
>
> - *Prohibit* discrimination based on sexual orientation and gender identity.
>
> - *Safeguard* freedom of expression, association and peaceful assembly for all LGBT people.[77]

In 2015, the UN High Commissioner for Human Rights issued a significant report on the status of SOGI human rights and of the treatment of

LGBTQ people with regard to human rights. "Discrimination and Violence against Individuals Based on Their Sexual Orientation and Gender Identity" documents that seventy-six countries criminalize same-sex sexuality, seven nations make same-sex sexuality a capital offense, and violence based on actual or perceived SOGI is often more brutal than violence against other minority or persecuted groups.[78] Finally, in 2016, the UN's Human Rights Council appointed Vitit Muntarbhorn to serve as the first independent expert on sexual orientation and gender identity, a position whose broad mandate includes investigating and reporting discrimination and violations of human rights based on SOGI.

The Barack Obama administration publicly announced its support for SOGI human rights in the last days of 2011 and effectively began to implement its policy and programming outlined in Geneva by Secretary Clinton in early 2012. Among nations, and by standards set by UN statements, resolutions, and reports, the US government was a late adopter of SOGI human rights. By the time Clinton delivered her remarks, some European nations—especially the Netherlands and Sweden—already had moved purposefully in the direction of embracing SOGI rights, domestically and internationally. As many scholars have pointed out, "Europe" comprises a diverse collection of states that have pursued very different policies and practices with regard to SOGI rights and LGBTQ people. Still, as Phillip Ayoub notes,

> If any world region can boast the establishment of an international norm concerning sexual minority rights, it is Europe. European actors—the European Union (EU), the Council of Europe, and a transnational network of activists—have fostered change by propagating lesbian, gay, bisexual, and transgender (LGBT) rights and by introducing the issues into the domestic discourse of various European states.[79]

A key concept in the study of human rights is "norm diffusion": the process by which "international human rights regimes and the principles, norms, and rules embedded in them are internalized and implemented domestically and, thus, affect processes of political transformation."[80] Typically, scholars have traced the diffusion of human rights norms on SOGI and with regard to other target populations from the West or global North to the global South. However, human rights norms also have diffused within the global South and within the West/global North, including from

Europe to the United States on issues such as the conditions of criminal sentencing. The United States lagged behind other Western nations in its policies with regard to SOGI, but by the time Donald Trump took office in early 2017 the United States was considered by many SOGI human rights defenders to be an important force—and perhaps even the "biggest player"—in international SOGI human rights advocacy and assistance.[81] Those who have referred to the United States as the biggest player in international SOGI human rights refer primarily to the State Department's Global Equality Fund but also to a human rights community in government and in CSOs whose members are globally active at all levels of SOGI advocacy.

## A Map of the Book

Of the chapters that follow, chapters 1 and 3 are empirical, and I set out the basic outlines and trajectory of US government pro–SOGI human rights interventions outside the domestic United States and some particular examples of these interventions. Political scientists will not be surprised to see that US government SOGI advocacy has not merely been conceived by and directed from Congress or the White House. Instead, it has emerged from within executive branch agencies, through revisions of policy, and sometimes by way of coordination between civil servants and civil and human rights activists outside the government. Only relatively recently has support for SOGI human rights been mandated by the president (Obama) and the Secretary of State (Clinton). In 2017, at a time when the US government's continued commitment to human rights is far from assured, this story of the path to support and advocacy for SOGI human rights provides a resource to remind citizens that although some commitments can be undone, the potential for resurrecting and protecting human rights can remain.

Chapter 1 begins with the 1990s, the decade in which the Department of Defense's "Don't Ask, Don't Tell" policy was implemented. The debate over that policy was accompanied by an escalation of public discourse about the unassimilable nature of nonheterosexuals into the US military. On the other hand, the decade also saw a fruitful organizing of LGBTQ federal employees and the first US government–sponsored projects to assist foreign LGBTQ citizens. The chapter surveys projects associated with the Department of State from the time of the late Bill Clinton administration until President Obama's December 6, 2011, "Memorandum for the Heads of Executive Departments and Agencies" on the subject of "International Initiatives to Advance the Human Rights of Lesbian, Gay, Bisexual, and Transgender Persons." The memorandum, released on the same day that Secretary of State Clinton delivered her International Human Rights Day address in Geneva, is included in this book as Appendix A. For narrative purposes, I take this period from 1999 to 2011 to be the "early" period of US government pro-SOGI policy.

In chapter 2, I focus on Clinton's speech, "Remarks in Recognition of International Human Rights Day." The most public US intervention on SOGI human rights to date, the speech has been interpreted by critics on the political left and right in ways that converge and produce unanticipated agreements on the cynicism and foreign policy duplicity understood to motivate official SOGI human rights advocacy. I include the full text of Clinton's speech in Appendix B and begin the chapter with an analysis of the speech's principal aims: enunciating the moral and legal foundations of human rights, identifying SOGI rights with the historical work and cross-cultural understandings of human rights, explicitly rehearsing and refuting standard grounds of anti-LGBT prejudice, admitting the limitations of the United States' own confrontation with LGBT people and their human rights struggles, and pledging to work with LGBTQ people around the world as allies in the struggle for SOGI human rights.

Finally, I sample reviews and reactions to Clinton's speech, sorting them into categories that demonstrate that key indictments of hypocrisy and political calculation unite conservative and left-progressive critics. The convergence of left and right critiques of US support for SOGI human rights isn't only a feature of the responses that Clinton's speech elicited from diverse constituencies. As I show in chapter 5, left-progressive opposition to US support for SOGI compromises US advocacy by delegitimizing it before programs and their effects can even be identified and assessed.

In chapter 3 I take up the period after Clinton's speech and examine commitments and programming dedicated to SOGI human rights from early 2012 to early 2017. I begin by surveying ongoing US government programs and initiatives such as the Global Equality Fund, embassy engagement programs, the LGBTI Global Development Partnership, and the appointment of the first Special Envoy for LGBTI Human Rights. Through a case study, I look more closely at some applications of these policies and practices and provide some evidence of how they are received by US government partners and grantees abroad.

In contrast with the first three empirical chapters, chapters 4 and 5 address opposition to and critique of pro-LGBT interventions by the US government that are aimed at international audiences and in the service of human rights goals. I turn first, in chapter 4, to the political right and examine the opposition to the linkage between LGBTQ issues and human rights discourse. US Christian conservatives have long opposed LGBTQ legal and political rights and the linkage of LGBTQ social, legal, and political progress with the rubric of "human rights." Less public is the Christian right movement's deployment of the charge of cultural imperialism and the unforeseen consequences of the movement's new commitment to a particular kind of cultural relativism that furthers their anti-LGBTQ politics. For students of US politics who don't understand why the Trump campaign and administration have not been repudiated by Christian conservative supporters over charges of collusion with Russia and Vladimir Putin, I provide evidence of the Christian right's growing affinity with Russia over anti-LGBT oppression during the Obama administration.

In chapter 5, I turn to the academic critical humanist left and articulate a range of critiques of concepts and arguments that bear on US rhetorical, diplomatic, and policy interventions on or related to SOGI human rights. I begin this analysis with a critique of the monolithic and widely shared conception of "the state" that prevails in much critical humanist scholarship on politics and foreign policy, and why such a conception misleads critical humanists in their quest to stake out a position on human rights that opposes cynical US government acts and interests. My goal is to present and examine the criticisms of US government human rights intervention abroad that have been developed under a variety of theoretical rubrics, especially in humanities disciplines such as philosophy, literature, cultural studies, ethnic studies, and women's studies. Because disciplinary discourses are less bounded now than ever before, there is considerable sharing and migration of key theories, concepts, assumptions, and political commitments by scholars and students across disciplines. To the extent that this sharing has lowered barriers to cross-disciplinary intellectual conversations, it has enhanced our opportunities to learn and talk across research questions and bodies of knowledge. However, at times the sharing has fostered an unfortunate tendency for practitioners and students who are learning the theoretical ropes of academic life to take theoretical precepts and political convictions as settled facts and underestimate the importance of assessing the empirical data of each case.

Finally, in the afterword, I make a case for openness to US government involvement in international efforts to assist LGBTQ-identified people, people who engage in same-sex relations, and transgender/gender-nonconforming people. Here my goal is to articulate the stakes in debates about SOGI human rights. As I explore in chapter 4, not all critics of SOGI human rights are invested in the safety and flourishing of LGBTQ people. For those who are so invested, I believe it makes sense to gather and analyze information on the efforts of US government officials and agencies to advance LGBTQ interests.

In making these arguments, it's important to highlight linguistic choices I make throughout this book. First, with regard to the central terminology of human rights in this study, many scholars, lawyers, and human rights professionals who work in the area of rights related to sexuality and gender use the term "sexual orientation and gender identity," abbreviated as SOGI, to modify "human rights." The advantage of this phrase is that it focuses attention on sexual and gender diversity while avoiding reifying particular linguistic categories of identity that people in global communities may not embrace. The alternative is to use some variation of an abbreviation that begins with LGBT and directs attention to the groups of people who are likely to be targeted for their minority sexuality or gender identity. An advantage of LGBT, LGBTQ (queer), LGBTI (intersex), LGBTA (asexual), or some combination of these or other identity markers is that such abbreviations are recognizable to and often embraced by audiences outside the human rights community. In the chapters to come, I use "sexual orientation and gender identity" or SOGI to refer to the category of human rights on which I focus. I use LGBTQ—or some related term or abbreviation that makes sense in the context—to refer to the people whose human rights are at issue when SOGI human rights are invoked and to the organizations that organize under that label. It's useful to note that for many US scholars and students of sexuality who problematize identity categories related to nonnormative sexualities and genders, terms such as "sexual orientation and gender identity" are themselves problematic. Unfortunately, I don't have space in this book to fully engage that debate.

Second, different intellectual communities make quite different uses of the term, "intervention." In discourse in and on foreign policy, "intervention"—often modified by particularistic national terms such as "American" or "US"—connotes a diplomatic statement or some use of diplomatic, economic, or military incentive, pressure, or coercion applied to bring about a desired result. In general, the Secretary of State, US diplomats and Foreign Service officers abroad, and others in policy positions in the US government engage in human rights interventions when they speak about human rights problems in public forums or in more private meetings with other government officials or human rights community actors. Less rhetorical and discursive human rights interventions occur when the US government integrates human rights concerns and conditions into its diplomacy, foreign aid, foreign policy, and immigration policy. By contrast, in intellectual discourse in the humanities, "intervention" connotes an act of analysis or interpretation of an object. Hence, in addressing these diverse intellectual settings, distinctions of usage must be differentiated from each other, and in this project I try to be as careful as possible not to elide these distinctions.

Many students and observers of the state of SOGI rights and the status and well-being of LGBTQ people in the world have noted declining support in many regions and jurisdictions for previously common forms of anti-LGBTQ harm and exclusion, and rising support for LGBTQ/SOGI rights. However, as many sources document, support for LGBTQ people, MSM, WSW, and people who express gender nonnormatively is uneven. Social exclusion, physical abuse, discrimination, and the threat of judicial penalties remain too common in much of the world. Given these realities, I would like to proffer what political theorist Jeffrey C. Isaac characterizes as "a qualified defense of the discourse of human rights and human rights interventionism" in the particular arena of SOGI rights.[82] In the chapters that follow, I use material obtained from formal and informal conversations with officials at the State Department and the US Agency for International Development. I make extensive use of scholarly texts as well as documents generated by US government agencies (especially the Department of State). I rely on information provided by organizations that work in the area of SOGI human rights, designing and executing programs to advance the cause as they understand it.

In literatures on LGBTQ identity and/or sexuality, it is easy enough to discern something like a left-right divide in opinion on support for minority sexualities and gender identities: social liberals and progressives generally support SOGI human rights, and Christian social conservatives generally oppose them. However, when we factor in the US government—its history, policies, resources, and standing as a world power—this relative simplicity breaks down. A deep distrust of government that no new information can allay threatens liberal-democratic institutions and some fragile commitments to human rights. The Christian right and the criti-cal humanist left aren't allies on SOGI human rights, but the conclusions these groups reach about US government support for SOGI human rights and the implications of those conclusions for human rights advocacy are depressingly similar. In 2017, at a time when support for human rights may become a quaint artifact of US history, a predisposition against assistance on the left and right can have deleterious effects on the lives of people outside the United States.

Some parts of the story of the inception and continuation of the US government's participation in efforts to support SOGI human rights abroad have been told, but so far those accounts have been piecemeal. In the chapters that follow, I fill in some of the blanks in this ongoing story. I think there are important questions to be asked: is it *possible* that some US government program or intervention might serve the needs or interests of LGBTQ people outside the United States? If so, what would count as a successful intervention? How would we know? To begin to answer such questions, we need to have more information; we need to understand the passionate opposition or ambivalence with which many Americans approach this subject and these questions. As a theorist, I am interested in articulations of values, beliefs, and principles of explanation that aim to influence political thought and practice, both within in the United States and for those who are affected by US power. I hope that such conversations, and the disagreements they inevitably bring to light, can help us be better stewards of our government's power and more responsible citizens, of both the United States and the world. This book is an attempt to engage in just such a conversation.

# Chapter 1

# The US Government and
# SOGI Human Rights Abroad

## The Early Years

## The Clinton Administration

In many respects, the story of SOGI human rights and the US government abroad begins in the 1990s during the Bill Clinton administration. However, in one important respect, the story begins before Clinton—either much earlier, in the McCarthy era, or in the modifications to federal government personnel policies in the 1970s and 1980s. Historians have documented the investigations and purges of civil servants in the federal government who were or were suspected to be gay in the 1950s. David K. Johnson's *The Lavender Scare: The Cold War Persecution of Gays and Lesbians in the Federal Government* is a key text for this dark period in US history. Relying on government documents and other sources, Johnson analyzes the tactics and the consequences of the "lavender scare"—also known as the "purge of the perverts"—and demonstrates that this institutional moral panic predated and outlasted the better known "red scare" of the same era.[1]

A particular focus of the efforts to identify and root out homosexuals in the federal government began with the Department of State in 1950 after a high-ranking official there testified before a congressional committee to his agency's dismissal of ninety-one homosexuals on the basis of their status as national security risks. The threat of a US government infiltrated by homosexuals whose allegiance to the nation might be compromised because of their underground lives set off the purges that forced thousands of state and federal government employees from their careers.[2] The firings and the rhetoric about homosexuals and same-sex sexuality that emerged in the 1950s reinforced the moral undesirability of homosexuals in ways that resonated well beyond the scope of government employment. Supplementing the historical evidence, Gregory B. Lewis relies on answers to questions about homosexuality and political tolerance on the General Social Survey throughout the 1990s to investigate an alternative explanation—besides the anxiety about blackmail of closeted gay people—for decades of antigay government employment practices. Lewis finds that respondents who scored high on attitudes of disgust for homosexuals and saw homosexuality as a "filthy secret" were more willing to support the investigation of prospective employees' private relationships and the denial of security clearances to people who engaged in same-sex relations than those who did not share those negative attitudes.[3] Such an analysis helps explain the formulation and maintenance of antigay politics in the absence of supporting evidence for the blackmail hypothesis.

Although homosexuals were not the only group expelled from government service, the Department of State scrutinized potential employees on the basis of homosexuality and denied security clearances to those who engaged in same-sex relations. Repeal of the antigay employment policies and practices didn't occur all at once. Instead, these changes took place in a piecemeal fashion throughout the Ford, Reagan, and George H. W. Bush administrations by way of personnel guidelines developed by the Civil Service Commission, which became the Office of Personnel Management.[4] The policy of federal government nondiscrimination on the basis of sexual orientation was formalized in 1998 by President Clinton's Executive Order 13087. Nearly twenty years later, on January 9, 2017, Secretary of State John Kerry acknowledged his agency's ugly history of antigay bias by offering a public apology to those who were harmed by its practices. Christian conservative organizations responded quickly to the apology, painting it as a desperate act of "cultural extremism" from a defeated political left.[5]

When scholars of LGBTQ politics and public attitudes narrate the history of LGBT issues and civil rights just before and during Clinton's terms in office, they usually begin with his campaign promise to end discrimination based on sexual orientation in the US military and the promulgation and institutionalization of the disastrous "Don't Ask, Don't Tell, Don't Pursue"—quickly abbreviated to "Don't Ask, Don't Tell (DADT)"—policy.[6] Clinton's foray into military policy and LGBTQ politics bitterly disappointed LGBT activists and many gay, lesbian, and bisexual citizens, some of whom were serving in the military at that time.

I begin to explore the early stages of programs of assistance to LGBTQ people outside the United States with a somewhat different focus: the founding of organizations of, by, and for LGBTQ federal employees that occurred in the years after the last vestiges of explicitly antigay employment practices were ended. It would be difficult to imagine the kind of open conversations about LGBTQ people as members of a marginalized population that have occurred in US foreign policy contexts in recent years if those prohibitions on their employment still prevailed. Hence, while the ending of discriminatory federal government labor practices isn't a sufficient condition for the emergence of a pro-SOGI human rights foreign policy orientation, I regard the change in labor practices as a necessary condition for the emergence of that orientation.

In 1992, just before Clinton took office, two such federal organizations were founded to advocate for and represent the interests of LGBTQ federal employees. Both began to function at a time when vociferously antigay and antilesbian arguments were being aired by figures outside the armed forces and up and down the military chain of command, and both are still in existence and active today. One of these is the Gay, Lesbian, Bisexual, Transgender Employees of the Federal Government (Federal GLOBE). The second, and the one most salient for our purposes, is the organization founded under the name Gays and Lesbians in Foreign Affairs Agencies (GLIFAA). GLIFAA was organized to represent LGBT federal employees in the Department of State, the US Agency for International Development (USAID), and several other agencies and work groups engaged in foreign affairs. Today, GLIFAA underscores its inclusiveness by substituting the motto "LGBT + Pride in Foreign Affairs Agencies" for the phrase "gays and lesbians" in its original title.[7]

While Federal GLOBE and GLIFAA came into existence during the final moments of the George H. W. Bush administration, the first milestone of Clinton's presidency with implications for LGBTQ people outside the United States was Attorney General Janet Reno's Order 1895–94. In it, Reno affirmed the right of immigrants to apply for asylum in the United States because of persecution or a well-founded fear of persecution related to identifying (or being identified) as gay or lesbian. The Board of Immigration Appeals had granted asylum to one such claimant in 1990. In 1994, Reno explicitly established the 1990 case as a precedent to be followed in situations where immigrants sought asylum based on persecution of same-sex sexuality.[8]

The next official action in the foreign affairs sector of the US government with regard to LGBT issues was Bill Clinton's 1997 nomination of gay philanthropist—and Hormel Foods Corporation heir—James Hormel to serve as the US ambassador to Luxembourg. Clinton nominated Hormel, a Democratic Party donor, but the usually routine process of Senate approval of ambassadorships hit a snag. Hormel's openness about his sexuality was the basis for opposition to his appointment from some congressional Republicans and from Christian right organizations such as the Family Research Council and the Traditional Values Coalition. The campaign against his nomination depicted Hormel as a gay activist, which he was; he was a founder of the Human Rights Campaign Fund and the funder of a collection of gay and lesbian materials that bears his name at the San Francisco Public Library. In the end, a 1999 recess appointment allowed Hormel to assume the position for which he had been nominated, and he became the first openly gay US ambassador in US history.

President George W. Bush nominated the first openly gay ambassador to be confirmed by the Senate in 2001.[9] Career foreign service officer Michael Guest, who became the ambassador to Romania, was also opposed by Christian right groups, who were particularly incensed when Secretary of State Colin Powell recognized Guest's partner at Guest's swearing-in. Guest, who was a critic of US government employment policies that discriminated against LGBT employees, is now a senior adviser at the Council for Global Equality.

When Hillary Clinton became Barack Obama's Secretary of State in 2009, she directed her staff to review departmental policies on domestic partner benefits to determine what benefits the agency could grant to same-sex domestic partners without running afoul of the Defense of Marriage Act (DOMA), which her husband had signed into law in 1996. In June 2009, Obama issued the "Memorandum on Federal Benefits and Non-Discrimination," which directed heads of executive branch agencies to extend same-sex partner benefits for federal employees to the extent possible under federal law at that time. Relying on the memorandum, Clinton's State Department extended benefits to same-sex partners of Foreign Service personnel abroad and modified its equal employment opportunity policies to add protection based on gender identity to already-existing protection based on sexual orientation for employees and job applicants.[10]

Openly gay ambassador nominees in the Obama administration did not attract the kind of opposition from conservative members of Congress that obstructed Hormel's nomination in 1997. For example, when Daniel

Baer, who had served at the State Department as Deputy Assistant Secretary for the Bureau of Democracy, Human Rights, and Labor under Hillary Clinton, was confirmed to serve as the ambassador to the Organization for Security and Cooperation in Europe in 2013, there was no congressional opposition to his appointment. The State Department even produced a video, available on YouTube, of the new ambassador discussing his post and his partner, Brian Walsh.[11] A final note on LGBT embassy personnel: the existence of a new organization with a low profile and a circumscribed membership testifies to an emerging community of international embassy staff in official Washington. Gays and Lesbians International, is a "cross-Embassy initiative connecting LGBTIQ people working in Embassies in [the] Washington D.C. area."[12]

For the link between reversal of official government discrimination based on sexual orientation and gender identity and pro-LGBT human rights foreign policy, consider Secretary of State John Kerry's remarks at the June 19, 2013, Pride @ State event. Pride @ State was held in the Dean Acheson Auditorium and was sponsored by the Office of Civil Rights and GLIFAA, and besides Secretary Kerry, speakers included Congressman John Lewis and Mara Keisling, executive director of the National Center for Transgender Equality.[13] Keisling delivered a speech on transgender issues in the United States and abroad. Lewis's remarks emphasized the continuity of race, sexuality, and gender-based forms of civil rights violations and demands. Invoking Martin Luther King Jr.'s ideal of a "beloved community," Lewis argued that the goal of civil rights struggles was to "let everybody live with dignity and with pride." Secretary Kerry, whose tenure at the department was still young at the time, was introduced by Kenneth Kero-Mentz, then the president of GLIFAA, as a friend of the LGBT community and one of only fourteen senators to vote against DOMA in 1996.

In his address, Kerry explicitly connected three contexts: the Department of State's repudiation of discrimination toward LGBTQ personnel, struggles for LGBTQ rights in the United States, and the role of agency personnel in advancing the human rights of LGBTQ people elsewhere in the world. Alluding to the history of discrimination within the Department of State and in other government agencies, Kerry asserted that in 2013 the agency "does not discriminate [against employees] on the basis of sexual orientation and gender identity." He lauded the Obama administration's refusal to "defend the constitutionality of DOMA," and he acknowledged continuing LGBT struggles over discriminatory immigration laws and policies and marriage equality. In spite of the fact that the United States had not ended all disparate treatment on the basis of nonnormative sexuality and gender identity, Kerry argued that the nation could and should work to set a global example for LGBT human rights and that the country would use the "tools of development and diplomacy" in support of "universal values" and "universal rights." As this brief discussion suggests, some preconditions for US government interest in and commitment to SOGI human rights abroad began to be sown over a decade before the State Department began to engage in pro-SOGI discourse and interventions.

## The Early Years: SOGI Before 2009

Reconstructing the story of US government advocacy on behalf of SOGI human rights abroad shows that these interventions didn't commence as a result of explicit direction from Congress or the executive branch. Instead, support for SOGI human rights emerged within the State Department as an extension of its commitment to human rights for a range of marginalized populations. This support operated in much the way it does today: through networks of US government officials, international actors (other governments and civil society organizations, or CSOs), and LGBTQ activists and organizations. SOGI interventions are different today in degree—that is, their scale and complexity has increased over time—but they are also different in kind. To investigate these differences, we must begin with interventions that occurred before President Obama and Secretary of State Hillary Clinton announced official US support for SOGI human rights in 2011.

### The Nazi Persecutee Relief Fund

The first initiative from within the Department of State on behalf of LGBTQ people's SOGI human rights outside the United States occurred quietly in 1999 and 2000, in the final years of the Clinton administration. The initiative emerged from the US role in a transnational movement to pursue concealed Holocaust-era assets and compensate survivors and heirs. In 1996, the Jewish World Congress persuaded Senator Al D'Amato (R-NY) to investigate the matter of assets seized and stolen by the Nazis between 1933 and 1945 without restitution, as well as restitution for slave labor and other forms of persecution. By the end of 1996, the Clinton administration had appointed Stuart Eizenstat as Special Representative of the President and Secretary of State on Holocaust-Era Issues and established a federal Interagency Group on Nazi Assets to investigate and issue reports on stolen assets. The goal was to provide restitution to Holocaust survivors and their heirs before the last survivors of the Nazi regime's mass murders vanished.[14] In addition, Holocaust survivors and heirs filed suit against Swiss banks in US and Swiss courts to recover assets held—and in many cases actively hidden—by the banks since the end of World War II. From these simultaneous challenges and investigations, a variety of reports, litigation, settlements, and new funding institutions ensued.[15]

One result of this movement was that the United States and United Kingdom established the international Nazi Persecutee Relief Fund (NPRF), launched in 1997 at the London Conference on Nazi Gold. The fund was created, first and foremost, to identify victims of Nazi expropriation and provide resources to needy survivors of Nazi persecution. The NPRF also outlined related purposes: first, cultural preservation of persecuted communities; second, commemoration and memorialization of victims.[16] Other countries were invited to join and contribute to the NPRF, and in 1999 the US Department of State announced that seventeen countries had pledged $61 million toward the goal of "bring[ing] justice to Holocaust survivors."[17] Under the rules that governed the NPRF, participating countries could select CSOs and projects to fund, and these CSOs would execute the projects in ways that were consistent with the goals of the NPRF. The United States pledged $25 million to the fund to be disbursed over a three-year period from 1998 to 2000; in 1998, the first $4 million was disbursed by the Department of State, which administered US NPRF funds, to the Conference on Jewish Material Claims against Germany (also known as the Claims Conference).

In 1998, in the midst of these international dialogues and legal advocacy on behalf of Holocaust victims, LGBTQ advocates and organizations founded the Pink Triangle Coalition in Berlin as an umbrella organization made up of LGBT advocacy organizations "working on behalf of gay and lesbian victims of the Nazis."[18] A key motivation for establishing the Pink Triangle Coalition was ensuring compensation for any gay and lesbian Holocaust survivors who could be identified and located. But the organization's mandate was broader:

- To ensure representation of the homosexual victims of the Nazis in the various international funds that are being or have been created (such as the Swiss Humanitarian Fund

and the Nazi Persecutee Relief Fund) with a view to maxi-
mizing resources for humanitarian aid to the few surviving
homosexual victims and for educational projects and ensuring
fair distribution of any such resources.

- To collect and disseminate information about the Nazi
  persecution of homosexuals with a view to involving other
  non-governmental organizations (NGOs) in efforts to document the history of this persecution, to commemorate the
  victims, and to support survivors.[19]

In 1999, Patricia Davis—now director of the Office of Global Programs
of the Bureau of Democracy, Human Rights, and Labor (DRL)—was the
program officer for Human Rights and Democracy in Europe.[20] Davis
knew that in addition to Jewish victims of Nazi persecution, there were
other groups of victims, such as homosexuals and Roma. She researched
organizations that might be capable of using funds to assist less high-
profile survivors and engage in projects of commemoration that would be
consistent with the intentions of the NPRF. In the course of her research,
she learned about the Pink Triangle Coalition and contacted them to invite
them to apply for funding.[21]

The Pink Triangle Coalition applied to the State Department for
a portion of the US funds allocated for the NPRF to materially support
projects related to Nazi persecution of gay men and lesbians. For the 1999
funding cycle, Davis chaired a committee that selected the Pink Triangle
Coalition's proposal and allocated $72,000 for the coalition to distribute
to seven gay men who had been identified as survivors of Nazi antigay
persecution during the Holocaust. In 2000, the Pink Triangle Coalition
partnered with the Astraea Lesbian Foundation for Justice to request
additional monies from the NPRF. In the next round of allocations, Davis
chaired the committee that selected the coalition's proposal for a total of
$528,000. Of these funds, $212,000 went to the Magnus Hirschfeld Gesellschaft in Berlin to document the destruction of the Institute for Sexual
Sciences[22] in 1933; $238,000 went toward distribution of the Holocaust
documentary *Paragraph 175*, which focused on Nazi persecution of gay
men, lesbians, and their communities during the Third Reich; $30,000 went
to Berlin's LGBT Schwules Museum to financially support an exhibition
and book on underground gay community in Berlin from 1933 to 1945;
and $14,000 was directed to gay survivors of the Nazis.[23] The funds were
approved by Special Representative Stuart Eizenstat.

US government funding related to LGBT Holocaust survivors and projects related to Nazi persecution of LGBTQ people encouraged other countries to direct some restitution to the Pink Triangle Coalition. In this sense, the US distribution of NPRF funding helped raise the profile of Nazi persecution of gay men and lesbians who, after the war, were the most stigmatized of all groups targeted by the Nazis. A postscript to this story is that in 2001 the Pink Triangle Coalition initiated legal action to secure 1 percent of settlement funds that had been created as a result of class action suits against Swiss banks.[24] A *cy pres* distribution provides a method for distributing funds from, for example, class action settlements when direct claimants are not available. The justification request for a *cy pres* distribution was that "for a series of historical reasons, extremely few victims of Nazi persecution [could] be identified."[25] The coalition proposed to use settlement funds for gay Holocaust education, commemoration, and research and prevention of persecution on the basis of sexual orientation. Based on the existence of other needy Holocaust survivors, the special master for the US District Court for the Eastern District of New York and the US Court of Appeals ruled against the Pink Triangle Coalition's request. The funding of projects related to Nazi persecution of lesbians and gay men in 1999 and 2000 proceeded without political backlash in the United States. Indeed, it was only in the early 2000s that assistance related to sexual orientation human rights came to the attention of a small audience of critics in the United States. The episode was a scandal over "gay billboards" in the Balkan nation of the Republic of Macedonia.

### The "Gay Billboards Scandal"

President George W. Bush took office in 2001, and from 2001 to 2008 his administration did not publicly defend policies or practices specifically intended to advance SOGI human rights. However, in 2003, the willingness of some US officials to consider LGBTQ people as a group vulnerable to human rights violations set the conditions for a SOGI intervention in the Balkans that sparked controversy and embarrassed the US ambassador to Macedonia: the Macedonian LGBT billboard campaign, referred to in retrospect by one commentator as the "gay billboards scandal."[26]

Although some aspects of the intervention are disputed, what is clear from various published accounts is that the Center for Civil and Human Rights (CCHR), a Macedonian LGBTQ organization that at the time was the only one of its kind in the country, received $20,000 from the US government that was part of a tranche of funding for human rights programming. With those funds, the CCHR erected a number of billboards in the capital, Skopje, and other cities. The billboards featured pictures of same-sex couples and read: "Face Reality, The Campaign to Promote the Rights of Sexual Minorities." The most controversial element of the public education campaign? Typically, grantees who receive congressionally appropriated foreign assistance are required to "mark" or "brand" any product of US government assistance to designate it as US-funded.[27] In accordance with this marking policy, the lower right corner of each billboard featured the seal of the US embassy in Skopje.

The billboard campaign received no public attention in the United States until early 2004, when the conservative *National Review* reported on it and described it as a noxious example of the Department of State "work[ing] for the American left in Macedonia." Juxtaposing putatively genuine problems in the Balkan nation to the LGBT campaign, the article held that

> against th[e] backdrop of critical economic and identity development as well as ethnic unrest, the vast majority of Macedonians think that homosexuality is a disease. Therefore, the U.S. embassy in Macedonia is using U.S. taxpayer dollars to erect billboards promoting the homosexual agenda.

Blame for this intervention was assigned to the State Department and to Lawrence Butler, who was then the US ambassador to Macedonia. The *National Review* cast Butler as having "vast European experience, particularly in the Balkans" that made his "egregious and ill-advised" decision to sponsor the billboards more perplexing. Alluding to a group of Macedonian women with whom the article's author, Kerri Houston, met to talk about politics unrelated to the billboards, the article concludes with an argument for respecting cultural differences: "The Macedonian women have it right—America's greatest gift to their nation should be the export of economic and individual liberty, wrapped in respect for the country's historic and deeply held cultural and religious beliefs."[28]

Immediately after the *National Review* expressed outrage over the billboards as an example of US liberals exporting "the homosexual agenda of the American left," State Department spokesperson Kurtis Cooper defended granting funds to the CCHR while denying that either the Department of State or the US embassy in Macedonia sanctioned the billboards. Instead, he said, the grant to the LGBTQ group was a reflection of the State Department's "policy of supporting tolerance and human dignity" and was allocated to provide "legal assistance and counseling to victims of discrimination."[29]

Reports of the affair of the Macedonian LGBTQ billboards diverge on significant points such that it's not clear whether the billboards were erected with the approval of the US ambassador or other embassy personnel. It may be that US officials didn't approve the use of the funds for a public information campaign and that the CCHR used funds intended for legal assistance and counseling for the billboards. Conversely, it may be possible that the US embassy did greenlight the billboards. Interestingly, two accounts of the incident assume the ambassador's approval but situate the intervention in very different contexts. In *Balkanalysis*, Chris Deliso emphasizes the animus of Ambassador Butler—a Clinton administration appointee—toward Macedonian President Boris Trajkovski, the Bush administration's "family-values agenda," and the International Republican Institute, an international prodemocracy CSO with a board of prominent Republicans chaired by Senator John McCain.[30] By contrast, writing for the *Institute for War and Peace Reporting*, Ana Petruseva describes Macedonia in terms of pervasive discrimination and hostility against LGBT people and argues that the billboards "sparked a fresh debate over homosexual rights" that evoked some domestic support for sexual diversity.[31]

Either way, the State Department appropriated funds to an LGBTQ rights organization abroad for a purpose related to SOGI human rights. Hence, it appears that the funding process that resulted in the Macedonian billboard scandal was an early example of "embassy engagement" in SOGI human rights before such engagement was institutionalized as part of the mission of US embassies during the State Department tenure of Hillary Clinton. In her *National Review* article, Houston argued that "It seems that in Macedonia at least, support for the homosexual agenda has become the official position of the U.S. State Department." In spite of the questions that remain about this episode, it is possible to conclude with confidence that although that day would come, in 2003 support for the homosexual agenda had not yet become the official public position of the US Department of State. This state of policy with regard to SOGI and LGBTQ people was evident in the early 2000s in the President's Emergency Plan for AIDS Relief. The program, which is still in operation, quickly became better known among US LGBTQ activists for what it didn't do than for what it did.

*The President's Emergency Plan for AIDS Relief*

A high-profile international US government program began in 2003 when Congress passed and President George W. Bush signed into law the United States Leadership against HIV/AIDS, Tuberculosis, and Malaria Act, also known as the Global AIDS Act. The law wasn't originally implemented in a way that was directly related to SOGI human rights; however, both criticisms and modifications made over time to associated programs necessitate its inclusion in a comprehensive history of US government advocacy for SOGI human rights.

Beginning in the mid-1990s, the Clinton administration implemented domestic US initiatives and the UN initiated international initiatives to confront the global AIDS pandemic. From 2001, the George W. Bush administration also engaged in other HIV/AIDS initiatives, including one aimed at reducing mother-to-child HIV transmission in Africa. The Global AIDS Act dwarfed these efforts in scope and funding. The law, supported by a broad coalition of Democrats and Republicans in Congress and a range of liberal and conservative CSOs, created the office of Global AIDS Coordinator within the State Department and the US President's Emergency Plan for AIDS Relief (PEPFAR).[32] Bush appointed and the Senate confirmed Randall L. Tobias, a former CEO of pharmaceutical giant Eli Lilly, to be the first Global AIDS Coordinator. Later, Tobias was promoted to be the Bush administration's first director of Foreign Assistance, a position that included serving as the administrator of USAID, but Tobias resigned in 2007 for "personal reasons" after he was named as a client of Deborah Jeane Palfrey, the "D.C. Madam."[33]

In the years since its creation, PEPFAR has been credited as being as "the largest international health initiative in history for a specific disease."[34] The program has been divided into phases that reflect a series of five-year plans. Phase one, which ended in 2007, was the emergency response phase; phase two, 2008 to 2012, focused on sustainability; and phase three, 2013 to the present, is focused on "transparency and accountability for impact, as well as accelerating core interventions for epidemic control."[35]

There have also been many criticisms of PEPFAR. Some of these, such as accusations of fiscal mismanagement (including aggrandizing pharmaceutical companies) and concerns that unilateral US programming undercuts multilateral approaches, are not directly related to concerns about gender, sexuality, and SOGI policy. More directly related to SOGI, HIV/AIDS advocates and scholars in the United States have criticized PEPFAR, the Bush administration, and later the Obama administration over specific aspects of the planning and execution of the program. Criticisms include the charge that the Bush administration made PEPFAR an instrument to extend American conservative moral views about sexuality outside the United States. This conservative policy orientation had many results, including an emphasis on sexual abstinence, marginalizing condoms as a means of HIV prevention, and stigmatizing (and silencing) sex workers.

The most consistent criticism of PEPFAR from advocates and scholars of sexual health was the commitment to sexual abstinence education and programming embedded in the law: the approach known as "ABC" for "abstinence, be faithful, use a condom." ABC predated PEPFAR, but critics pointed out that "the Bush administration redefined the 'ABC' approach as a preference for abstinence-until-marriage programming," an approach that constituted an extension abroad of abstinence-only sex education in the United States.[36] Critics explicitly characterized this approach as heteronormative, that is, supporting "institutions, structures of understanding, and practical orientations" that privilege heterosexuality and render same-sex sexuality invisible.[37] For example, scholars argued that millions of dollars of funds were disbursed to "severely afflicted regions" under PEPFAR by "insinuating the heteronormative, conjugal, and procreative model of sexuality so dear to the hearts of the US Christian Right into the criteria for receiving funding."[38] However, for critics, even the assumed heteronormativity of ABC was better for fighting HIV/AIDS transmission than exemptions tendered to faith-based providers funded through the law to reject condom distribution as a strategy for preventing HIV transmission.[39]

In addition to expressing Christian conservative morality through its emphasis on abstinence/fidelity, PEPFAR conflated sex work with sex trafficking, explicitly denied funding for sex worker advocacy, and instituted an antiprostitution pledge that organizations had to sign in a grant application or agreement to receive PEPFAR funds and other US assistance. From the inception of the program, health and other advocacy organizations resisted and protested the pledge while Christian conservative organizations lobbied to retain it. It was not until 2013 that the Supreme Court ruled the antiprostitution pledge unconstitutional on First Amendment grounds in *Agency for International Development v. Alliance for Open Society International*. Even then, some government agencies interpreted the decision as applying only to domestic organizations, not to foreign CSOs or foreign affiliates of domestic groups. It wasn't until early 2015 that a federal court ruled in effect that "the First Amendment doesn't stop at the U.S. border."[40] Until it was struck down, the pledge was a contentious issue in SOGI human rights advocacy for many reasons, including because the policy contributed to stigmatizing sex workers as morally defective; because many rights groups practice simultaneous LGBTQ and sex worker advocacy; and because sex workers, disproportionately at risk for HIV/AIDS, are a key constituency in treating and preventing the disease.

As John W. Dietrich reminds us in his succinct 2007 analysis, PEPFAR is "a public health program" that is "also a political program."[41] In this, PEPFAR isn't unique; indeed, different political processes brought to bear during the Bush and Obama administrations shaped the terms and implementation of PEPFAR in these different political moments. In their famous analysis of the "social construction of target populations," Anne Schneider and Helen Ingram demonstrate that government policies and the programs they create do not merely serve particular target populations. Instead, every part of the policy process is shaped by the political influence of groups and the social attributions—from negative to positive—by which groups are defined in their social context.[42] Such an approach can help us understand how the administration of PEPFAR has changed over time as a result of the influence of Christian conservatives during the Bush administration and the ascendance of LGBTQ political voices during the Obama administration. This shift from Christian conservative to LGBTQ political influence in the White House set conditions for policy changes that were more significant than Christian conservatives would have liked and less decisive than LGBTQ people had hoped. To understand these changes, we can begin by examining the relationship between the Democratic Party and LGBTQ citizens.

## The Obama Years: 2009–2011

Since lesbian, gay, and bisexual (LGB) voting behavior began to be studied systematically in the 1980s, LGB people have been known to be such a loyal Democratic Party voting bloc that in recent years this loyalty has raised concerns of political scientists about LGB electoral capture. Analyzing a broad literature on LGBT voting and polling data from the 2000 election, Gregory Lewis, Marc Rogers, and Kenneth Sherrill confirm multiple factors that motivated high percentages of LGB voters to identify as politically liberal across policy domains and support Democratic candidates for president at a higher rate than did straight voters. These factors included interest in LGBT civil rights and political socialization within the LGBT community. Indeed, the stable political liberalism of LGB voters in the United States is striking because even without the intergenerational transmission afforded in ethnic families, "LGBs [are] as consistent a Democratic voting bloc as Jews, Latinos, and the non-religious, and nearly as consistent as African Americans."[43] In the presidential election of 2000, researchers determined that 71 percent of LGB voters voted for the Democratic candidate, Al Gore, and 25 percent voted for George W. Bush.[44]

Eight years later, 70 percent of voters who identified as LGB supported Obama, while 27 percent voted for the McCain/Palin ticket. In 2012, 76 percent of LGB voters supported Obama over his rival, Mitt Romney, and analysts from the Williams Institute on Sexual Orientation and Gender Identity Law and Public Policy at UCLA argued that this bloc was decisive in Obama's reelection.[45] This means that although LGBTQ people and activists were widely reported to be unsatisfied with Obama's performance on LGBTQ issues at the conclusion of his first term, Obama won an equivalent or slightly higher percentage of the measurable LGB vote in his reelection campaign than he had in 2008.

When Obama ran for president in 2008, he endorsed LGBT civil rights and civil unions (not marriage) for same-sex couples. By 2012, it was well known that Obama, who had represented his perspective on same-sex marriage as "evolving," was closer to endorsing marriage equality. However, it was Vice President Joe Biden who came out in support of same-sex marriage in an unscripted moment on *Meet the Press*.[46] Obama's endorsement followed soon thereafter. In the 2012 presidential election campaign, white and African American Christian conservatives vowed to leverage Obama's endorsement of same-sex marriage against him during the campaign. That effort ultimately failed to derail the president's reelection. But the issue of Obama's views on marriage equality was revived in 2015 when his close aide, David Axelrod, revealed that he and other advisers had encouraged the president to misrepresent his position on same-sex marriage during the 2008 presidential campaign for political advantage and that Obama had accepted this advice.[47] Obama contested Axelrod's interpretation of his views.[48] This brief public transcript of the relationship of Obama and his administration to LGBTQ communities in the United States can be understood as a context for the policy debates and revisions that occurred thereafter, including those surrounding PEPFAR.

## PEPFAR Redux

PEPFAR was a legacy of the George W. Bush administration to the Obama administration. After the transition from the Republican to the Democratic administration, critics of PEPFAR—including Democratic and progressive constituencies and HIV/AIDS researchers—began to exert pressure to modify the program in ways that would repair some of what these critics understood to be its deficiencies. In 2010, the Center for American Progress and the LGBTQ CSO Council for Global Equality coproduced a report written by Scott H. Evertz titled "How Ideology Trumped Science: Why PEPFAR Has Failed to Meet its Potential." The preface to the report identifies Evertz as

> the former director of President George W. Bush's Office of National AIDS Policy and an openly gay Republican [whose] analysis reflects a degree of experience and honesty that is too often obscured by the rigid ideology and partisan policymaking that have—up until now—been the cornerstones of PEPFAR and the Bush administration's bilateral funding strategy.

Evertz's report is indeed critical of PEPFAR. The first paragraph of the preface acknowledges the positive health impact of the program while bluntly stating the major criticisms against it as costs that had damaged PEPFAR's efficacy:

> The President's Emergency Plan for AIDS Relief has saved many lives and profoundly shaped the global response to HIV. But like the proverbial Trojan Horse, it has been let into the gates with a belly full of hidden contradictions—insufficient attention to marginalized communities, earmarks for unscientific programming, and forced "pledges" that both undermine sound reproductive rights programming and challenge basic rights to freedom of expression.

Early in the report, Evertz cites the enthusiasm and goodwill PEPFAR originally engendered across the political spectrum from the Christian right (Rick Warren) to the international activist left (Bono). He acknowledges the diverse ways large-scale public programs can fail under the best of circumstances, from the stages of legislative negotiation and bureaucratic

interpretation to implementation. However, the report focuses most attention on the details of Evertz's indictment of PEPFAR's "flawed framework"
"that placed ideology [specifically, "religious ideology"] above science." It's
no surprise that as a result of his support for condoms and his criticisms of
abstinence-only provisions, Evertz served only a little over a year (2001–2)
as director of National AIDS Policy. When the report was published in 2010,
Evertz expressed hopefulness that the Obama administration's approach
to PEPFAR would be evidence-based and that the administration would
"infuse PEPFAR with its own vision and principles."[49]

Indeed, the Obama administration presented an opportunity for
researchers and activists to revise PEPFAR to meet their specifications. In
early 2011, 146 LGBT, HIV/AIDS, and global health CSOs collaborated
on a letter to Global AIDS Coordinator Dr. Eric Goosby that called for
modifications to PEPFAR to recognize the specific needs and risk factors of
men who have sex with men (MSM) to better serve this population.[50] Before
Goosby was appointed to head the Global AIDS Office, he had decades
of experience with HIV/AIDS as a physician in San Francisco and as a
government official administering the Ryan White Care Act. Working with
the LGBTQ, HIV/AIDS, and health communities, Goosby's office modified
the administration of PEPFAR in 2011 by developing and disseminating a
Technical Guidance on Combination HIV Prevention, a "guidance document
[that] addresses prevention programs for Men Who Have Sex with Men."

The technical guidance is a fascinating policy document that can
be read as an incisive commentary on how to think about the disease
as well as the social, legal, medical, behavioral, and policy challenges
that interventions must confront. It begins by reframing the HIV/AIDS
epidemic as "multiple epidemics within diverse populations and social
networks," some of which are stigmatized populations, "marginalized
and discriminated against." The document calls for all parties engaged
with PEPFAR—US government agencies, US embassies, country teams,
and other implementing partners—to commit to "evidence-based HIV
prevention with MSM" and details services, modes of outreach, and best
practices for "optimiz[ing] HIV prevention with MSM." The document
also explicitly ties its mandate to serve MSM with the protection of the
human rights of this stigmatized and marginalized group, arguing that

> reducing HIV risk among MSM will require rapid introduction,
> scaling up and strengthening of comprehensive HIV preven-
> tion programs for MSM and their sex partners as well as the

expansion of laws, regulations and policies that support the
human rights of MSM, improve the ability of MSM to access
HIV care and treatment[,] and enhance HIV prevention (4).[51]

In December 2013, in response to critiques of the program and new
evidence garnered from its operation, PEPFAR published an "Updated
Gender Strategy" that focused on the significance of sex, gender, and
gender identity for preventing and treating HIV/AIDS. The Updated
Gender Strategy was:

> designed to help programs recognize the critical role gender
> norms and inequality play in the HIV epidemic, ensure equity
> in access to HIV programs and services, and take concrete
> steps to respond to the unique needs of different populations.
> It emphasizes the importance of understanding the needs of
> populations whose sex (women and girls), gender identity
> (transgender persons), sexual orientation (lesbian, gay and
> bi-sexual populations—LGBT), and/or sexual behavior (men
> who have sex with men, sex workers) make them vulnerable
> to HIV.[52]

The strategy is one of several cognate studies, reports, and statements
intended to strengthen PEPFAR research, monitoring, and implementation
with regard to gender equality, gender-based violence (GBV), sexualities,
and transgender identity. It addresses the extraordinary vulnerability
of women and girls to HIV infection and GBV, as well as how gender
scripts and expectations may enhance risky behaviors among men and
boys. Integrated with these concerns are issues of sexual orientation and
gender identity that were ignored or discounted in PEPFAR's early years.

It's common for federal programs to survive the administration
in which in which they were first implemented. As a headline in the
*Washington Post*—"Bush's Legacy on AIDS Trails Obama in Africa"—
suggests, such policy legacies can create problems and opportunities
for new administrations. For example, HIV/AIDS activists and medical
professionals expressed concern during the Obama administration about
budget constraints from the Great Recession that seemed to signal that
the United States was "retreating from AIDS."[53] And dimensions of the
law and its administration that are relevant to SOGI have been challenged
by US critics under the Obama administration in a way that would have

been unlikely during the Bush administration. This includes critics who have exposed and criticized some organizations that have received PEP-FAR aid as homophobic and as withholding US government funds from LGBTQ communities.[54] As criticisms and challenges to PEPFAR illustrate, activism can have an effect on the interpretation and implementation of government policies.

Another policy legacy of previous administrations to the current administration is the annual Country Reports on Human Rights Practices, now forty years old. Beginning in 1977, in a context of debate over the place of human rights in US foreign policy, Congress required the State Department to produce and submit annual country reports beginning in 1977 (for human rights conditions in 1976). President Jimmy Carter famously aspired to infuse his administration's foreign policy with a moral and humanitarian perspective.[55] The country reports on human rights conditions were an instantiation of this emphasis on the values and prac-tices of nations, although they also represented a culmination of years of efforts by some policy makers and citizens to commit the United States to taking human rights into account in foreign policy.

### Country Reports on Human Rights Practices

A public sign of the increased salience of SOGI human rights in the Obama administration was a revision to the State Department's annual Country Reports on Human Rights Practices. In the early 1970s, most attention to human rights conditions abroad originated in Congress and CSOs and was resisted (for different reasons) within the executive branch by presidents and by the State Department. With regard to the latter, scholars identify one potential pitfall of diplomacy as "clientitis," an effect of perceived "patron–client relations" between United States and foreign officials that may encourage US officials to promote "good relations" with countries with which they work and interfere with officials' ability to confront foreign states or officials with criticisms.[56] By contrast, the integration of human rights into the foreign policy of states sometimes calls for a demarch, which the State Department's Foreign Service Institute defines as "a request or intercession with a foreign official, e.g., a request for support of a policy, or a protest about the host government's policy or actions."[57]

Congress responded to executive branch resistance to human rights policy by inserting human rights provisions into legislation (such as the 1973 Foreign Assistance Act) and passing "country-specific legislation" that would "put the president and abusing states on notice that their behavior would not go unnoticed." As Clair Apodaca argues in her account of the evolution of US human rights policy, members of Congress, human rights CSOs, and public opinion all contributed to the development of this policy, often over the objections of presidents, State Department officials, and foreign policy "realists."[58]

Besides publicizing human rights conditions generally, the country reports have more specific effects; they enhance the information about human rights conditions that policy makers and diplomats use to formulate policy, and they complicate the ability of presidents and legislators to formulate foreign policy without taking human rights into account.[59] The process by which country reports are produced illuminates the changing contents and focuses of the reports over time. By September of each year, all US embassies produce and forward a draft of their report of human rights practices in the country in which they serve for that current year. Embassies send the drafts to the DRL, which uses the drafts to produce a final version of each country report. The format of the reports changes over time; embassies are only required to report on human rights categories identified by DRL, and DRL communicates updates to categories for which information will have to be collected and reported. Until DRL categories are revised, embassies may report on human rights issues that go beyond the scope of DRL requirements, although it's likely that some such reports have been rejected in the past as not fitting defined categories of human rights jeopardy. One State Department informant suggested to me that an attempt to report the climate for SOGI human rights in one country in the late 1990s was rejected for just this reason. In recent years, major category additions include human rights related to LGBT issues and internet freedom.

For most of their history, country reports haven't captured threats, violence, and discrimination based on SOGI. Before 2010, some harms perpetrated against LGBTQ people were listed under a miscellaneous category of "Other Societal Abuses and Discrimination" for each country, but there was no required category for assessing the human rights situation of LGBTQ people. Looking at the 2008 country reports (published in 2009), the entry for the Republic of Serbia provides an example of including LGBTQ human rights in the miscellaneous category. The report on Serbia details national attitudes toward same-sex sexuality as measured by survey research ("homosexuality is a disease and represents a threat to society"); the role of neo-Nazi and right-wing groups in supporting anti-LGBT activities and attitudes; street violence and threats against LGBT people; a court decision upholding the right of LGBT people to be free of threats (and the failure of some authorities, including police, to recognize the decision); and underreporting of HIV and discrimination against people with AIDS (including refusal of medical care).[60]

Beginning with the 2009 country reports—published by the State Department in early 2010—the targeting of LGBTQ people was denoted in a distinct category: "Societal Abuses, Discrimination, and Acts of Violence Based on Sexual Orientation and Gender Identity." This addition of a dedicated category for SOGI human rights was instated under Secretary Clinton and Daniel Baer, then Deputy Assistant Secretary for DRL. For the published volume of 2009 country reports, a general heading of "Discrimination or Harassment of Vulnerable Groups" in the introduction begins in this way:

> Members of vulnerable groups—racial, ethnic and religious minorities; the disabled; women and children; migrant workers; and lesbian, gay, bisexual and transgender individuals—often were marginalized and targets of societal and/or government-sanctioned abuse.[61]

In the individual reports that followed, information regarding a wide range of issues related to human rights practices was delivered in concrete prose with little editorializing.

For Albania, a country not usually included in lists of the worst anti-LGBT human rights abuses, under the heading "Section 6: Discrimination, Societal Abuses, and Trafficking in Persons," the subheading "Societal Abuses, Discrimination, and Acts of Violence Based on Sexual Orientation and Gender Identity" consists of two paragraphs. The first makes note of the state of criminalization of same-sex sexual behavior (none in Albania), the status of LGBT-oriented organizations ("few"), and the "repeated reports" of violence and employment (and other) discrimination on the basis of SOGI. The second paragraph expounds on these themes, giving examples of disparate treatment of LGBT and non-LGBT people, charges of societal and police discrimination, and the absence of specific legal protections for LGBTQ people.[62]

Human rights professionals and other US citizens have been critical of the official country reports because they focus attention outside the United States instead of on violations of human rights within the nation or violations abroad by agents of the US government. A concern with elisions of official US actions that violate human rights is well taken and was acknowledged by the Department of State in the introduction to its 2009 reports.

> Some critics, in the United States and elsewhere, also have challenged our practice of reviewing every other country's human rights record but not our own. In fact, the U.S. Government reports on and assesses our own human rights record in many other fora pursuant to our treaty obligations. . . . We are reviewing our reporting, consistent with President Obama and Secretary Clinton's pledge that we will apply a single universal human rights standard to all, including ourselves. . . . And in the fall the U.S. Government will appear before the United Nations Human Rights Council for the first Universal Periodic Review of our domestic human rights situation.

This set of reports was produced in early 2010, at the conclusion of Obama's first year in office and Clinton's first year as Secretary of State, and may be read as a rhetorical expression of the administration's public commitment to respect human rights.[63]

Although the Department of State has not been authorized to report on human rights conditions inside the United States or human rights violations committed abroad by the US government in its country reports, that oversight function has been assumed by nongovernment CSO human rights actors. For example, beginning not long after its founding in 1978, Human Rights First began to publish annual responses to the country reports by reporting on US human rights practices. Amnesty International's germinal 1997 global report on SOGI human rights, *Breaking the Silence*, documents antigay laws and hate crimes based on sexuality or sexual identity in the United States, just as it does anti-LGBT laws and hate crimes in other nations.[64] HRF, Amnesty International, and other human rights organizations also publish reports challenging human rights violations inside the United States related to a range of issues that include discrimination based on SOGI, police profiling and violence, capital punishment, and mass incarceration.

As we shall see in chapter 2, a common critique of US foreign policy and human rights discourse from the progressive left and critical humanists is of US hypocrisy: the claim that the US government uses, for example, human rights discourse or interventions to further its own interests while committing similar or worse violations with impunity. Domestic human rights CSOs, journalists, scholars, and others have used a variety of tools to publicize official wrongdoing and harms. Taken together, these reports, publications, and forums present a valuable picture of human rights within and committed by the United States. However, as the introduction to the 2009 reports points out, a newer international strategy for assessing the human rights record and conditions of nations now exists; under the imprimatur of the UN, this strategy is the Universal Periodic Review.

### UN Universal Periodic Review

In addition to academic scholarship on violations of human rights and human rights oversight by voluntary-sector groups in the United States, in recent years there is an institutionalized international mechanism for reporting and evaluating the human rights record of all UN member states: the UN's Universal Periodic Review (UPR). Established by the UN General Assembly in 2006, the UPR is a "peer review–based initiative" conducted under the auspices of the Human Rights Council.[65] Through the UPR, member states submit a report of human rights conditions in their nations to the Human Rights Council approximately every four and a half years. In 2010, US government representatives first appeared before the Human Rights Council to participate in a review of US human rights policies and practices from the perspective of compliance with international human rights law. In preparation for its UPR review, the US officials engaged in a Civil Society Consultation process that entailed holding town hall meetings in major cities, soliciting testimony from citizens and groups, and preparing a report to submit to the council.

An important feature of UPRs is that human rights CSOs in the country whose government is undergoing the review may submit "shadow reports" that can do any or all of the following: provide information about human rights conditions omitted from a country's official record, challenge the official state account, or highlight conditions that reporting organizations believe should be incorporated into a government's human rights assessment and action plans. Human rights groups have produced shadow reports on conditions in many nations, including the United States. For example, in 2010, the Council for Global Equality, an umbrella organization of nineteen human rights groups, collaborated to produce a shadow report for the US UPR that surveyed the state of LGBTQ human rights across several categories. These included hate crimes, employment discrimination, family recognition, immigration, and state ballot measures.[66]

In response to the 2010 UPR, the United States received 228 international recommendations on human rights issues from UN member states, 3 of which—recommendations 86, 112, 116—were related to the human rights of LGBTQ people. The passage below, from the State Department's UPR Working Group, lists these recommendations and a single "US Position" statement that restates the recommendation and appears to qualify the suggestion contained in Recommendation 86 to undertake public service campaigns to raise awareness of and counter stereotypes and violence against LGBT people and sex workers.

> **Recommendations 86 and 112**: (86) Undertake awareness-raising campaigns for combating stereotypes and violence against gays, lesbians, bisexuals and transsexuals, and ensure access to public services paying attention to the special vulnerability of sexual workers to violence and human rights abuses; (112) Take measures to comprehensively address discrimination against individuals on the basis of their sexual orientation or gender identity.

> **U.S. position**: We agree that no one should face violence or discrimination in access to public services based on sexual orientation or their status as a person in prostitution, as these recommendations suggest. We have recently taken concrete steps to address discrimination on the basis of sexual orientation and gender identity, and are engaged in further efforts.

> **Recommendation 116**: Continue its intense efforts to undertake all necessary measures to ensure fair and equal treatment of all persons, without regard to sex, race, religion, colour, creed, sexual orientation, gender identity or disability, and encourage further steps in this regard.[67]

It's important to note that although LGBTQ rights organizations criticized the human rights situation for LGBTQ people in the United States, conservatives excoriated the Obama administration for supporting the Human Rights Council and for participating in the UPR process at all.

For conservatives, the UPR provided a process by which the United States could be inappropriately "targeted by human rights abusers."[68]

More recently, in early 2015, the United States submitted its second UPR report. In preparation for this review, the Williams Institute delivered a statement on LGBT human rights in the United States to the Department of State as a component of the Civil Society Consultation and published the statement online. The "Universal Periodic Review of the United States: Sub-group on Civil Rights and Racial and Ethnic Discrimination Issues" statement establishes continuity with the previous UPR recommendations and responses. Addressing UPR Recommendations 86, 112, and 116, the statement points to failures and deficiencies in these areas and prescribes policy solutions. This SOGI-focused agenda clarifies that intersectional issues of "race, gender, disability, homelessness, religion, and criminal justice" are "of central importance to the lives of many LGBT people" and thus must be addressed simultaneously.[69] As an additional contribution to the UPR consultation process, the Williams Institute called for the formation of a National Human Rights Institution that "would have the powers to investigate all types of human rights violations, including discrimination against LGBT people in the workplace, schools, public benefits programs, healthcare systems, and at the hands of police." Such an institution would have adequate independence and resources to research, monitor, investigate, and facilitate remedies for "systematic and structural disparities."[70] If it were to be created, its mandate would be complicated by a federal system in which states are responsible for many domains of law implicated in human rights violations.

Under the category of "Civil Rights and Discrimination," the 2015 US UPR report enumerates forms of legal and other progress in resolving "discrimination against lesbian, gay, bisexual, and transgender individuals." These forms of progress included the Supreme Court decision in *United States v. Windsor* and policy changes compatible with the partial nullification of the Defense of Marriage Act (struck down in 2016); efforts to resolve discrimination and harassment against LGBT students in public schools; transgender training for law enforcement officers; efforts to prohibit SOGI discrimination in federal employment; the extension of the federal ban on sex discrimination in employment to discrimination based on gender identity and transgender status; and final repeal of Don't Ask, Don't Tell.[71]

The UPR process for each country engages citizens, CSOs, and government agencies to document and engage in advocacy and contestation over SOGI/LGBTQ rights. According to some transnational SOGI human rights activists, the process also offers opportunities for SOGI human rights advocates to "promote, protect and advance SOGIE rights."[72] Attendees of the ILGA World conference held in Bangkok in late 2016 were invited to join "UPR experts, LGBTI activists and diplomats" at a side event on the promise of the UPR process as "a political tool to advance SOGIE Rights."[73] Conferees received a booklet produced by ARC International, the International Bar Association's Human Rights Institute, and ILGA. The booklet, "Sexual Orientation, Gender Identity and Expression, and Sex Characteristics, at the Universal Periodic Review," informs readers about the activist uses of the UPR and characterizes it as "a crucial platform to make visible a wide array of human rights violations against LGBTI persons worldwide and to hold states to account."[74]

Between the first UPR of the United States in 2010 and Hillary Clinton's SOGI human rights speech in 2011, DRL launched a human rights emergency assistance program to provide "legal representation, security, and, when necessary, relocation support" to human rights defenders endangered in their own countries. This program is Lifeline: Embattled Civil Society Organizations Assistance Fund. Unlike other human rights assistance programs, Lifeline incorporated SOGI activists and CSOs from the very beginning of its operations.[75] Thus, the program occupies a place in the timeline of US government SOGI human rights interventions.

### Lifeline: Embattled Civil Society Organizations Assistance Fund

As Secretary Clinton prepared to attend the 2011 Community of Democracies meeting in Vilnius, Lithuania, Patricia Davis and Michael H. Posner, then Assistant Secretary of State for DRL, conceived of Lifeline. Clinton announced the new program in Vilnius. Before Lifeline, the Department of State had provided emergency assistance to some individual human rights defenders operating under dangerous conditions in their own countries, but the practice hadn't been formalized. As a fund and partnership, Lifeline effectively institutionalized several practices: extending emergency aid to human rights advocates, dedicating more funding and diplomatic resources to human rights defenders, and expanding the scope of assistance to include CSOs and individual activists. The new program affirmed that threats to human rights defenders were included in the mandate to advocate for the human rights of marginalized populations.[76]

Fundamental precepts of Lifeline include support for civil society and a "commitment to the fundamental freedoms of association and assembly."[77] More specifically, if NGO members are arrested on trumped up charges, we can provide funds for bail and legal representation; if an NGO is evicted without valid grounds from its offices, we can help that NGO get set up again with new office space. Lifeline also provides small amounts of funding to NGOs that want to raise awareness of the difficult, often hostile environments in which they operate and to address barriers to their fundamental freedoms of assembly and association.[78]

By its launch, organizers had formed a consortium of twelve partner governments for the international effort, and by 2016 the program grew to eighteen government partners: Australia, Benin, Canada, Chile, Czech Republic, Denmark, Estonia, Latvia, Lithuania, Luxembourg, Mongolia, Netherlands, Norway, Poland, Sweden, United Kingdom, United States, and Uruguay. In addition to governments, foundations such as the Ford and MacArthur Foundations support Lifeline. A consortium of international CSOs led by Freedom House disburse Lifeline funds for purposes that are consistent with program criteria. An example of the kinds of groups and activists served by Lifeline is provided by the Iraqi Civil Society Solidarity Initiative, which informs human rights defenders about Lifeline, what the program's emergency funds may be used for, eligibility criteria, and instructions on applying for grants (in English, Spanish, French, Arabic, Russian, Farsi, or Amharic).[79]

Between 2012 and 2016, advocacy for SOGI human rights expanded from one program to a set of programs and became more institutionalized in US human rights policies and assistance than ever before. A major difference between earlier SOGI interventions and those after Obama's and Clinton's public declarations is that in the period after late 2011, the advocacy and interventions became more deeply embedded in the mandate and functioning of the State Department and other executive branch agencies. The extent to which SOGI human rights advocacy is institutionalized is a subject of some interest and concern to professionals in human rights CSOs; foreign government officials who partner with the United States in human rights programs; and local, grassroots activists outside the United States who work with DRL and rely on the US government's commitment to SOGI human rights. A common question I've heard raised in every SOGI human rights venue I've been in since 2013, in the United States and abroad, is some variation of the following: what will happen to the US commitment to SOGI human rights when the next president takes office in 2017? The answer to that question is as yet unknown.

## Coming Out on SOGI Human Rights

Given its high profile, Clinton's 2011 speech in Geneva attracted more public attention than other, closely related SOGI statements and programs. One of these was coordinated with her speech: President Obama's "Memorandum for the Heads of Executive Departments and Agencies" on the subject of "International Initiatives to Advance the Human Rights of Lesbian, Gay, Bisexual, and Transgender Persons," released on December 6, 2011, and included in this book as Appendix A. Whereas Clinton's speech was addressed to an international audience, Obama's memo was addressed to US officials—presidential appointees and members of the civil service—and delivered instructions to foreign affairs agencies about implementing the commitments Clinton outlined in Geneva.

US presidents have various means of wielding executive authority at their disposal, including executive orders, executive proclamations, presidential memoranda, signing statements, and national security directives, all of which are customary, rather than constitutional, in origin and come from "implied constitutional and statutory authority." Like executive orders, memoranda may have "the force and effect of law" as long as they reflect "a valid claim of authority" and are published in the *Federal Register*. As questions have arisen about distinctions between executive orders and presidential memoranda, federal government attorneys have clarified that while executive orders must be published in the *Federal Register*, presidential memoranda need not be.[80] Obama's critics pointed to his frequent use of memoranda instead of executive orders as proof of his interest in evading limits on executive power.[81] This is not true of the Presidential Memorandum on LGBT Human Rights, the final line of which "authorize[s] and direct[s]" the Secretary of State to publish the memorandum in the *Federal Register*.

In his Presidential Memorandum, Obama calls on US government foreign affairs agencies to confront the "global challenge" posed by egregious violations of SOGI human rights. Citing "violence and discrimination" against LGBTQ people, Obama generally "direct[s] all agencies engaged abroad to ensure that U.S. diplomacy and foreign assistance promote and protect the human rights of LGBT persons." More specifically, agencies are charged with "combating criminalization of LGBT status or conduct abroad" (Section 1); "Protecting Vulnerable LGBT Refugees and Asylum Seekers" (Section 2); using "foreign assistance to protect human rights and advance nondiscrimination" (Section 3); ensuring "swift and meaningful

U.S. responses to human rights abuses of LGBT persons" (Section 4); "engaging international organizations in the fight against LGBT discrimination" (Section 5); and "reporting on progress" (Section 6). Through the memorandum, the Obama administration extends the mandate to attend to the human rights of LGBTQ people beyond the Department of State and its collaboration with USAID to advance SOGI human rights abroad.

Like other government institutions, from the 1950s to the present the Department of State and other foreign affairs agencies have changed enormously in their orientation and policies toward LGBTQ people. These changes have not been linear and predictable, and they probably have been overdetermined by changes in, for example, public attitudes, periods of conservative retrenchment, legal and political strategies of LGBTQ activist organizations, Democratic and Republican party politics, institutional dynamics and practices within federal government agencies and their workforces, and other factors such as the goals and interests of particular US officials in particular roles that intersect with SOGI issues.

Researchers who investigate an administration's policies and practices in an area such as human rights promotion abroad may reasonably raise many questions. For example, with regard to pro-SOGI policies and practices during Obama's terms in office we might wonder whether (or how much of) the administration's foreign policy support for SOGI human rights was driven by domestic political considerations such as the goal of mollifying LGBT activists and political donors who were dissatisfied by the president's first-term record on LGBTQ issues. To investigate what has been done—to say nothing of what can and should be done in the future—researchers might investigate particular events, decision makers, agency goals and cultures, policy histories, and governmental activist networks.

Careful investigation is necessary because establishing motives for government practices and policies is a deceptively complicated enterprise. Even though critics may impute motivations and goals to political actors that appear facially accurate in the context of news reports and their own political convictions, policy histories often excavate complex motives, unanticipated alliances, political compromises, institutional norms and processes, and unintended consequences that play unpredictable roles in policy development and outcomes. Nevertheless, constituencies of the right and left often apply shorthand understandings of motivation that fit preconceived political schemas. On the right, US conservatives attribute to liberals, progressives, Democrats (and Democratic administrations), and

LGBTQ people/activists a set of motives that include replacing capitalism with socialism, stigmatizing and punishing religious belief and worship, destroying the natural family, and valorizing sexual perversion. For
conservatives, pro-LGBT interventions by the US government epitomize
all of these goals even if the relationship between socialism and gender
diversity/same-sex sexuality is usually assumed rather than spelled out by
right-wing moral entrepreneurs.

On the critical humanist left, quite different and widely accepted
explanations for the US government's formulation and execution of pro-
LGBT projects emerge from the intersection of queer, postcolonial, antine-
oliberal, anti-imperialist, and other forms of critique. Despite the variety
of theoretical paradigms brought to bear on foreign policy, explanations
and accounts of US interventions generally rely on simplistic understandings of how "the state" functions to produce and perpetuate racism,
militarization, neoliberal privatization, deregulation, and imperialism. A
common assumption is that pro-LGBTQ/SOGI projects and policies on
the part of the US government are intended to function as evidence of
an "American exceptionalism" that consolidates empire by simultaneously
exposing human rights abuses by other states and deflecting attention
from racist abuses of human rights within the United States and abroad.
The arguments of many critical humanists explain and link a wide variety
of phenomena from progressively positive attitudes in the United States
toward LGBTQ people, to same-sex marriage (in the United States and
Europe), to the general contours of and specific phenomena that constitute
the War on Terror.[82]

Human rights violations don't occur in a social, political, and economic vacuum. There are many issues and phenomena that complicate
the task of conceptualizing human rights and efforts to support human
rights. These include links of correlation or causation between human
rights violations and conditions such as poverty, official corruption, and
the suppression of civil society. Furthermore, SOGI human rights violations may occur in the same contexts as other kind of violations of human
rights and civil society. Because human rights jeopardy can follow from
or mutually reinforce poverty, sexism, political corruption, the suppression of civil society, and broader geopolitical events and dynamics, US
government officials who monitor human rights violations and develop
and implement programs and initiatives to support human rights are well
advised to take these factors into account.[83] Indeed, judging from public
and private statements, one thing academics, activists, and government

officials seem to agree on regarding SOGI human rights assistance and programing is the need to listen to and work closely with indigenous activists to understand their needs and the sources and histories of sexism, homophobia, and transphobia in cultures and nations. Mechanisms that help institutionalize such commitments include meetings at which issues can be discussed confidentially and reports from activists and LGBTQ people such as one I describe in chapter 3.

I return to the claims and assumptions Christian conservatives make about left and pro-SOGI human rights interventions in chapter 4, and I take up progressive, critical humanist critiques in chapters 2 and 5. For now I suggest that neither of the critiques I've outlined should be taken for granted as a sufficient or even adequate explanation for the US government's involvement in SOGI human rights.

I devote the next chapter to a close examination of the public declaration of support for SOGI human rights by the Obama administration. The declaration was delivered in Geneva by Secretary of State Hillary Clinton in the form of a speech in honor of International Human Rights Day 2011, and it remains the most public intervention of the US government on SOGI human rights. I introduce the speech with an account of the background to the event at which Clinton unveiled the administration's support for LGBT human rights.

What follows is a reading of her speech, "Remarks in Recognition of International Human Rights Day," the full text of which is available as Appendix B. Clinton's speech inspired a variety of reactions and received a range of reviews, including from foreign officials, in the US press, from LGBTQ civil rights activists and organizations, and from domestic US political constituencies. I give particular attention to reactions and reviews of the speech from the US political right and left because of the ways these critiques converge and produce unanticipated agreements on the cynicism and foreign policy duplicity understood to drive official SOGI human rights advocacy. My extensive reading of her speech in the context of the empirical chapters is meant to demonstrate that there are alternative interpretations of the speech (and, by extension, advocacy) that don't lead ineluctably to the conclusions reached by critics of human rights interventions on the political right or left.

Chapter 2

# SOGI Rights Are Human Rights, and Human Rights Are SOGI Rights

## What Happens in Geneva Doesn't Stay in Geneva

In December 2011, Secretary of State Hillary Rodham Clinton delivered an unprecedented speech in Geneva in honor of International Human Rights Day.[1] Established by the General Assembly of the United Nations in 1950, Human Rights Day recognizes and celebrates the 1948 adoption of the Universal Declaration of Human Rights. Human Rights Day has been celebrated widely through a variety of events and themes. Clinton's speech can be distinguished from other addresses by US officials on the subject of human rights in two key ways. First was its exclusive focus on the human rights of lesbian, gay, bisexual, and transgender (LGBT) people, and indeed its assertion that, as Clinton put it, "gay rights are human rights, and human rights are gay rights." Second, most of the dignitaries who assembled for the address did not know the topic on which Clinton would speak. The fact that she would deliver an address on SOGI human rights was a closely held secret among those who were involved in planning the event. To preserve the element of surprise and ensure that officials wouldn't absent themselves in protest against the speech's topic, the invitations sent to ambassadors, international public officials, and other guests didn't disclose the topic of the speech or mention SOGI/LGBTQ human rights.

Although "Remarks in Recognition of International Human Rights Day" has received wide attention from news and partisan sources, the background, staging, and logistics of the speech have been reported piecemeal.[2] As a matter of political convention, the speech is credited only to Hillary Clinton; however, we know that like many addresses by prominent public figures, this speech was produced by Clinton and a small group of authors close to her. (Information about authorship was revealed as a result of the Clinton emails released by the State Department pursuant to an inquiry of her private email server during her State Department tenure.) One coauthor was Daniel Baer, in 2011 the Deputy Assistant Secretary of the State Department's Bureau of Democracy, Human Rights, and Labor (DRL). Also cited as people who contributed to drafting the address were speechwriter Megan Rooney, Assistant Secretary of State for DRL Michael Posner, and advisers Jacob J. Sullivan and Cheryl D. Mills.[3] DRL Program Officers Jesse Bernstein and Emily Stanfield helped implement the speech by providing information "building blocks" and arranging travel for the international activists who attended.[4]

For some time before December 2011, Clinton had sought a venue outside the United States for a speech centered on LGBT human rights. She approached UN organizers of the International Human Rights Day events and offered to deliver an address. She delivered the speech in the Palais des Nations before the UN mission in Geneva, Undersecretary General and head of the UN office in Geneva, and UN ambassadors. It is apparent from the later comments of some officials present that not everyone was pleased with the contents of the remarks. However, no national representative walked out of the speech, and at its end Clinton was rewarded with a standing ovation from most attendees.[5]

From the beginning of her tenure as Secretary of State, Hillary Clinton traveled widely and held strategic meetings with government officials and more informal dialogues with citizens that focused on civil society and human rights. These meetings were dubbed "Town Halls" and, more awkwardly, "Townterviews."[6] DRL partnered with the nonprofit Jefferson Institute to perform some travel agency functions to support these foreign Town Hall programs. In 2011, in preparation for the International Human Rights Day speech, DRL again turned to the Jefferson Institute to help carry out travel arrangements for thirteen invited guests: activists from countries where the human rights situation of LGBTQ people is perilous who would have to be transported from geographically diverse locations. The LGBT human rights defenders who became Secretary Clinton's guests in Geneva hailed from Cameroon, Colombia, Croatia, Kenya, India, Jamaica, Lithuania, Malawi, Moldova, the Philippines, Russia, Uganda, and Ukraine.[7] The State Department also invited other LGBTQ activists as guests, including members of the International Lesbian, Gay, Bisexual, Trans, and Intersex Association (ILGA)—Europe and US activists such as Julie Dorf, founder of the International Gay and Lesbian Human Rights

Commission (IGLHRC, now OutRight Action International) and currently a senior adviser at the Council for Global Equality (CGE), and Mark Bromley, founder and chair of CGE.

The activists met with the secretary before the speech, and Clinton delivered brief private remarks—later posted to the Department of State website—thanking them for "making the case for dignity and human rights for all people" even in circumstances that might be "challenging or dangerous." In this private meeting, Clinton stated her conviction that LGBT rights are the "human rights issue for the 21st century" and that the task ahead would be to "keep evolving the consensus on behalf of LGBT rights for all."[8] For the speech itself, the international LGBTQ guests were seated in the front row.

The full text of Clinton's "Remarks" is available on the Department of State website and appears in Appendix B in this volume. For the sake of analysis, I have divided the text of Appendix B into four parts and added paragraph numbers. A video of the entire speech is available on YouTube.[9] Here I interpret the speech and highlight key elements, including moral and legal foundations of human rights, the case for SOGI human rights, an engagement with standard grounds of anti-LGBT prejudice and enmity, an account of US struggles with group prejudices, and an agenda for realizing fairer societies that respect SOGI human rights throughout the world. Finally, I cite a number of reviews, responses, and rejoinders to Clinton's speech. I am particularly interested in striking similarities between conservative and left-progressive responses to the speech, which represent differences in domestic US constituencies' orientations toward human rights discourse, nonnormative sexuality and gender identity, and US government interventions on behalf of human rights abroad.

## Unpacking the Speech

There are many ways to read and interpret Secretary Clinton's speech, but in what follows, I argue that each section does different rhetorical work. Part one (paragraphs one through five) consists of pedagogy on human rights; part two (paragraphs six through eighteen) identifies the endangered community and issues the indictment; part three (paragraphs nineteen through twenty-nine) defines aspirations for the global community; and part four (paragraphs thirty through thirty-six) imagines a covenant between LGBTQ people and "people around the globe." Another way to conceptualize the speech is to trace it from a statement of norms—in this case, norms of human rights—to a "series of condemnations" and then to "a prophetic vision that unveils . . . promises" and "announces the good things to come." This movement from an indictment of wickedness to a vision of its correction is consistent with what Sacvan Bercovitch describes as the "American jeremiad."[10] It is a form of moral rhetoric shared by New England Puritan sermons and contemporary US "prophetic politics" of both the political right and left.[11]

If interpreting the speech partly through the lens of the jeremiad helps us make sense of its form and message, such a reading inevitably casts Clinton as a kind of prophet. Clinton herself may acknowledge this identity implicitly by humbly reporting her evolution—"the deepening of [her] own convictions"—on the subject of LGBTQ rights as universal human rights. Like the nation she serves, she says, she has been a party to harms toward LGBT people by being insufficiently committed to eliminating them. Recognizing that she and others will be judged by what Hannah Arendt calls the "backward glance of the historian," Clinton exhorts her audience to allow "dialogues" and "relationships" to do the work of transforming their attitudes toward LGBT people.[12] Clinton's admission of evolution from relative indifference to staunch commitment to SOGI human rights is open to interpretation. It's plausible to see her support for SOGI human rights as a calculating bid to establish her progressive bona fides, to attract the support of a voting demographic, or to further US imperial interests. It's also plausible to interpret her support for SOGI human rights as, at least in part, an ethical response to a sense of guilt and the desire to see justice for a vulnerable minority.[13]

In interpreting the speech as a jeremiad, I don't argue that Clinton (or her coauthors) deliberately casts the call to respect SOGI human rights in a Christian form or that such a form automatically discredits the call by parochially Westernizing it or ineluctably associating it with a missionary impulse toward ethnic, national, or cultural "others." Instead, such an interpretation merely provides a heuristic for reading and making meaning of a speech that contains an indictment of widespread human rights failures and a public call for responsibility and progress. In the following subsections I unpack the four parts of the speech, emphasizing particular strands of argument and analyzing what the speech as a whole communicates about SOGI human rights and a US commitment to those rights.

*Part One: Just Human Rights*

Part one establishes the provenance and normative force of human rights ideals in the adoption and application of the Universal Declaration of Human Rights, adopted by the General Assembly of the United Nations in 1948. In her introduction, Clinton asserts the "inherent dignity and humanity of all people" as an incontrovertible ideal that is "the birthright of all people," rather than being "conferred by government," either arbitrarily or along the lines of distinctions between favored and disfavored groups. This universality of natural rights entails a responsibility of states to protect these rights and indeed Clinton traces a progress narrative in which obstacles to the achievement of human rights that reflect race-, sex-, and religion-based exclusions "have fallen away" "in many places" since the adoption of universal standards of human rights. However, after articulating this passive version of progress, Clinton emphasizes in paragraph five that the progress that's been achieved has been hard won—that "people fought and organized" to transform "laws[,] . . . hearts and minds" and that the resulting changes enhanced the freedom of those individuals and the flourishing of their communities.

In this introductory part of the speech, Clinton strategically presents a brief narrative about the Universal Declaration of Human Rights (UDHR), its promulgation, and its effects. On the promulgation, she cites "the delegates" of "many nations" on "six continents," an account that emphasizes the multinational investment in and embrace of the fundamental principles of human rights doctrine. Omitted in this account are two features of the UDHR that it might well be politic to elide in a speech on SOGI human rights delivered by a US Secretary of State on foreign soil: the key role of US delegate Eleanor Roosevelt in bringing the declaration into existence and the formulation of critiques by scholars and national representatives who allege Western bias in the declaration and in other human rights instruments.

Considering the brevity of Clinton's account of the UDHR and the global commitment to human rights, excising Roosevelt from the account is interesting on two counts. The first is Roosevelt's quite public role in chairing the Human Rights Commission and writing some parts of the declaration that resulted from the commission's work. The second is Clinton's personal identification with and admiration of Roosevelt, which is evident in her autobiography, *Living History*, and in many public statements.[14] Roosevelt is important enough a figure to Clinton, however, that she does make an appearance in part three of the speech, when she is called into service to remind listeners that "human rights" is not only a matter of laws and institutions but is also instantiated in "small places close to home" and interpersonal relations.

A more telling elision is that Clinton does not acknowledge critiques of the UDHR—and by extension, of international human rights doctrine—by many scholars, citizens, and officials of noncompliant groups and nations. Many scholars have developed or embraced a critique of human rights discourse and US government interventions in that discourse. With regard to the former, they argue that cultural differences are reflected in widely varying notions of "rights" that may be quite different than those that are widely subscribed to in Western societies. With regard to the latter, they argue that US government interventions on behalf of purported universalisms are likely to enact—or invariably do enact—forms of power that reflect great power interests and that instantiate cultural, political, or economic imperialism.

Perhaps to avoid weighing in on contentious debates over culturally specific ideals or instantiations of human rights, Clinton's rendering of the values expressed in principles of human rights is vague and general rather than robust and specific: "the full measure of liberty, the full experience of dignity, and the full benefits of humanity." The benefits of citizens enjoying these values are both personal—"to live more freely"—and political—"to participate more fully in the political, economic, and social lives of their communities." For Clinton, these values and benefits are unambiguous goods that are not up for debate. Their assertion constitutes a prelude to naming the population whose members belong in the ranks of people deprived of human rights on the basis of race, sex, and religious belief and practice.

## Part Two: SOGI/LGBTQ Human Rights

In part two of the speech, Clinton introduces the more specific subject matter: an often "invisible minority," members of which are not only "denied opportunities" routinely extended to other citizens in many nations but also "arrested, beaten, terrorized, even executed," often with the complicity of police and other public officials. Only after she starkly lays out the forms of harm to which this "invisible minority" are subjected does she introduce, in paragraph seven, the principals of the speech as "gay, lesbian, bisexual, and transgender people, human beings born free and given[,] bestowed equality and dignity."[15] In reading the transcript of the "Remarks," it's useful to bear in mind that only at this juncture did the ambassadors and other assembled guests learn that Clinton intended to address the global vulnerability of LGBT people to egregious human rights violations.

However, in the brief preamble to part two, the list of human rights violations and the catalog of brutality against LGBT people is not complete. In this section alone, Clinton includes the following terms and phrases that construct an indictment of the world's enmity to LGBT people: "arrested," "beaten," "terrorized," "executed," "treated with contempt and violence," "authorities . . . look the other way," "[authorities] join in the abuse," "denied opportunities to work and learn," "driven from their homes and countries," "forced to suppress or deny who they are to protect themselves from harm," "endured violence and harassment," "bullying and exclusion," "beaten or killed because of their sexual orientation," "[beaten or killed] because they do not conform to cultural norms about how men and women should look or behave," "governments declare it illegal to be gay," "[governments] allow those who harm gay people to go unpunished," "lesbian or transgendered [sic] women are subjected to so-called corrective rape," "[lesbian or transgendered women] are forcibly subjected to hormone treatments," "people are murdered after public calls for violence against gays," "forced to flee their nations and seek asylum in other lands to save their lives," "life-saving care is withheld . . . because they are gay," "equal access to justice is denied," "public spaces are out of bounds," "inflicting violence on LGBT people," "criminalizing their status or behavior," "expelling them from their families and communities," and, finally, "tacitly or explicitly accepting their killing."

Although it might have been more politic here to have soft-pedaled the range of harms to LGBT people, the speech is explicit—even relentless—in capturing harms from stigma and ostracism to judicial execution and extrajudicial murder. A feature of this recital is that some elements in the list are delivered in the passive voice, which obscures the source of the actions being narrated. One effect of this ambiguity is to suggest accurately that anti-LGBT acts are carried out by a wide range of actors in diverse geographic contexts. The closest Clinton comes to acknowledging family members as a source of harm to LGBTQ people is in paragraph six, where she notes that LGBTQ people are "driven from their homes," and in paragraph sixteen, where the fact that many LGBTQ people are "expel[ed] . . . from their families and communities" is explicitly linked to anti-LGBTQ "religious or cultural values" that at times motivate "violent practices towards women like honor killings."

From the philosophical statement that LGBT people are no less than human beings with a right to dignity and equality, Clinton immediately pivots to a concession: because the US "record on human rights for gay people is far from perfect," Americans cannot speak on this subject from a position of moral or juridical superiority. Clinton characterizes the plight of LGBT people in the United States as vulnerability to "violence and harassment" as well as "bullying and exclusion." In this passage and others later in the speech, Clinton softens the criticism that she—a high-ranking US government official in a high-profile international venue—makes of the denial of human rights to LGBT people by acknowledging US failures.

But the most intriguing rhetorical move in this section of the speech occurs in paragraph seven: "Until 2003, it was still a crime in parts of our country." Here the nonspecific pronoun "it" could refer to desire, identity, or identification if not for the obvious referent to the Supreme Court's decision in *Lawrence v. Texas*, a constitutional ruling with which many international dignitaries might be unfamiliar. This deployment of "it" in place of a more specific term such as "sodomy," "same-sex relations or intimacy," "nonnormative gender expression," or even "nonprocreative sexuality" is unusual in a speech otherwise notable for its clarity. "It" allows Clinton to avoid, or to mention only obliquely, the criminalized or merely stigmatized sexuality with which LGBT people are likely to be identified, especially by those who hold them in contempt or mean them harm.

The single oblique reference to sexuality here contrasts with Clinton's direct references to the continuum of harm and the specific forms harm toward LGBT people can take. Sexuality studies scholars have taken up and sometimes disagreed about the value of detailing harms to LGBT people, especially how an emphasis on feelings, victimization, and what Dawne Moon calls "gay pain," can and often does depoliticize the identities and claims of stigmatized group members.[16] In *Tough Love*, I argue that although a focus on "gay pain" can have the depoliticizing effect Moon and others worry about, there are also political circumstances when it's necessary to make the pain suffered by members of stigmatized groups publicly legible. With regard to harms against gender and sexual minorities, I find Shane Phelan's notion of "credentialing by pain" a useful approach to the problem of widespread anti-LGBTQ bias and punishment. For Phelan, credentialing by pain is a political strategy by which LGBTQ people and their allies relate painful episodes and effects related to anti-LGBTQ bias to establish standing and credibility on the issue. Although she regards this credentialing to be a kind of assimilationist political strategy, Phelan doesn't reject it, noting that the move is an attempt "to 'put a human face' on a social problem. . . . [by] appeal[ing] to the heterosexual reader who thinks of homosexuals as 'them.'"[17]

Besides detailing the harms and human rights violations to which LGBTQ people are often subjected, the principal task of this second part of Clinton's speech is to respond directly and forcefully to common justifications for singling out LGBTQ people for ill treatment or judicial punishment. These justifications are: first, the belief in many parts of the world that same-sex sexuality, and nonnormative gender identity and expression are products of licentious, decadent Western nations; second, the idea that protecting the human rights of LGBT people would prove too expensive a goal for poorer and developing nations to aspire to; third, the existence of strong religious or cultural objections to human rights for LGBT people; and finally, the belief in pejorative stereotypes of sexual and gender minorities that, for many, vitiate the possibility of regarding same-sex-loving and gender nonnormative people as deserving of human rights protection.

Of these, the argument against SOGI human rights that's rarely heard in public is based on the cost of protection, although it's possible that this concern is raised among elites who may consider the relative costs and trade-offs of different uses of government resources, including the "cost" of such symbolic resources as citizens' attention and the possibility that public officials might suffer disapproval for supporting SOGI rights. However, the other justifications of bias and harm against LGBT people have constituted a common transnational discourse of opposition to nonnormative sexuality and gender identity. In some respects, at least, this is not surprising. Justifications for cultural differences between the amoral West and putatively more morally virtuous cultures, nations, ethnic groups, faith traditions, and nationalist movements can take a variety of forms that speak to local conditions and to the cultural payoffs that might accrue to those who stigmatize and demonize gender and sexual minorities. Similar justifications work within national boundaries to identify distinctions between, for example, virtuous Americans who reject same-sex sexuality and amoral groups and the elites that enable them. These comparisons have been amply documented and analyzed by students of the US Christian right.

Hence, in spite of their differences, there are remarkable similarities between arguments deployed in recent years in such diverse contexts as Russia, Eastern Europe, and Israel against public celebrations of LGBTQ identity and against the formation of political solidarity with LGBTQ people. In 2007, during a question-and-answer session after a speech at Columbia University, Iran's former President Mahmoud Ahmadinejad invoked the moral distinction between the West and non-West to explain that homosexuality is an unknown sexual phenomenon in Iran. In response to a question about the status and treatment of gay people in his country, Ahmadinejad said, "In Iran, we don't have homosexuals like in your country. We don't have that in our country. In Iran, we do not have this phenomenon. I don't know who's told you we have it."[18] After this demurral, it was a logical step for journalists to investigate the accuracy of the claim; indeed, it turns out that there are LGBT people, men who have sex with men, and women who have sex with women in Iran, however discreet they must be to avoid identification and potential prosecution.[19]

Of the four types of justification for discriminating against and targeting LGBT people to which Clinton responds, the one defended most vociferously by US social conservatives and representatives from many nations consists of religious and cultural reasons for repudiating LGBT human rights. These justifications Clinton deems "most challenging" because passionately held religious and cultural beliefs are matters of personal conscience and are often understood to constitute a bedrock foundation of belief that binds and constitutes cultural groups and nations. Clinton deals with this justification by reminding her listeners that religious precepts provide grounds for respecting and securing human rights as well as challenging and undermining them:

> rarely are cultural and religious traditions and teachings actually in conflict with the protection of human rights. Indeed, our religion and our culture are sources of compassion and inspiration toward our fellow human beings. It was not only those who've justified slavery who leaned on religion, it was also those who sought to abolish it. And let us keep in mind that our commitments to protect the freedom of religion and to defend the dignity of LGBT people emanate from a common source. For many of us, religious belief and practice is a vital source of meaning and identity, and fundamental to who we are as people.

Finally, Clinton points out that people in many parts of the world reject and violate the human rights of LGBT people because they embrace pejorative stereotypes that they believe excuse—or even necessitate—harsh treatment and punitive public policies. One example of such a stereotype that has proved ubiquitous and functional as a justification for anti-LGBT laws and attitudes is the argument that same-sex-attracted people target and "recruit" children to homosexuality. This particular stereotype has been a durable feature of anti-LGB sentiments, political arguments, and public policies across cultures and nations, including in the United States. An example is the 2013 Russian law that forbids "propaganda of nontraditional sexual relations to minors," a law that observers point out effectively requires that LGB/same-sex-attracted people and their allies refrain from any public discussion or recognition of same-sex sexuality. As concerns about the safety of LGBTQ athletes and visitors mounted leading up to the 2014 Sochi Winter Olympics, Russian President Vladimir Putin made a statement that queer people from abroad didn't need to worry about being in Russia if they agreed to "just leave kids alone, please."[20]

Following the indictment against the global vulnerability of LGBTQ people, Clinton turns to the more positive work of outlining aspirations for the treatment of LGBTQ people and their flourishing in communities.

### Part Three: What Is to Be Done

Part three consists of an affirmative framing of the work to be done to support and protect SOGI/LGBT human rights. Here Clinton outlines a range of recommendations from the legal/institutional—"changes in laws"—to the personal, including imagining how it would feel if those who are not LGBT stood in the place of LGBT people, what Hannah Arendt referred to as "representative thinking."[21] Clinton introduces this section of the speech with a declarative statement of the crucial distinction in morally loaded debates about the proper attitude toward and treatment of LGBT people: the difference between belief and expression, on one hand, and action, on the other. "While we are each free to believe whatever we choose, we cannot do whatever we choose, not in a world where we protect the human rights of all."

Clinton's argument here maps something of a levels-of-analysis approach to an agenda for SOGI human rights worldwide, but the argument doesn't begin with the personal and build to the legal/political/institutional level of action. Instead, Clinton propounds a different trajectory for achieving recognition of SOGI human rights. Beginning in paragraph twenty with the legal/political/institutional level of analysis, she asserts that "progress [in extending human rights to disfavored groups] comes from changes in laws." A theoretical rendering of this perspective is "jurisgenerativity," which Seyla Benhabib explains as "the law's capacity to create a normative universe of meaning that can often escape the 'provenance of formal lawmaking' to expand the meaning and reach of law itself."[22] Clinton's examples of the power of law to advance human rights are drawn from US history and from a single institution, the US military: the integration of African Americans into the armed forces after World War II and the repeal of the antigay "Don't Ask, Don't Tell" policy. However, she expresses a broader confidence that "in many places"—and not only in the United States—"legal protections have preceded, not followed, broader recognition of rights." The sanguine effects of legal protection that she points out include the pedagogical influence of laws on attitudes and the mitigation of fear that occurs when people discover that their worst misgivings about a disfavored group aren't vindicated.

However, Clinton isn't naive about the ability of minorities to enact laws whose purpose is to protect themselves against the will of majorities: "Acting alone, minorities can never achieve the majorities necessary for political change." Once again Clinton compares violations of LGBT human rights to those based on differences of sex, race, and religion. Such a comparison, which might be read as a naive idea that these categories of identity function legally and socially in the same way may instead be a kind of "adjacency claim" that ties a "new normative claim" to "more established" human rights.[23] What Clinton doesn't say directly in this context is that human rights–securing laws create penalties for behavior that violate the human rights of others and, ideally, bind citizens as well as government officials from engaging in human rights violations without fear of punishment. Hence, at this point Clinton downplays the punitive dimension of laws that not only secure the human rights of gender and sexual minorities but also rescind the impunity of those who deliberately violate the rights of members of those groups.

Finally, it's useful to note the understanding of sexual desire and gender identity encoded in Clinton's speech, revealed in the question, "How would it feel to be discriminated against for something about myself that I cannot change?" The question of the immutability of sexual desire or orientation frequently has created counterintuitive cleavages within political movements, including the antigay Christian conservative movement and the LGBTQ-affirming left. Clinton takes as her position an assumption that something like sexual orientation exists and that, at least for many people, is more or less immutable. This position has created fascinating correspondence between political liberals, LGBTQ activists, and some sectors of the ex-gay movement in which same-sex-attracted people are encouraged to practice celibacy and strive for "holiness."[24] Here, as has often been the case in political debates in the United States, Clinton's position on the immutability of sexuality underwrites her case for sexual autonomy and for state action and states' responsibility to transnational human rights norms to protect the lives and well-being of LGBT people.

### Part Four: To LGBTQ People Worldwide

Finally, in part four Clinton addresses LGBTQ people directly and at some length: "to LGBT men and women worldwide, let me say this: Wherever you live and whatever the circumstances of your life, whether you are connected to a network of support or feel isolated and vulnerable, please know that you are not alone." Here Clinton lists the US actors and institutions she claims are dedicated to protecting the human rights of LGBT people outside the United States, including "millions of friends" among Americans that include President Barack Obama, the State Department, US government agencies operating abroad, and US diplomats and embassy personnel. Clinton delivered her remarks against the background of anti-LGBT US Christian right and missionary activity in Russia, Eastern Europe, and much of the developing world. She doesn't directly address this global anti-LGBT preaching, teaching, organizing, and lobbying by Christian conservative Americans, but she firmly repudiates it by rhetorically redefining what it means to be an American through a statement directed to a transnational LGBTQ community: "you have an ally in the United States of America and you have millions of friends among the American people."

As she has already, in this part of the speech Clinton acknowledges that the United States is vulnerable to charges of having violated the human rights of its own citizens, not only in the area of proscribed LGBT identity and practices but also in terms of race and gender. Instead of asserting US superiority in recognizing and securing the human rights of LGBT people, the speech offers a statement of official and unofficial ("millions of friends") US resolve. Clinton delivered the speech in her role as a high-ranking public official, but she shifts the source of the resolve to protect

SOGI human rights from herself and her State Department to President Obama and the executive branch of the US government more broadly. The speech offers other nations as exemplars of good practices in the arena of SOGI human rights: South Africa, Colombia, Argentina, Nepal, Mongolia, and India. Although more recent events in India undermine this favorable assessment, it is significant that none of these nations are European; hence, the audience is not presented with a contrast between Western/European states and developing nations or states in the global South.

The absence of such a contrast suggests that the speech was crafted deliberately to displace the United States as a self-appointed leader in the area of SOGI human rights or at least to do so as much as possible given Clinton's positions as a prominent citizen and a member of the Cabinet. However, this refusal to present such a global North/South distinction is also consistent with realities of US and Christian right-led transnational anti-SOGI politics and anti-LGBTQ/SOGI beliefs and advocacy in and originating from other pro-LGBTQ nations. As Katherine Browne and Catherine J. Nash point out, resistance to LGBTQ beliefs and advocacy continues in, for example, Canada and the United Kingdom as well as in the United States. This resistance plays a role in mobilizing transnational anti-SOGI movements in the global South.[25]

In the final passage of the speech, Clinton invokes immutability for a second time, directly and in a phrase that gestures to natural law and to liberal political thought, if not liberal political practice: "the truth, the immutable truth, that all persons are created free and equal in dignity and rights." Inviting the assembled guests to join those who have fought for LGBTQ and other human rights "on the right side of history," she ends the speech in the role of the prophet of the jeremiad. Instead of the dour Methodist scold that has constituted one depiction of Clinton by her domestic critics, here she is upbeat and optimistic—expressing "great hope and confidence" in the work to come protecting the human rights of LGBT people around the world.

In the speech, Clinton acknowledges that SOGI human rights are "new" in one sense: like the human rights of indigenous people, children, and people with disabilities, sexuality and gender identity were not considered in the deliberations of those who drafted and ratified the UDHR. However, she denies that SOGI human rights are "new" in the more important sense that rights for members of these groups and on these bases have been merely fabricated and are not grounded in the fundamental agreements made by nations to respect and protect human rights. In paragraphs nine and ten, Clinton argues that "members of these groups are entitled to the full measure of dignity and rights" because "they share a common humanity." This is why protecting human rights on the basis of indigenous or LGBTQ identity is not tantamount to creating "new or special rights" but "honoring rights that people always had," even if we—members of national communities and the global community—didn't realize it.

On the same day Clinton delivered her remarks in Geneva, the White House released a Presidential Memorandum on "International Initiatives to Advance the Human Rights of Lesbian, Gay, Bisexual, and Transgender Persons." Together, Clinton's remarks, the programs she announced in her speech, and Obama's memorandum constitute a set of interventions that have symbolized the coming out of the Obama administration and the United States on SOGI human rights. Having delivered her speech in such a public, international setting, Clinton became the face of US advocacy for SOGI to the many journalists, activists, CSOs, nations, and scholars who responded to and analyzed her speech.

## Reviews, Responses, and Rejoinders

In the aftermath of Clinton's address, many representatives of news outlets, nonprofit organizations, and political perspectives in the United States and elsewhere responded to the speech and the related initiatives. Most of these responses reflect the political perspectives and agendas of the outlets and organizations in predictable ways. What is less predictable is how some of the agendas and perspectives relate to each other to form political-intellectual alliances that don't reflect a traditional left-right/liberal-conservative binary. Mainstream media outlets generally coded as "liberal" on the right, human rights groups, and LGBTQ rights organizations approvingly reviewed the speech and accompanying initiatives as commendable individual rights–respecting developments. On the other hand, in spite of differences I note later, conservative and left-progressive/critical humanist reviews converged on criticisms of the speech that fit into two general categories: charges of US hypocrisy and charges of political calculation. As I will show, the latter category can be further subdivided into calculations regarding domestic political (especially electoral) interests and calculations regarding US domination of other nations (imperialism).

This cleavage between mainstream/culturally "liberal" media and opinion leaders and those closer to both ends of the traditional left/right political spectrum is significant. As we shall see, the convergence of progressive left and socially conservative Christian right on state actions and human rights isn't limited to repudiating Clinton's speech.

## Liberal Responses

Mainstream media, mainstream human rights organizations, and LGBTQ organizations characterized the speech and Clinton's mission on behalf of LGBT human rights abroad in favorable terms. In the *Washington Post*, the speech was described as "blunt, yet inspiring," and in the *Post* column "PostPartisan," Jonathan Capehart quoted liberally from the speech and called it "phenomenal."[26] A *New York Times* article by Steven Lee Myers and Helene Cooper was similarly positive but raised a number of issues related to the announcement that the US government would "use all the tools of American diplomacy, including the potent enticement of foreign aid, to promote gay rights around the world."[27] Besides offering an overview of the speech and its related projects and initiatives supporting of LGBT human rights, the issues integrated into the *Times* analysis include the absence of modes of international enforcement for human rights standards; the symbolic value of official US dedication to human rights principles; the possible effects—positive and negative—of the initiative for domestic 2012 presidential electoral politics; and the possible complications for US relations with some allies.

Human rights community reviews of the speech were celebratory. Human Rights First characterized it as a "breakthrough policy speech." A press release put out by the organization, titled "LGBT Rights Are Human Rights, Clinton Says," begins: "Human Rights First today commended Secretary of State Hillary Clinton as she seized another opportunity to establish the principle that LGBT rights are human rights and human rights are LGBT rights." Human Rights First used the opportunity presented by the speech to call for the United States to "continue to lead by example at home and strengthen its own protections for LGBT Americans." With regard to the kinds of human rights violations Clinton enumerated, the press release especially emphasizes the plight of LGBT refugees who may confront violence and discrimination in their countries of origin, during flight, and in countries in which they are resettled.[28]

Similarly, Amnesty International USA (AIUSA) "welcome[d] the Obama administration's continued enhanced commitment to protecting the rights of lesbian, gay, bisexual and transgender people, and urge[d] swift action to match the Administration's articulated vision." Much of the work of Amnesty International is mobilizing public pressure on regimes for violating and failing to protect human rights. Consistent with this mandate, AIUSA highlights Clinton's challenge to strengthen legal protections for LGBT people, noting that although "open and honest discussion" on LGBT human rights is valuable, "it is the duty of the government to ensure progress" in protecting human rights. As the news item begins by affirming the Obama administration's "continued . . . commitment" to LGBT human rights, it ends by urging the United States to continue "to be a world leader in the fight for LGBT equality." An AIUSA blog post affirmed the importance of a "concrete action" item associated with Clinton's speech: the "*first ever U.S. government strategy* dedicated to combating human rights abuses against LGBT persons abroad," a reference to the Presidential Memorandum.[29]

The most prominent Western and US-based LGBT rights organizations endorsed Clinton's speech and the Secretary's and President Obama's pro–SOGI human rights agenda as it was announced in December 2011. ILGA-Europe posted articles developed for other LGBT rights organizations and linked to the websites of groups whose activists had been invited to the speech. Jessica Stern, acting executive director of what was then IGLHRC, issued a statement that noted IGLHRC's longtime support for the integration of SOGI human rights into US foreign policy. Of Clinton's speech and the Presidential Memorandum, Stern wrote, "We are deeply gratified by today's historic development. Under the leadership of President Obama and Secretary Clinton, we now see a strategic approach to LGBT human rights and the most affirming LGBT rights foreign policy in the nation's history." Julie Dorf, the founder and first director of IGLHRC, attended the speech in Geneva and reported her perspective on it in an essay for Huffington Post's "Gay Voices," "An Unforgettable Night in Geneva." Dorf casts the speech as an outcome of a long process of persuading the US government to include LGBT human rights in its foreign policy and human rights reporting, a process in which she had played a key role starting in the George H. W. Bush administration.

Of the speech itself, Dorf describes Clinton as having acknowledged the "imperfect record" of the United States on LGBT rights while also "us[ing] the power of her position brilliantly as she invited everyone to join her on the right side of history."[30] Celebrating the speech and its associated initiatives, the Council for Global Equality posted on its website an extensive list of leads and links titled "Global Press and Organizational Statements on Secretary Clinton Human Rights Speech and the Presidential Memorandum." CGE's affirming stance toward Clinton's speech was predictable since the organization had worked with the State Department to identify and transport the guest activists from diverse locations to Geneva to attend the speech and other LGBT human rights meetings.

US LGBTQ organizations and news sites that cover domestic LGBTQ-related issues affirmed the administration's commitment to LGBT human rights abroad and Clinton's speech as a manifestation of that commitment. Sources included the Human Rights Campaign, the National Gay and Lesbian Task Force (NGLTF), GLAAD (formerly Gay & Lesbian Alliance Against Defamation), the *Washington Blade*, the *Advocate*, and the online LGBT magazine *Queerty*. A statement by Rea Carey, executive director of NGLTF, "thank[ed] Secretary Clinton for taking to the world stage to send the unequivocal message that LGBT people everywhere should be able to live freely and with dignity."[31] GLAAD's report on the speech and Obama's memorandum opened with this statement: "Yesterday marked a historic moment in lesbian, gay, bisexual, and transgender history as the Obama administration expressed its commitment to ensuring the human rights of all people."[32] As is clear from their titles, both the *Advocate*'s and *Queerty*'s reporting focused attention on the reactions of attendees who disapproved of Clinton's LGBT human rights message: "Negative Reaction among Some Ambassadors Following Clinton U.N. Speech" (*Advocate*) and "Most of Africa Not Such Big Fans of Obama and Clinton's LGBT Human Right Speech" (*Queerty*). However, unlike similar reporting by conservatives about foreign opposition to a pro-LGBT human rights agenda, US LGBT organizations approved that agenda while publicizing opposition to it.

### Conservative Responses

By contrast with mainstream media, human rights organizations, and LGBTQ groups, coverage was less favorable among conservative news services, secular and religious. Differences emerge among conservative criticisms, among progressive/critical humanist criticisms, and between conservative and left-progressive/critical humanist criticisms of the speech.

However, certain thematic patterns emerge within each of the categories. The most obvious link between right and left criticisms consists of the regular deployment of one or both of the following arguments: first, that the United States censures other nations for transgressions equivalent to those of which the United States is also guilty (hypocrisy); and second, that the pro-LGBT human rights moves of presidential administrations are motivated by undisclosed political interests (political calculation). These interests may be domestic electoral interests or they may disguise a motivation of imperialism: the United States forcing or pressuring other nations to adopt its practices or obey its dictates, especially in ways that benefit the United States and/or extend its power. I sample conservative responses to the speech first, followed by left responses, especially those produced by progressive, critical academics.

The *National Review* online reviewed the speech as a "global gay-rights crusade" that combined the "commendable" with the "pernicious." The pernicious element is the regrettable liberal tendency to link the natural right to be free of violence with same-sex sexuality as a putative cause of human rights violation.

> When Clinton says, "It is a violation of human rights when people are beaten or killed because of their sexual orientation," no recourse is required to a gay right. The words "because of their sexual orientation" are superfluous. When she says that the horrors of "corrective" rape against women who are suspected of being homosexual are violations of a right, to what right could she be referring besides the right not to be raped, *simpliciter*?

In addition to repudiating "liberal ideology," the editors trace Clinton's speech and the associated initiatives to "domestic political concerns—President Obama is not long out of the doghouse among the gay-rights crowd." *National Review* mocks Clinton's admission of the imperfection of the United States on LGBT rights, but it also puts the initiatives down to political calculations of the Obama administration.[33]

Townhall, a website that perhaps too ambitiously dubs itself the "leading source for conservative news and political commentary and analysis," announced the speech and the introduction of the government's pro-LGBT human rights agenda with an article that casts "gay rights" in ironic quotes. Core criticisms of the speech are two: the first is that "religious or cultural objections" to LGBT conduct and human rights inappropriately are treated as equivalent to other justifications for human rights violations.

> Mrs. Clinton had the audacity to compare religious or cultural objections to homosexual practice to "the justification offered for violent practices towards women like honor killings, widow burning, or female genital mutilation," as if the religious and moral objection to men having sex with men is somehow equivalent to the Muslim practice of honor killings or the Hindu practice of burning widows.

Townhall's second criticism is the account of US "hypocrisy" cited in the title, which alludes to US moral degeneracy and lack of standing to criticize other nations' standards of "sexual morality": "when it comes to sexual morality we should be hanging our heads in shame, not lecturing others."[34] A key feature of both secular and Christian conservative denunciations of the speech is the citation of foreign nations and their officials on the legitimacy of anti-LGBT beliefs and policies and the inappropriateness of US intervention on behalf of values that many—within and outside the United States—regard as depraved.

Conservative Christian sources also were critical of Clinton's speech and the pro-LGBT human rights initiatives associated with it. Like Townhall, both the *Christian Science Monitor* and the *Christian Post* specifically cite disapproval of some African representatives of Clinton's speech. In the suitably titled, "World Reacts to Clinton's Pro-Gay Rights Speech," the *Christian Post*'s Amanda Winkler enumerates disapproving nations' responses to Clinton's speech and the call for recognition of LGBT human rights, focusing especially on nations in Africa and South and Central America. Although it doesn't spell out an argument that links the speech with US imperialism, the article lists without comment the thirty African nations with antigay laws and quotes an adviser to Ugandan President Yoweri Museveni, a popular figure among US Christian conservative moral entrepreneurs, saying of Clinton, "I don't like her tone at all." Winkler quotes at length from a Venezuelan news article that explains the speech in terms of Obama's domestic political calculations: "Obama has taken several policy measures to please the gay rights activists, a key group among voters in the Democratic Party."[35]

Peter Sprigg, Family Research Council (FRC) senior fellow for policy studies, often speaks for the FRC on issues related to "homosexuality." In an interview on Christian Broadcasting Network News, Sprigg directly characterizes Clinton's speech and the announcement of a pro-LGBTQ human rights US foreign policy as cultural imperialism.

> It is startling that President Obama is prepared to throw the full weight and reputation of the United States behind the promotion overseas of the radical ideology of the sexual revolution. If he did the same on other issues, his own liberal allies would undoubtedly accuse him of cultural imperialism. Threats to withhold foreign aid from poor countries unless they conform their laws to the views of Western radicals are unconscionable.[36]

The FRC has had to contend with criticisms in the United States of its praise for Museveni since the introduction of the Anti-Homosexuality (a.k.a. "Kill the Gays") Bill in Uganda in 2009. While repudiating a death penalty provision, FRC President Tony Perkins consistently has praised Museveni for standing "often alone—for traditional values, abstinence, and families despite tremendous pressure from the West."[37]

*Progressive/Critical Responses*

A final category of responses to the speech and the US government's pro-LGBT human rights initiatives are those of academic and other left-progressives. Writing for *Workers World* (the newspaper of the Workers World Party), Leilani Dowell uses Audre Lorde's famous dictum that "the master's tools will never dismantle the master's house" to rebut Clinton's "outrageously hypocritical remarks" on LGBT human rights in Geneva. In fact, Dowell's brief analysis combines the charges of hypocrisy and political calculation and both versions of calculation: electoral interests at home and imperialism abroad.

> Clinton's statement would be laughable if it were not so dangerous at the same time. For the U.S. has consistently used the "championing" of human rights around the world to facilitate its imperialist goals, including imposing brutal sanctions and waging outright war against countries that the U.S. claims don't measure up to its own "standards." The U.S. picks which countries to attack on their human rights record not based on

their lack of human rights—which, of course, the U.S. has no moral standing to judge upon anyway—but on whether or not they bow down to U.S. imperialism. . . . Now, in an attempt to woo the LGBTQ vote, comes the announcement that the oppression of LGBTQ people in other places is wrong.[38]

As Dowell notes that "LGBTQ people in the U.S. continue to resist the numerous attacks against our lives," it appears that she identifies as LGBTQ and is not motivated by anti-LGBTQ beliefs or sentiment.

Other critiques of Clinton's speech rely on hypocrisy or political calculation. One example is the Huffington Post "Gay Voices" article, "Hillary Clinton Is Not Helping the Gay Civil Rights Movement," by Jim Downs, a professor of history and American studies. Downs outlines a set of criticisms of the speech that overlap with and exceed the arguments common to conservative and left critiques. However, his arguments are not as intelligible as they might be. In the passage below, Downs makes the charge of political calculation in the form of "cultural imperialism," but follows that charge with an argument that is more consistent with the charge of US national hypocrisy.

This is all to say that while Clinton wants to do the right thing and make a noble statement about people being beaten and tortured for their sexual choices, she invariably and unwittingly propagates many contradictions and posits a familiar strand of American cultural imperialism. Is the United States really in a position to make an international call for gay civil rights when the Obama administration, which Clinton represents, has failed to give any federal teeth to the gay marriage campaign? Gay people can marry in New York City, but if their partners are Russian, Canadian, or any other nationality, they do not quality [sic] for citizenship rights and are deported.

Interestingly, in making the alternative version of the argument for political calculation, Downs is actually more critical of Clinton than are conservatives and other critical humanists whose responses I've found. This is because he accuses Clinton of failing to realize the ways her speech would aggrandize US conservatives and undermine progress in LGBTQ civil rights in the United States. This complaint finds Clinton either engaging in faulty domestic political calculation or failing to engage in appropriate domestic political calculation. Finally, Downs repudiates Clinton's claim that "Being gay is not a Western invention; it is a human reality" and retorts, "Actually, being gay is a Western invention." For many critical humanists, Downs included, cross-cultural historical variations in sexuality and the nineteenth-century European categorizing of same- and opposite-sex desire into sexual identities render Clinton's anodyne generalization about same-sex sexuality as itself a form of Western imperialism.[39]

A final example of left critique of Clinton's speech: although the focus of his critique isn't exclusively Clinton's speech and its related initiatives, in "Under the Cover of Gay Rights," law professor Dean Spade characterizes the speech as an expression of US imperialism that fits a pattern of motivated duplicity in which putatively pro-LGBT interventions serve as a pretext for other national goals and interests:

> Hilary Clinton's 2011 speech declaring that "gay rights are human rights," along with the prevalence of references to same-sex marriage and gay rights at the 2012 Democratic National Convention (DNC) and Obama's reference to gay marriage in his 2013 inauguration speech, are examples of American pinkwashing. Clinton's speech evinces a relatively new logic in U.S. imperialism: that the U.S., regardless of failures to protect queer and trans people from state violence at home, will now use gay rights to exert pressure on countries where the U.S. has some ulterior motive. Clinton uses lesbian and gay rights to bolster the notion that the U.S. is the world's policing arm, forcing democracy and equality globally on purportedly backward and cruel governments.[40]

For Spade and many critical humanists, the charge of pinkwashing asserts a deliberate state deployment of LGBT-friendly policies or social climate to deflect attention from reactionary politics in other social, legal, or political arenas as well as a recruitment of LGBT people as a face of this reactionary politics, themes to which I return in chapter 5.

Combining conservative and progressive objections to Clinton's speech, Table 2.1 captures the core arguments of hypocrisy and political calculation that opponents levied against Clinton as well as other forms and instances of US advocacy on SOGI human rights. Since she was First Lady, Clinton has been a controversial figure, opposed by conservatives and fiercely criticized by progressives during her 2008 and 2016 presidential

Table 2.1. Christian Conservative and Progressive/Critical Humanist
Critiques of Hillary Clinton's International Human Rights Day Speech

|  |  | Conservative | Progressive/Critical Humanist |
|---|---|---|---|
| Hypocrisy |  | US government intervenes in the internal affairs of other nations under the guise of morality and human rights while perpetuating immorality and denigrating Christian faith | US government intervenes in the internal affairs of other nations under the guise of (SOGI) human rights while perpetuating discrimination and oppression against LGBTQ people, people of color, and poor people |
| Political calculation | Electoral | US government intervenes on SOGI human rights to attract and solidify the political support of LGBT people | US government intervenes on SOGI human rights to attract the political support of LGBT people and distract them from racism, imperialism, and/or failures to deliver other progressive goods and policies |
|  | Imperialism | US government intervenes in the internal affairs of other nations to force them to accept SOGI human rights and US standards of immorality | US government uses SOGI human rights as an excuse to intervene in the internal affairs of other nations, and enhance its own political and economic power over them |

campaigns. We might suspect that left and right resistance to her SOGI human rights declaration reflects resentment toward Clinton herself except that, as we shall see, the claims and arguments reappear in other contexts and constitute persistent threads of reproach toward official US advocacy for SOGI human rights.

For now, I set aside the charge of political calculation—and especially the subindictment of imperialism—and take up the claim of hypocrisy: that US failures to fully recognize civil and human rights protections for LGBTQ people, same-sex sexuality, and gender nonnormativity disqualify the US government or its representatives from speaking out against or taking up the cause of SOGI human rights outside US borders. At a fundamental level, there are circumstances in which the charge of hypocrisy against Clinton's public affirmation of US government support for SOGI human rights would be well leveled. One would be if, for example, Clinton had called for other nations to reform their legal and political systems while investigations into her or her agency's practices exposed breaches of support for SOGI or a climate of discrimination toward LGBTQ people. Another circumstance that would vindicate the charge of hypocrisy would be if Clinton and Obama were found to have conspired to suppress LGBTQ rights in the United States while scolding poorer, weaker nations about their lack of commitment to SOGI human rights. However, no such practices have been brought to light. Indeed, State Department officials involved with human rights assistance programs point out that in 2009 Obama's presidential transition team expressed interest in working with DRL and the CGE to coordinate SOGI assistance.[41]

Another response to the charge of hypocrisy leveled against the US government can be found in Jeffrey Isaac's rejoinder to Noam Chomsky's repudiation of the Clinton administration's military intervention in Kosovo. Using the political thought of Hannah Arendt to set the stage for his reply to Chomsky, Isaac argues:

> Arendt refused to dismiss the discourse of human rights. She knew as well as anyone that this discourse was the source of enormous hypocrisy. But she also understood that hypocrisy is not the ultimate vice, and that the exposure of hypocrisy is not the ultimate task of intellectual work. She saw that the relentless exposure of the human rights idea only strengthened the hands of dictators who were the only true believers in the dispensability of human rights. And she also saw that the limits of the human rights idea, and the hypocrisies surrounding its rhetorical deployment, did not fatally damn this idea.[42]

With regard to Chomsky and Kosovo, Isaac argues, "it is irresponsible to make the exposure of official hypocrisy the ultimate public intellectual project" because to do so represents the "real issue [a]s not what might be done to relieve the suffering, but rather how certain (American) officials can be caught in their own verbal contradictions."[43]

Isaac's analysis is powerful and salient precisely because he takes the perspective that to determine whether a particular official intervention is helpful or harmful, good or bad, "one would have to examine what was actually happening in Kosovo in 1999, the historical and political backdrop of those events, and the range of options that might have been undertaken then and there." In other words, to return to my own concern with SOGI human rights: the question of whether a particular SOGI human rights intervention is helpful or harmful is not only a matter of assigning a particular quotient of hypocrisy to it. Rather, this is an empirical question that requires careful empirical research that yields data that can be applied to—but not substituted for—answers to similar questions in other cases.

## Political Values and Political Reason

There are several possible explanations for the very different responses to US SOGI human rights discourse of, on one hand, liberal/mainstream government, media, CSOs, and LGBTQ rights groups and, on the other hand, critical humanists who are extremely skeptical of US government intervention in human rights. Here I suggest four explanations: first, liberal/mainstream government, media, and human rights professionals may be unaware—or may discount the significance—of historical and contemporary abuses of US government power. Second, liberal/mainstream agents in institutions such as government, the media, and CSOs may be too coopted by their status and cooperative enterprises or too complicit in these enterprises to recognize the pernicious effects of official US support for SOGI human rights. These are both plausible conditions that may account for some part of the consistent split between readings of Clinton's speech that prevailed among different constituencies of the political left, although I doubt they account for most of the split.

A third explanation is the existence of working relationships between members of human rights CSOs, US government officials, and local/regional human rights advocacy groups. One way of theorizing these relations is in terms of the contact hypothesis that has been applied to relations between ingroups and outgroups with regard to such differences as race and sexuality. Conditions that predict positive relations between ingroups and outgroups can also facilitate positive contact between those who work to achieve common goals.[44] A corollary to "contact" is that, in fact, many human rights professionals take up roles in different CSOs or in both CSOs and government. For example, before he was appointed Assistant Secretary of State for DRL in 2014, Tom Malinowski served as the Senior Director on Bill Clinton's National Security Council and as Washington Director for Human Rights Watch. Close working relationships can contribute to positive regard for the tasks on which human rights professionals jointly labor. At least sometimes, people take up different roles in different institutions in ways that contribute to stabilizing particular conceptions of human rights tasks and goals.

I believe that the final explanation accounts for much of the difference in reactions to official US support for SOGI human rights abroad. This explanation, one that Christian conservatives call "worldview" and academics often understand as "ideology," helps make sense of what groups regard as the unusual, obdurate, uninformed, delusional, or counterfactual beliefs of those with whom they disagree. A less judgmental perspective is offered by scientist and philosopher of science Ludwik Fleck, who would conceptualize groups such as Christian conservatives and academic humanists as "thought collectives," or "communit[ies] of persons mutually exchanging ideas or maintaining intellectual interaction" in a shared conceptual language that is inaccessible—or makes little sense—to outsiders. A thought collective produces and in turn is reproduced by a "thought style," which Fleck defines as "the readiness for directed perception and appropriate assimilation of what has been perceived." Fleck describes the experience of a thought style as one in which the interpretation of the thought collective "appears imperative" to those within the collective while other, "alien" interpretations seem "like a free flight of fancy."[45]

Senator Daniel Patrick Moynahan—a policy maker whose views have been understood to straddle the political spectrum from liberalism to conservatism—asserted that everyone is entitled to their own opinion but not their own facts. We may not be entitled to our own facts, but we still hold them—from what Randall Balmer has called the "ruse of selective [biblical] literalism" among Christian conservatives to the particular political convictions that guide much critical humanist research on political phenomena.[46] Scholars of political psychology have generated fascinating insights into shared belief systems and their cognitive and emotional/affective correlates, challenging the notion that political values proceed for most people unimpeachably from objective political reasoning.[47] Generally speaking, social and political psychology demonstrate that even the perception of facts is mediated by partisanship and/or political belief systems.[48] Such a challenge applies not only to those with whom we disagree but also to our own convictions and the facts we reconcile with those convictions.

Hillary Clinton's speech is not the only target at which critical humanist US critics have leveled charges of LGBT-related hypocrisy. Indeed, these charges are common as a response to US criticisms of other nations' anti-LGBTQ attitudes, policies, and acts. For example, days before the opening of the Winter Olympics in Sochi, Russia, in early 2014, Yale law professors Ian Ayres and William Eskridge contributed an opinion article to the *Washington Post* titled "America's Gay Hypocrisy." In it, the authors excoriate the United States for "ignor[ing] its own anti-homosexual statutes" while criticizing Russia's 2013 law prohibiting propaganda of nontraditional sexual practices. Ayres and Eskridge explicitly compare US state and local "no promo homo" statutes with the Russian law, but the analysis is as interesting for what it does not do as it is for what it does. The authors compare the similar language of US and Russian statutes but note consequences only of US statutes, which they argue have "contributed to classroom bullying and to the high level of suicides among gay teens." Ayres and Eskridge appear to have no interest in the context for or consequences of the Russian law for LGBTQ Russians (or visiting Olympic athletes) even though there was, by the time they wrote their exposé, abundant evidence for widespread violence and threats of violence for which no analogue existed in the United States at the time. The asymmetrical nature of the analysis is captured in a full paragraph that directly compares the US and Russian statutes and notes the deleterious consequences of US anti-LGBT laws:

> Putin has assured the International Olympic Committee that the law is merely symbolic. But in the United States, officially sanctioned anti-gay prejudice has contributed to classroom bullying and to the high level of suicides among gay teens.

Ayres and Eskridge alert readers that while the Russian law is symbolic ("Putin has assured"), US statutes kill. No wonder the authors find that US hypocrisy generates worse consequences for LGBTQ people than Russia's official hostility and antigay legislation.[49]

A brief riposte to Ayres and Eskridge is "Americans Aren't Hypocrites for Criticizing Russia's Homophobia," by *Slate*'s Mark Joseph Stern. Stern sums up Ayres and Eskridge's argument by noting that "there is an irritating strain of soft-core cultural relativism that runs through this op-ed, but the bigger problem is the sheer inaccuracy of the central comparison." By way of correction, Stern notes the legal consequences of the Russian law and the virulence of public anti-LGBTQ bias legitimized by it, including the message to "homophobes that they can beat, rape, torture, and murder gay people with no consequences."[50] In his closing argument, Stern points to a key distinction in the Russian and US cases by alluding to the significance of fragmentation of US law and policy making, a point I return to later when I criticize critical humanist indictments of the singular "state": "We needn't overlook another country's vicious homophobia merely because some of our states remain lodged in a bygone era of bigotry."[51] Framed another way, Yale law professors surely know the difference between the executive branch of the US government and Texas. A consequence of ignoring differences between the most persistently biased jurisdictions of the United States and its more potentially rights-respecting institutions is that such critique leaves little basis for recognizing and leveraging important differences that may prevail between political parties, movements, and presidential administrations.

I conclude this discussion for the moment by introducing an academic consideration of Clinton's speech that's nested in a broader analysis of SOGI human rights violations and what can, or should, be done about them. In the essay that introduces their edited volume *Global Homophobia*, political scientists Michael J. Bosia and Meredith L. Weiss raise the subject of US hypocrisy but push well beyond it to make a case regarding SOGI human rights that's quite different than what emerges from much critical humanist scholarship on politics, as we will see. Indeed, from one perspective, I regard the essay (and others in the volume) as an attempt to suture a critical humanist critique of US intervention as hypocritical and/or imperialist to a defense of the importance of Western assistance in combating the forms of violence and impunity that Clinton enumerated in her Geneva speech. Bosia and Weiss briefly invoke the charge of hypocrisy as US government officials exhort foreign nationals and governments to respect LGBT human rights when the United States in many respects still makes LGBTQ people "sexual strangers."[52] For them, Clinton's "strident declaration" that " 'gay rights and human rights . . . are one and the same' is undercut by the fact of LGBT citizens' dubious *de jure* and *de facto* equality in the United States itself."[53] However, in their analysis of the phenomenon of transnational "political homophobia," Bosia and Weiss go on to call explicitly for respect for SOGI human rights and forcefully make an empirical case for Western aid to endangered gender and sexual minorities. I return to these claims and concerns, and to Bosia and Weiss's essay, in chapter 5.

In my analysis of Clinton's speech, I acknowledge the unusual level of detail she gives to the harms visited on people as a result of discrimination and violence based on sexual orientation and gender identity. One plausible reading of this passage is that it functions as a victim impact statement delivered on behalf of those who are not in a position to speak for themselves. Another possibility was suggested to me in a casual conversation with a US-based human rights professional: that in using this level of detail Clinton may have meant to inform a European audience of officials who don't work directly with SOGI issues and thus aren't well informed about the real effects of anti-LGBT bias an understanding of what's at stake in human rights concerns in this arena. In this interpretation, the speech could have been aimed at Europeans as much as at diplomats, regimes, and citizens outside Europe.

The speech is one intervention among many taken by US government officials with the goal of advancing SOGI human rights abroad. What differentiates it from many others that have been or are being taken is that it was a discrete event and a public one to which many interested parties around the world responded. For now, I merely argue that the categories of responses I've sampled rely on preexisting political commitments regarding universal human rights, LGBTQ identity and rights, and/or US government intervention. These commitments are activated by the invocation of, in this case, US government intervention in the arena of international (SOGI) human rights. A full account of any intervention, including Clinton's "Remarks in Recognition of International Human Rights Day," would include multiple elements, including close analysis of the intervention itself and, as much as possible, of its effects.

An example of such an analysis is Elise Carlson-Rainer and Jacqueline Dufalla's "The Foreign Policy of LGBT Rights: Russia's Reaction and Resistance to US Policy." The article takes into account the history of LGBTQ activism in Russia, some aspects of the history of US government advocacy for SOGI human rights, public attitudes in Russia toward the West and US LGBTQ advocacy, Russian cultural beliefs about sexuality, the Putin regime's strategic policy and priming on the subject of LGBTQ rights, and local activists' strategic judgments about the consequences of receiving external assistance and the changing conditions that influence such judgments. Carlson-Rainer and Dufalla also evaluate likely short- and long-run consequences of US and other transnational advocacy for LGBTQ activism in Russia. In the short run, "withdrawing from their relations with Western organizations seems to be the safest option" for Russian LGBTQ activists. However, the authors note that withdrawing from these relationships "could prove disastrous for the Russian LGBT movement" in the long run because "powerful outside voices can, and will, amplify their call for equality." Finally, the authors advise transnational SOGI advocates to "focus more on localizing their efforts more specifically to the Russian context."[54] Such analyses, and the activist and academic conversations they provoke, are intellectually and politically productive because, with their careful empiricism, they suggest that the landscape for human rights advocacy may change over time and require different kinds of policies, strategies, and interventions. By contrast, conclusions about US human rights advocacy from the political right and left are relatively static in their convictions about the consequences that issue from official US involvement in human rights.

In the next chapter, I return to an empirical account of US government SOGI human rights programing and interventions, beginning with the Global Equality Fund announced in Clinton's speech in Geneva and ending with advocacy by the State Department's Special Envoy for the Human Rights of LGBTI Persons. Most of what interested US citizens know about the administration's SOGI human rights dates from the period I address in chapter 3: from 2012 to the end of the Obama administration in early 2017. Even so, scholarship, official documents, interview material, and participant observation can inform our understanding of this period in which US government support and international advocacy for SOGI human rights was consolidated.

Chapter 3

# The US Government and SOGI Human Rights

## *After Geneva*

### The Global Equality Fund

In her speech in Geneva, Hillary Clinton announced a new initiative, the Global Equality Fund (GEF), to support organizations and programs "that advance the human rights of lesbian, gay, bisexual and transgender (LGBT) persons around the world."[1] Although it was intended to foster changes in programs and practices within the purview of executive branch agencies, Barack Obama's Presidential Memorandum doesn't mention the GEF by name. However, Section 3 (Foreign Assistance to Protect Human Rights and Advance Nondiscrimination) and Section 5 (Engaging International Organizations in the Fight Against LGBT Discrimination) are closely related to the goals of the program, which the Bureau of Democracy, Human Rights, and Labor (DRL) began to administer in early 2012.

The GEF is an umbrella fund that supports three kinds of assistance programs. These programs perform different functions and in some cases serve different populations. The three categories of assistance are emergency support; long-term technical assistance and organizational capacity building; and small grants. The GEF is not the only US government funding source that has been available to groups and individuals involved with SOGI human rights, and it isn't the only initiative that currently exists to serve members of the LGBTQ community whose human rights are in jeopardy. With its three distinct categories of assistance and many partners and grantees around the world, the GEF is the best known of the SOGI human rights programs and initiatives of the US government.[2] It is also a set of programs familiar to many LGBTQ activists affiliated with the African LGBT organization I address below.

The idea for the GEF emerged from planning within DRL by "a group of committed policy advisers" that included Daniel Baer, Jesse Bernstein, Patricia Davis, and Mira Patel in the run-up to Clinton's speech in 2011.[3] Since it was activated in 2012, the GEF has been administered by Davis, DRL's Director of Global Programs, who manages foreign assistance programs for the State Department. She hires and manages the GEF staff; from early 2015 to early 2017, she worked closely with the Special Envoy for the Human Rights of LGBTI Persons, Foreign Service officer Randy W. Berry.[4] As a Program Officer in DRL, Jesse Bernstein helped launch the GEF; met with activists in Washington, DC, and in their home countries; designed funding solicitations; and monitored SOGI projects.[5]

With regard to the GEF and similar programs situated within the State Department, some institutional vocabulary is necessary because particular terms denote the relationship of the US government to outside entities. For example, *implementing partners* are grantees who receive US government funding. The difference between implementing partners and other *grantees* is that implementing partners receive US government funding and then subcontract services and resources to other grantees. *Partners* are organizations, including other governments, that provide resources to implementing partners and grantees.[6]

The first category of assistance in the GEF is the emergency support provided by Dignity for All. Dignity is a "rapid response" subprogram of GEF that provides emergency funds, advocacy support, and security assistance to LGBTQI individuals or groups under threat or attack due to their sexual orientation or gender identity.[7] The State Department's implementing partner for the Dignity grants is a consortium of international organizations led by Freedom House, a US-based nonprofit and "independent watchdog organization dedicated to the expansion of freedom around the world." Freedom House and its consortium partners disburse emergency funds directly to LGBTQ organizations, human rights defenders, and vulnerable LGBTQ people for such forms of emergency assistance as security training, medical or legal assistance, trial monitoring, prison visits, and temporary relocation of threatened activists or organizations.[8]

The second category of assistance in the GEF is for long-term capacity building and technical assistance grants that either directly fund programs of local, in-country LGBTQ organizations or fund grants to international groups to work with local organizations. Programs help enhance the capacity of pro-LGBTQ civil society groups to support their constituencies through, for example, supporting legal challenges and legal reforms, working to expand allies in civil society, and fostering the ability of civil society groups to monitor, document, and respond to human rights violations.

The third category of assistance under the GEF consists of small grants (under $25,000) disbursed to local organizations through US embassies for high-impact programs. Because working closely with local groups and advocates can enable embassy personnel to learn about the needs of local LGBTQ groups and advocates, the GEF confers discretion to disburse small grants to those groups and advocates for purposes like creating educational curricula and training materials and developing civil society networks. Every US embassy has a human rights officer whose responsibility is to investigate allegations of human rights violations where they serve, as well as represent human rights as they have been defined by the Universal Declaration of Human Rights (UDHR) and other treaties and declarations. At the 2015 conference I discuss later, US State Department officials encouraged the human rights advocates in attendance to contact US embassy human rights officers for assistance with SOGI human rights violations.[9]

As of 2017, fifteen countries are GEF partners of the United States: Argentina, Australia, Chile, Croatia, Denmark, Finland, France, Germany, Iceland, Italy, Montenegro, the Netherlands, Norway, Sweden, and Uruguay. Prominent by its absence from this list is the United Kingdom, which engages in its own outreach abroad on SOGI human rights but is not a member of the GEF. Other partners include the Arcus Foundation, the John D. Evans Foundation, LLH: the Norwegian LGBT Organization, the MAC AIDS Fund, Deloitte, Royal Bank of Canada, Hilton Worldwide, Human Rights Campaign, Out Leadership, and USAID. The outlook for the GEF under the Trump administration is unclear, but if the fund continues to operate and the State Department continues to administer it, the GEF may enroll new members over time. For now, the GEF welcomes members regardless of the size of their financial contribution. Indeed, members may make in-kind contributions such as providing expertise for GEF projects.[10]

While officials in DRL manage the fund, twice a year GEF partners meet and establish themes for SOGI human rights assistance that emerge from conversations, consulting, and outreach to LGBTQ activists and communities.[11] Themes that reflect these communities' current needs are discussed at meetings between funders and human rights activists like those

I highlight later in this chapter. These themes are publicized to potential grantees and implementing partners in solicitations for proposals such as those advertised on Grants.gov, which "provides a unified site for interaction between grant applicants and the U.S. Federal agencies that manage grant funds."[12] Assistance themes and opportunities are also conveyed to potential grantees through networks and personal contacts between funders and grantees. A 2012 theme was documentation of human rights abuses, and themes for 2013 included combating violence against transgender people and legal/decriminalization strategies where those would be appropriate given local conditions. For 2015, themes included "friends and allies" and "protecting and promoting the rights of transgender persons."[13]

The GEF small grants program is only one of the many ways that US embassy officials work with LGBTQ advocates and grassroots organizations to support vulnerable populations. But the role of US embassies in supporting SOGI human rights isn't limited to the GEF; embassy engagement has been one prong of official US government support for LGBTQ human rights in recent years. Indeed, embassy personnel document and report human rights conditions, engage in "private" or "quiet"—that is, nonpublicized—diplomacy, and sponsor events and programs whose purpose is to advance SOGI human rights.

## Diplomatic Initiatives/Embassy Engagement

As Secretary of State, Hillary Clinton initiated a requirement for all US embassies around the world to devise programs to support the human rights of LGBTQ people. What Clinton's State Department referred to as "innovative public diplomacy" to advance SOGI human rights didn't begin all at once in after her speech in Geneva.[14] Just as US embassies could report on the human rights situation for LGBTQ people in their annual Country Report before 2010 and were required to do so in 2010 (for conditions in 2009), before 2012, embassies could engage with members of LGBTQ communities to support human rights, but they were required to incorporate LGBTQ outreach and engagement beginning in 2012. In her 2011 remarks in Geneva, Clinton announced that in the early months of 2012 officials at the State Department would be developing a "resource toolkit" for US embassies abroad to help embassy personnel whose knowledge of LGBTQ human rights was limited implement such initiatives as embassy engagement and Dignity for All emergency programs.

State Department officials developed and distributed the resource toolkit to embassies in 2012.[15]

To complement the official internal State Department toolkit, in 2012 the Council for Global Equality developed and published a guidebook for non-US LGBTQ activists and human rights defenders: "Accessing U.S. Embassies: A Guide for LGBT Human Rights Defenders." The guide is formulated "as a resource for our human rights colleagues internationally who share our mission of encouraging U.S. embassies to stand in support of fundamental human rights for all individuals, regardless of their sexual orientation or gender identity." It contains information for indigenous human rights activists on, for example, how US embassies are organized, what forms of assistance are available from the embassies, how to seek and frame requests for that assistance, how to gather information relevant to SOGI human rights abuses, and how to engage embassies in human rights emergency situations. The guide even makes recommendations for contacting and meeting embassy officials to people who may need to protect their identities because of threats based on sexual orientation and gender identity.[16]

Because all US embassies were expected to develop programs suited to the country context in which they are located from 2012 to 2016, there are many more examples of SOGI embassy engagement than it is possible to address. Some of these are rhetorical or symbolic; some are public and visible, while others are insider events or programs that aren't widely advertised to people and officials outside of human rights and LGBTQ communities. For example, ambassadors and embassy staffs have released video statements on LGBT issues, screened films with LGBTQ themes for invited guests, hosted dinners and receptions, staged talks or roundtables on issues of interest to LGBTQ communities, and participated in Pride marches or other events. Many embassy events have been planned to coincide with Gay Pride Month activities (usually in June or July) or with the International Day Against Homophobia, Transphobia, and Biphobia (IDAHO, in May).

Clinton's State Department encouraged diplomatic personnel to be innovative while taking into account the country context for SOGI issues. For example, consider the embassy dubbed "the world's gayest U.S. embassy" by the Huffington Post in June 2013. On May 17, in recognition of IDAHO, US officials in Sarajevo, Bosnia, lit up the US embassy in the stripes of a rainbow flag. The embassy was bathed in rainbow colors for twenty-four hours while hosting LGBTQ-related activities and programs.

In June 2014, the US embassy in Kigali, Rwanda, invited Rwandan artists to decorate the embassy's outer wall with messages of support for LGBT human rights. Rwandan media organization IGIHE reported that more than forty people participated in the event, including artists and "representatives from Rwanda's LGBT community." Quoting Clinton's Geneva speech, acting public affairs officer Benjamin Roode noted of the event that "Gay rights are human rights. The U.S. Embassy wanted to make sure through this art event that everyone knows all people deserve to enjoy human rights." IGIHE reported that:

> The event was also a great way to show that art and expression can be positive reinforcements in society. Graffiti is a form of street art that can be used to express social or political messages for the world to see. The U.S. Embassy proudly supports arts development in Rwanda and was happy to share its walls as a canvas for important public messages.

IGIHE quoted Tony Cyizanye, leader of the Yego Arts studio: "We came to show our unity as artists and to support human rights universally. We're using our talents as weapons to change the world."[17]

Of the hundreds of examples of SOGI human rights embassy engagement since 2012, most haven't engendered controversy and thus have gone unremarked. However, both the policy of embassy engagement on SOGI human rights and particular forms this engagement takes have been controversial. Disagreements over US embassy participation in LGBTQ/SOGI events and programming in countries where they operate are of different kinds. First, there are disagreements within LGBTQ communities over goals, strategies, and modes of advocacy such that even programs or events crafted by embassies in cooperation with LGBT allies may not meet the needs or satisfy the political aspirations of all those who identify as sexual or gender minorities.

For example, in 2013, Embassy Tokyo hosted a booth at Tokyo Rainbow Pride to signal support for LGBTQ people and rights in Japan. In a post on Masaki Matsumoto's *Gimme a Queer Eye* blog a few days later, Masaki cast Tokyo Rainbow Pride as "the very first pride in Japan that is shamelessly commercialist, neo-liberalism friendly, war-friendly, and corporate-friendly." Among the national and corporate interests Masaki identifies as commercializing and undermining indigenous LGBTQ activism at Tokyo Rainbow Pride is the US embassy.[18] LGBTQ activists often note that SOGI activism in many countries isn't homogeneous but consists of a diversity of politics, philosophies, priorities, and interests among LGBTQ people, advocates, and organizations on the ground. Such diversity reflects a robust and vital civil society. It also means that even consultation among indigenous LGBTQ activists and between international allies and funders doesn't guarantee universal approval for SOGI human rights programs and interventions.

Second, there are disagreements that divide LGBTQ individuals and communities from fellow citizens and authorities in their nations. One such disagreement resulted in violent protests and received attention in the United States as well as in Pakistan, where it occurred. In June 2011, before Clinton's State Department mandated that US embassies integrate LGBTQ programming into their operation, Embassy Islamabad hosted a Pride Celebration for embassy and other US personnel, foreign dignitaries, and representatives of Pakistan's LGBT communities. The embassy reported that the "gathering demonstrated continued U.S. Embassy support for human rights, including LGBT rights, in Pakistan at a time when those rights are increasingly under attack from extremist elements throughout Pakistani society." The press release posted to the embassy on the day of the event included a statement of support for "equal rights for all, regardless of sexual orientation or gender identity."[19] The statement was reposted elsewhere and publicized, and extremist Islamic parties held protests against the event in several Pakistani cities. Extremist Islamic leaders decried the promotion of LGBTQ human rights as "cultural terrorism" and LGBTQ—including indigenous—people as "the curse of society and social garbage."[20] The State Department acknowledged the protests and posted a statement on its website noting that the government of Pakistan did not issue a formal complaint to the US embassy or ambassador over the event.[21]

Finally, there are disagreements in the United States over official endorsement of SOGI human rights, domestic or global. Such an example of embassy engagement was the response of US conservative media to Embassy Tel Aviv flying the rainbow flag beneath the US flag to signal support for LGBTQ people during Pride Week in 2014. Reporting on the symbolism of the US and rainbow flags, a Fox News report combined conservative US (and Israeli) distaste for the display with a pointed comparison of Israeli tolerance and official intolerance in Arab states for SOGI rights. A caption below a photo of the two flags flying at Embassy Tel Aviv, reads:

"The gay pride flag flying under the Str [sic] Spangled Banner above the U.S. Embassy in Tel Aviv has generated mild controversy, but all observers concede Israel's Muslim neighbors would never condone such a display."[22]

Not all conservative reporting paired distaste for the rainbow flag with a statement of Arab or Muslim bias against SOGI; Fox News's Todd Starnes and RedState only registered disapproval of the pro-LGBTQ gesture.[23] Aside from composing a provocative title—"American Embassy in Israel Does Something with a Flag It Has Never Done Before"—Glenn Beck's news website, *The Blaze*, reported the episode so objectively that Beck's readers were enraged. Many who left comments threatened to seek their news and commentary elsewhere.[24] Although Pride festivals in Tel Aviv have not been marked by violence or threats of violence, Pride demonstrations in Jerusalem have been contentious and violent, with members of Orthodox Jewish communities decrying moral degeneracy and seeking to ban public LGBTQ events. In 2015, six Pride marchers were stabbed by an ultra-Orthodox man who had been imprisoned for years after stabbing marchers in 2005. One victim, a sixteen-year-old girl, died of her injuries.[25]

Ambassadors and embassy personnel in nations where LGBTQ people are marginalized and vulnerable are often involved in advocacy on behalf of LGBTQ people in discreet ways that they and other members of the foreign affairs establishment regard as intrinsic to their diplomatic mission. Here, I offer two vignettes: the first, a meeting at the State Department to discuss human rights violations against LGBTQ people in a nation I'll call Country NPH (No Promo Homo), provides some insight into internal US embassy considerations in situations of human rights peril to LGBTQ people.[26] The second focuses on the Anti-Homosexuality Bill in Uganda and public discourse in the United States about the role of a US embassy in supporting SOGI human rights.

## A Tale of Two Embassies

### Country No Promo Homo

In early 2013, I attended a meeting at the State Department for members of the US human rights community who were concerned about the human rights situation for LGBT people in Country NPH. The meeting was an off-the-record discussion with an embassy official in Country

NPH attended by State Department officials and representatives of many US- and Western-based human rights organizations, including Human Rights First, Amnesty International USA, the National Endowment for Democracy, the Council for Global Equality, and the Robert F. Kennedy Center for Justice and Human Rights.[27]

The US embassy official, who had just returned from Country NPH, included a briefing on anti-SOGI policy initiatives and broader issues of the environment for human rights and LGBTI people in that country. The official described the formation of a SOGI human rights working group that included personnel from the US embassy and local activists and noted that embassy personnel were engaging in a variety of tasks. These included coordinating efforts of US and other international donors on LGBTI and other human rights; coordinating relationships between international human rights organizations and indigenous LGBTI CSOs and activists; providing private messages of support for human rights by way of social media; providing administrative (e.g., bookkeeping and financial accountability) and assessment assistance to indigenous LGBTI human rights groups; engaging with scholars, journalists, clergy, and other professional and intellectual sectors of society about the role that Western embassies and their personnel can play in strengthening civil society and respect for human rights; and responding when possible to anxieties of non-LGBTI citizens about LGBTI people, including the transnational charge that LGBT people "promote" homosexuality. These tasks suggest a wide scope of activity that encompasses LGBTI nationals, the human rights community in Country NPH, domestic civil society more broadly, other embassies in Country NPH, US government personnel, and the international human rights community.

The official outlined a number of obstacles and challenges embassy personnel in Country NPH face in their commitment to strengthen LGBTI human rights there. One was the challenge of operating in conjunction with human rights partners in the context of "a shrinking space for civil society" without endangering those partners, especially domestic activists or international groups that might face negative consequences for advocating human rights. A second challenge was brokering and coordinating relationships between local LGBTI organizations and those from outside the country with regard to one effect that occurred from time to time: prominent foreign nongovernmental human rights actors receiving outsized attention and influencing the human rights agenda in a way that undercut the agenda and perspectives of human rights groups and activists in the country. In response to this challenge, US embassy personnel worked to make outside human rights actors less conspicuous while facilitating the common efforts of a multiplicity of actors. US government advocates of LGBTI human rights believed that it was ideal for the LGBTI movement in the country to be "[indigenous]-led" and that outside assistance and support were key to the success of the indigenous-led movement.

The embassy official characterized a final problem as a cultural challenge, perhaps an unexpected one, especially from the perspective of many progressive Western critics of US human rights interventions. The speaker noted that many non-LGBTI nationals associate LGBTI human rights with Western imperialism. However, many young LGBTI nationals whose interests are served by human rights advocacy aspire to enjoy the civil rights and public freedoms they associate with LGBT people in the West rather than endure the cultural limitations of their native country. This disjuncture between the LGBTI-related attitudes of ordinary (presumed heterosexual) nationals and the aspirations of LGBTI nationals who advocate for their own human rights could—and sometimes does, the official reported—complicate the efforts of embassy personnel to advocate for them in a context of traditional attitudes about sexuality and social authority and skepticism about Western values and morality.

## Uganda

Uganda has been a focus of international attention for its anti-LGBT policy and public attitudes for many years. The Anti-Homosexuality Bill was first introduced in 2009 under circumstances I discuss in more detail in the next chapter. A somewhat less odious version of that bill was signed into law in early 2014. The bill (and subsequent law) received considerable international attention because of the severity of its provisions; when it was introduced critics renamed it the "Kill the Gays Bill." The bill criminalized same-sex sexual behavior, particularly by designating some acts of same-sex sexuality as a capital crime of "aggravated homosexuality," whereas others are designated merely as "the offense of homosexuality," punishable by life imprisonment. Additional provisions included criminal penalties for women having sex with women and for anyone "promoting" homosexuality, including through advocacy for LGBT rights. The latter provision criminalized the failure to report acts defined as homosexual offenses under the law but was deleted before the bill was passed into law.

Once the Anti-Homosexuality Bill became law, some human rights and social justice organizations in the United States called on the Obama administration to withdraw the ambassador to Uganda in protest.[28] Groups that so urged the administration included Human Rights Watch, Human Rights First, the Human Rights Campaign, and All Out, a US LGBTQ organization that engages in campaigns for equality worldwide.[29] Kapya Kaoma, an Episcopal priest from Zambia and senior researcher at Political Research Associates who frequently writes on LGBTQ issues in Africa, flatly rejected this option in a brief essay. In "Warning: U.S. LGBTQ Organizations Falling into Uganda's Anti-Homosexuality Trap," Kaoma argues that Western human rights organizations don't grasp how crucial the embassies of Western nations have been in "provid[ing] safe spaces for African LGBTQ persons": "not only major LGBTQ rights organizations, but the United States and the European Union . . . have for many years fought for the rights and dignity of LGBTQ persons on African soil."

Kaoma gives two reasons the US should not recall its ambassador to Uganda under these circumstances. One is the danger of "confirm[ing] the false claim that Western nations," such as the United States have as a primary goal "recruit[ing] young people into homosexuality." Kaoma argues that this inference about official US reaction to the law would bolster African anxieties about Western imperialism, consolidate support for African leaders like Ugandan President Yoweri Museveni, and intensify hostile attitudes about LGBTQ people. The second reason directly addresses what Kaoma regards as the benefits of Western embassies to LGBTQ Africans.

> Honestly, had it not been for the presence of the U.S. and European embassies, African gays would have been massacred years ago, without any fear of consequences. For LGBTQ organizations to now demand they pull out of Uganda perilously compromises the lives of LGBTQ persons—who will not have anyone to turn to for safety, and strip our ability to monitor persecution.[30]

Kaoma suggests alternatives such as pressing religious leaders with moral authority over Christian Ugandans to speak out against LGBT criminalization and working to end the exporting of anti-LGBTQ bias from prominent US Christian conservatives.

Although some US embassy engagement on SOGI human rights was in process by 2011, Clinton mandated systematic engagement on SOGI as of 2012. By then, another form of international cooperation and advocacy had emerged: international LGBT human rights conferences that bring together activists, donors, and officials from governments and multilateral organizations to advance SOGI human rights. As of 2017, there have been four of these international SOGI human rights conferences. Although it's not possible to discuss all the conferences at length, I provide some background information about these meetings and a more thorough account of the 2014 conference, held in Washington, DC.

## International SOGI Human Rights Conferences

The first international LGBT human rights conference, held in Stockholm in March 2010, was sponsored by European CSOs: the Swedish International Development Cooperation Agency (Sida) and the Dutch-based Humanist Institute for Development Cooperation (Hivos).[31] In December 2013, the conference was held in Berlin and was sponsored by the German Federal Ministry for Economic Cooperation and Development and a CSO, the Lesbian and Gay Federation in Germany (LSVD). In preparation for the second meeting, the Amsterdam Network, a coalition of LGBTI organizations from North America and Europe, produced a set of ethical guidelines for SOGI human rights advocacy in support of foreign activists and "on behalf of LGBTI communities abroad."[32] "The Amsterdam Network Guiding Principles" was distributed to all attendees, including the two US government representatives who attended: DRL's Patricia Davis and USAID's Claire Lucas, who at the time was Senior Advisor for USAID's Public-Private Partnerships in the Office of Innovation and Development.[33]

The next meeting, in Washington, DC, in November 2014, was cosponsored by the US State Department and USAID. DRL's Jesse Bernstein (in 2014, Senior Program Officer and Team Lead for Marginalized Populations) and Kerry Ashforth (Program Officer) were instrumental in organizing that conference.[34] I attended the Conference to Advance the Human Rights of and Promote Inclusive Development for Lesbian, Gay, Bisexual, and Transgender Persons, and here I provide a brief account of the meeting and the documents and agreements produced from it. The conference brought LGBTQI human rights activists from around the world together with representatives of human rights CSOs, multilateral organizations, and thirty governments.[35] GEF partners provided travel support so that indigenous LGBTQ activists could attend the meeting. Although the conference was conducted primarily in English, some speakers addressed the audience in their own language. For the benefit of non–English speaking presenters, simultaneous translation was provided for all sessions in Spanish, French, and another language, and the State Department provided translators for a small number of people who spoke other languages.[36]

The three-day conference was structured with a variety of themed plenary and breakout sessions, and the panels of most of these sessions included indigenous representatives of "civil society"—that is, grassroots activists—as well as a mix of funders, international human rights activists, and public officials from participant countries and multinational organizations. Exceptions were a plenary framing session on diplomacy, which featured only diplomat speakers and a set of breakout sessions on the final day that separated representatives of governments and multilateral organizations from private funders and activists/representatives of civil society. The purpose of the final breakout sorting of conference participants into government and nongovernment groups likely had two purposes: first, to facilitate open conversations among government representatives, and second, to enable private funders and grassroots civil society activists to convene away from public officials and formulate a set of recommendations for future SOGI human rights advocacy and the next international SOGI conference.

Conference results included brief media statements and three reports that mapped discussions and made recommendations for continuing engagement in SOGI human rights advocacy. The first report to be distributed to conferees and posted on the State Department website was "Joint Government and Multilateral Agency Communique" (November 20, 2014), which affirmed general commitments to SOGI human rights and specific commitments to integrate SOGI into development assistance and use diplomacy to advance SOGI human rights. On November 21, the State Department posted a brief media statement, "Key Outcomes from the Annual Conference," which provided bullet points that announced agreements and information such as an initiative of PEPFAR and the GEF "to document how stigma and discrimination, including discriminatory laws and policies, impede efforts to address HIV/AIDS" and new assistance from private donors "to strengthen assistance to transgender and intersex persons."[37]

Of the documents to emerge from the Washington conference, the second and third reports are the most important from the perspective of understanding transnational SOGI human rights advocacy. The second report summarizes the results of deliberations by SOGI human rights activists and representatives of local or regional LGBTQ people from around the world. Working in small groups as well as a group-of-the-whole, this CSO contingent produced the report "Civil Society and Non-State Donor Recommendations." Significantly, the civil society representatives added "Intersex" to their list of identities in the title of the conference—and thus in their report—with the understanding that subsequent references to the conference after its conclusion would augment LGBT identity with I. As unofficial rapporteur for the civil society group, Julie Dorf circulated the recommendations to conference participants, including government representatives, on December 16 "on behalf of the representatives of civil society and non-governmental donors."[38]

This document outlined priorities for SOGI human rights work and provided a detailed map of activist policy recommendations, interorganization coordination protocols, and guidelines for designing, implementing, monitoring, and evaluating human rights efforts in cooperation with local advocates and advocacy organizations. The report itself is divided into four sections: Introduction, Guiding Principles, Key Recommendations, and Key Recommendations for Next Conference in Early 2016 (originally scheduled for April 2016, the conference in Montevideo, Uruguay, was held in July). The brief introduction acknowledged progress on SOGI human rights organizing since the first international conference in Sweden in 2010, emphasized the importance of continued LGBTQ organizing and human rights advocacy, and pointed out that support from governments SOGI human rights has "financial" and "nonfinancial" components. Guiding principles that "underlie the recommendations" included a call for donors to "acknowledge intersecting marginalization," "recognise differential experiences," and "take into account global geopolitics."[39]

The final conference report from the US government sponsors performed a number of functions. One of these was to report key lessons from speakers and dialogue in the meeting's plenary and breakout sessions on topics that included the role of diplomacy in SOGI human rights, the role of multilateral organizations, inclusive development programming, responding to anti-LGBT laws, understanding intersex issues, "the invisible 'L'" (that is, attending to lesbian-specific issues that are frequently overlooked), safety and security, funding for HIV programs, gender identity and expression, judicial and legal reform strategies, and engagement with religious leaders and groups. The final conference report integrated

statements of affirmation of support for SOGI human rights from governments and the CSO recommendations that provided the basis for 2015
GEF grant themes. Finally, the report offered key recommendations for
the next SOGI international human rights conference.

The Global LGBTI Human Rights Conference: Nonviolence, Non-
discrimination, and Social Inclusion, sponsored by the governments of
Uruguay and the Netherlands, was held in Montevideo, Uruguay, in July
2016. US government representatives in attendance were Jesse Bernstein,
Randy Berry (then Special Envoy for LGBTI Human Rights), Kerry
Ashforth, and Todd Larson (then Senior Lesbian, Gay, Bisexual, and
Transgender Coordinator at USAID). US ambassador to the UN Samantha
Power was originally scheduled to speak but was unable to attend, so her
comments were delivered by video. A goal of the Montevideo conference
was to continue the process initiated at the Washington conference in
2014 of broadening the meeting's focus from SOGI human rights donors
to international diplomacy and the foreign policies of states. An example
of this expansion of focus is that both conferences featured ministerial-
level national participation in addition to activists and CSOs at all levels
of SOGI human rights advocacy.

The Montevideo conference also hosted the launch of a new partnership: the Equal Rights Coalition. Made up of forty nations, the coalition
has principles that affirm the applicability of the UDHR to LGBTI people
and pledges to "coordinate their diplomatic efforts, share information and
work together at the international level" for SOGI human rights. The initial
coalition fact sheet emphasizes its function as a diplomatic rather than a
funding partnership and stresses the importance for members of consulting
with civil society and being accountable to SOGI advocates and CSOs.[40]

International SOGI human rights advocacy now takes place in settings such as regular multinational, multilateral conferences and a variety
of other forums that represent different "tracks" of diplomacy and diverse
networks of advocates, representatives, and organizations.[41] Many of these
meetings aren't publicized or reported in press accounts of SOGI human
rights advocacy. Of course researchers rarely participate in quiet diplomacy
that consists of interactions between US officials and representatives of
regimes and civil society in places where people are discriminated against
on the basis of SOGI. Nor can researchers observe many situations in
which US officials meet with LGBTQ people and activists. To bridge this
gap between information about US government SOGI human rights advocacy and the reception of this advocacy by LGBTQ activists, individuals,

and organizations, I present a case study of participant observation at a conference organized by an African regional grassroots LGBTQ human rights organization. In what follows, I call this organization African Sexual Orientation and Gender Identity Human Rights Organization, or ASOGI-HRO—which conveniently can be pronounced "a SOGI hero"—for short.

## US–Indigenous SOGI Advocacy: A Case Study

ASOGIHRO is a pseudonym for an indigenous regional LGBTQ advocacy organization that functions as an umbrella group supporting civil society activism on sexuality, sexual health, and SOGI human rights in Africa. Besides a commitment to human rights, the organization's vision encompasses such values as gender equality, human dignity, and social justice. ASOGIHRO does not list names of individuals who are connected with the group on its website, a decision that is probably a response to threats that have confronted LGBTQ activists in many countries in recent years. As an umbrella organization, ASOGIHRO is a grantor that provides resources to sexual minority groups; it is also a grantee of the US government and other human rights and social justice funders.

Because some ASOGIHRO subscribers and conferees might suffer negative consequences if their affiliation or participation became public, the group does not advertise its conference online or publish lists of attendees. For that reason, I have given the organization a pseudonym, and in what follows I do not divulge information that would identify the group or the location of its meeting. In 2014, I learned about ASOGIHRO, its work, and its relationship with the State Department when I met the head of the organization in Washington, DC. In 2015, I was permitted to register for the conference and once there, I attended sessions, collected literature from the wide variety of groups with members at the meeting, and spoke informally with activists and funders. All other information in this chapter is drawn from my field notes for the 2015 meeting, conference literature (2013 and 2015), interviews with Patricia Davis (DRL Director of Global Programming), and formal and informal conversations with other sources. After attending the conference and collecting data about the group and its partnership with US government agencies, I hope to accomplish two tasks: first, to gain firsthand knowledge of how the US government engages in SOGI human rights advocacy with grassroots LGBTQ groups; and second, to use my own observations and information collected from the 2015 meeting to verify information about US government SOGI human rights advocacy provided by State Department officials, government documents, and other sources and thus enhance the reliability of this account.

## The 2013 ASOGIHRO Conference

In early 2013, the executive officer of ASOGIHRO visited Washington, DC, to meet with US government officials, including Davis and Bernstein.[42] In addition to conversations regarding the GEF, ASOGIHRO's representatives invited Davis and Bernstein to attend their 2013 conference. That meeting brought together activists and members of LGBTQ groups from across Africa and members of the international human rights community. The majority of attendees were citizens of African nations; a few were scholars at African universities or representatives of funding organizations. Davis and Bernstein attended as representatives of the US State Department—the first instance of US government participation in the conference—and were the only representatives of a foreign state present.

The conference opened with a preconference for donors from several organizations: Dutch and Norwegian CSOs, George Soros's Open Society Foundations, the MacArthur Foundation, the American Jewish World Service, the Ford Foundation, and Benetech. Of these, Benetech is less well known than many large human rights groups. Benetech is a nonprofit umbrella enterprise that, among other activities, hosts a Human Rights Program, hosts the Human Rights Data Analysis Group, and includes Martus, secure software for creating databases for human rights groups and reports that protects the identity of witnesses to human rights abuses. Benetech analysts have provided data analysis and expert testimony in many cases of human rights violations in Latin America, Asia, Africa, Eastern Europe, and the Middle East for such clients as the UN Office of the High Commissioner for Human Rights.[43]

A key goal for the ASOGIHRO preconference was determining which "priority populations" donors would serve among the groups of particular interest to the conference organizers: lesbians, gay men, bisexuals, transgender people, men who have sex with men, refugees, and sex workers. With regard to these groups, US policies prohibit international organizations that receive US funding from using those funds to advocate for sex workers' rights or for decriminalization of sex work, although US agencies can fund programs for sex workers on the basis of issues such as sex trafficking, anti-LGBTQ bias, or health (e.g., HIV/AIDS). These policies include the Trafficking Victims Protection Reauthorization Act and the United States Leadership against HIV/AIDS, Tuberculosis, and Malaria Act (known as the Global AIDS Act), both passed into law in 2003. The prohibition on US government funds being applied to sex workers' rights advocacy has been unpopular in the human rights community because it complicates transnational responsiveness to sex trafficking and sexual health threats.[44]

A session at the 2013 ASOGIHRO conference, scheduled for the afternoon of the second day, was "Donor Speed Dating," so denoted in the conference program.[45] Conference organizers placed conferees in about a dozen circles of approximately fifteen participants each so conferees could talk directly with donors about sources of funds and assistance and how to access them. Donors—representatives of human rights organizations and the US State Department—were limited to speaking to each group for seven minutes. Davis and Bernstein described to conferees the three ways the DRL could render financial and other assistance for LGBTQ people and groups by way of the GEF and then took questions. Many activists followed up with private or small group meetings with Davis, Bernstein, or both about how to access US assistance.

In describing the conference, Davis reported that many (perhaps most) of the activists in attendance had never met with US government representatives and that these activists responded positively to the message that LGBT Africans and human rights advocates were eligible to receive US human rights assistance. The human rights activists Davis described as having been "very welcoming" to the US delegation and other funders in 2013 were also welcoming in 2015.[46]

### The 2015 ASOGIHRO Conference

Between the 2013 and 2015 ASOGIHRO meetings, the State Department and USAID hosted the Conference to Advance the Human Rights of and Inclusive Development for LGBTI Persons in Washington, DC, and a few African activists attended both conferences. For the 2015 ASOGIHRO meeting, attendance had increased enough over the earlier meeting that plenary sessions were held in a large tent rather than an indoor space, as they had been in 2013.[47] The US delegation attending the conference expanded to five members: Bernstein, Davis, and Emily Renard from the State Department and Vy Lam and Todd Larson from USAID.

As in 2013, US officials were the only government officials to attend the 2015 conference, although a representative of a Norwegian CSO that works closely with its government attended. The donor preconference attracted representatives from organizations that grant funding for SOGI human rights, including Astraea, the Jewish World Service, Wellspring, and the Open Society Foundations. I did not attend the preconference, so my account begins with the conference proper. A plenary session on the first day of the meeting was titled "We Don't Know the Answers (But We Have a Few Explanations)." This donor-led session took its title from a statement Davis made at the 2013 international SOGI human rights conference in Berlin when she introduced herself by saying, "I'm from the United States, and we don't know all the answers." The 2015 ASOGI-HRO session featured Davis and representatives of three CSOs that fund SOGI human rights–related projects and programs: US-based Astraea, the American Jewish World Service, and the Deutsche Gesellschaft für Internationale Zusammenarbeit. The idea of the panel was for funders to explain to activists and representatives of LGBTQ organizations what specific conditions apply to funding from their organizations, to respond to questions about funding opportunities and constraints, and to suggest ways differently situated groups—such as those whose representatives were in attendance—could assist local LGBTQI human rights organizations.

In 2015, as in 2013, activists and panelists and attendees discussed the specific constraint on US government assistance that, according to Davis, was a subject of difficult conversations in 2013: US policies that prevent the funding of sex worker rights activism by agencies and officials. Davis explained that the constraint doesn't bar funding for assistance to sex workers as long as that assistance is not related to sex workers' rights or the decriminalization of sex work. Although some activists who attended the session pushed back against this constraint, Davis noted that the prohibition affects all US government assistance. She explained that the funds and assistance disbursed by the US to support SOGI human rights originate either from US tax revenue or from contributions of other governments, foundations, or funders. Whatever the source of these resources, when they are managed and disbursed by a US government agency, they are subject to specific internal processes of accountability and statutory requirements.

In her remarks, Davis set forth goals for cooperation between US government representatives and grassroots LGBTQI activists: to listen to

activists about their needs and issues, to travel to meet activists in locations around the world, to bring activists to meetings in donor countries
(including the United States), to deploy knowledgeable personnel to work
closely with activists to meet their needs, to protect the safety and security
of grantees and beneficiaries of human rights interventions, and to work
with grantee activists and organizations to adequately report what they
accomplish with the assistance they receive. Two questions addressed
to Davis as the US representative focused on the operational needs of
organizations. The first criticized a typical model of assistance as geared
to prioritizing and funding high-profile deliverables rather than meeting
the fixed and ongoing costs of advocacy organizations. Davis responded
that State Department human rights programs funded through the GEF
can in fact be used to pay fixed costs such as rent, personnel, and equip-
ment, so that human rights groups are able to function effectively over
time. The second operational question concerned the difficulties activists
often have with the reporting and administrative demands of managing
grants from international funders. Davis's response outlined a practice by
which the State Department funds a grant to a larger organization as an
implementing partner, and the implementing partner then subgrants to
the smaller group and agrees to take on the task of grant administration.
This practice provides a cooperative path to funding small LGBT human
rights organizations while shifting administrative tasks to groups with
more infrastructure and expertise in grant administration.

A key piece of information about US government resources and assistance dedicated to SOGI human rights was revealed in the "We Don't Know
the Answers" plenary session: under the US government's marking policy,
implementing partners and grantees must "mark," or brand, all products of
US government assistance at public meetings, on organizations' websites,
and on all other materials that might be produced from that assistance.[48]
DRL has received an exemption to this branding requirement because of
the sensitive nature of many of its human rights programs and because
association with the United States could place many human rights defenders at risk. This exemption is explained in grant agreements that grantees
(and implementing partners) sign when they receive aid. The exemption
means that grantees are free to reveal their cooperation with the United
States, but they are not required to publicize an assistance relationship
with the US government that may leave them open to charges of collusion.

LGBTQ organizations do make use of the exemption to the State
Department's marking policy. For example, even though ASOGIHRO is a

grantee of the US government, no information about its relationship with the United States appears on its website or in other materials produced by the organization. As I have researched US government interventions on behalf of LGBTQ human rights, I have discovered that many local advocacy groups have ties with the State Department that they do not reveal to the public. For example, at a recent LGBTQ human rights conference in a European city, I met one such DRL GEF grantee, who leads a Middle Eastern LGBTQ human rights organization that serves as a network hub for and regional partner with other Middle Eastern LGBTQ organizations. It does not advertise its relationship with the US State Department.

The second day of the conference included sessions of "Activist-Donor Speed Dating." The conference program promised activists "open engagement" with funders in the "Speed Dating" sessions and, indeed, the discussion was lively and informative in the sessions I attended. Organized differently than it was in the 2013 program, this version of "speed dating" featured two sets of four concurrent sessions. The first set of sessions concentrated on a region of Africa: north, south, east, and west. Representatives from the State Department, USAID, and other funding organizations spread out and formed a funder panel for each session. These regional sessions were followed by a brief break, after which a new set of topical sessions convened.

The topical session of "Activist-Donor Speed Dating" I attended focused on sexual health, and the US government panelist for that session was the DRL's Jesse Bernstein. Bernstein offered the session attendees a quick yet detailed overview of the three types of assistance that make up the GEF and represent opportunities for funding and assistance for SOGI human rights advocacy. He offered examples from funded projects that would be relevant to sexual health advocacy. One activist in this session asked how difficult or bureaucratic the process of applying for funding is, and Bernstein outlined a revised and streamlined grant process that had been designed to be more proposer-friendly than previous processes. In this process, advocates respond to a solicitation for proposals for particular programs by submitting a two-page statement of interest (SOI) without a budget. Donor representatives review the SOIs and request full formal proposals from activists or organizations for projects deemed competitive. At the formal proposal stage, potential grantees can receive further guidance from State Department personnel to complete the proposal, and DRL may encourage activists from smaller organizations to seek partnership with more experienced LGBTQ organizations such as ASOGIHRO.

SOGI human rights advocates attended the ASOGIHRO 2015 meeting from all across the African continent. Although I do not have a comprehensive list of delegates by nation, I know that activists from the following countries attended: Algeria, Angola, Botswana, Burundi, Cameroon, Democratic Republic of Congo, Egypt, Ethiopia, Ghana, Kenya, Liberia, Mozambique, Nigeria, South Africa, South Sudan, Tanzania, Uganda, Zambia, and Zimbabwe. As a whole, the conference incorporated presentations and discussions on a variety of topics germane to the concerns of LGBTQ people in different legal, social, and cultural positions in African nations, including the benefits and limitations of litigation; navigating conflict in and among LGBTQ human rights organizations; the role of young people in the movement; promoting transgender rights and awareness; migration, asylum seeking, and refugees; the role of art in the movement; addressing public health concerns of LGBTQ people (including but not limited to HIV/AIDS); international advocacy; employment and entrepreneurship for LGBTQ people discriminated against in labor markets; building movement sustainability; and LGBTQ people and religion. Many funders attended these sessions throughout the course of the meeting, no doubt learning more about the pressures, challenges, programs, and successes of LGBTQ movements on the continent.

My primary motivation for attending ASOGIHRO was to observe firsthand a conference to advance the cause of SOGI human rights that was planned and executed by indigenous advocates and incorporated US government representatives and US assistance. I didn't observe every event at the conference. I didn't participate in private meetings between funders and human rights defenders, although I was present for some meetings that took place in public spaces. Separate spaces at some meals were designated for the benefit of country and regional delegations, and I respected these boundaries. However, I observed all plenary sessions and as many breakouts as I could, met and spoke informally with many human rights activists and funders, and collected conference materials. From this participation, I have been able to subject accounts and comments regarding human rights assistance from informants in DRL and USAID to as much scrutiny as participant observation allows in such a context. Perhaps more important, I observed nothing at ASOGIHRO I would count as evidence to disconfirm information I received from other sources.

Although representatives from the State Department and USAID attended the ASOGIHRO conference, the agencies have diverse and overlapping mandates. USAID is the government agency whose official mandate is international economic development, poverty relief, and humanitarian assistance. The agency provides technical and financial assistance and has, for example, underwritten research and dissemination of research results on human development.[49] Under the Obama administration, USAID engaged in efforts to integrate SOGI human rights concerns into development programs. Instrumental in this effort was Todd Larson, before he retired after the election of Donald Trump. In 2014, USAID cohosted the Conference to Advance the Human Rights of and Inclusive Development for LGBTI Persons in Washington, DC. USAID has other projects that integrate economic development and SOGI human rights, most notably the LGBT Global Development Partnership, an initiative of USAID's Global Development Lab's Center for Transformational Partnerships.

## USAID and LGBTI Human Rights

USAID is an independent agency of the federal government led by an administrator, but the agency receives its guidance on foreign affairs from the President and the Secretary of State.[50] For purposes of coordination, USAID and the State Department operate under a joint Strategic Plan and a joint budget.[51] Appointed as the first—and as of early 2017, the only—USAID Senior LGBT Coordinator in 2012,[52] Todd Larson had among his responsibilities managing the agency's implementation of Obama's 2011 Presidential Memorandum. The memorandum does not call specifically for LGBT-inclusive development policy and programs; this focus emerged from within USAID and in its collaboration with DRL for SOGI human rights and LGBT-inclusive development.

Established in 2014 under the Obama administration, USAID's Global Development Lab was tasked with producing, sponsoring, and disseminating "development innovations" with an emphasis on "scientific and technological advances" and transnational partnerships. In the words of one bullet point that seems to sum up the initiative, USAID seeks to "improve millions of lives by speeding up the adoption of the most promising proven breakthrough innovations."[53] The Global Development Lab is made up of two offices and five centers, one of which is the Center for Transformational Partnership, which is tasked with "develop[ing] global partnerships with a wide range of public and private sector stakeholders to extend the impact and sustainability of global development programming."[54]

In organizational terms, the LGBT Global Development Partnership (GDP) is an initiative of the Global Development Lab's Center for Trans-formational Partnerships. The partnership was initiated during Clinton's State Department tenure by Claire Lucas, then a political appointee and USAID Senior Advisor. Lucas and her partner, Judy Dlugacz, founder and president of The Olivia Companies, are prominent Democratic Party and Hillary Clinton supporters. In 2016, the GDP, which promotes "global lesbian, gay, bisexual and transgender human rights, equality and economic empowerment," was administered by LGBT Coordinator Todd Larson. In the words of former USAID Administrator Dr. Rajiv Shaw, the goal of SOGI programming such as the GDP is "a world in which the basic rights of LGBT persons are respected and they are able to live with dignity, free from discrimination, persecution and violence."[55] According to Larson, the goal of USAID LGBTI programming has been to make "LGBTI inclusive development part of USAID's DNA."[56] Like the GEF, the GDP is a public–private partnership. While the GEF's partners are international, the GDP is a more US-focused partnership that includes LGBT CSOs such as Astraea and the Gay and Lesbian Victory Institute, as well as the LGBTQ research-focused Williams Institute.[57]

USAID's development policies and their implementation are appro-priate objects for criticism and political activism. However, even when the focus turns from development and economic policies and programming to integrating SOGI human rights into its programs and operations, it's clear that there are many potential problems for the agency to surmount. At times there are operational discrepancies between US policy and the goals and activities of groups funded by USAID as grantees or implement-ing partners. One example is the revelation that USAID has funded an Indonesian health organization, Lembaya Kesehatan Nahdlatul Ulama, whose parent organization, Nahdlatul Ulama, actively campaigns against SOGI human rights. Lembaya Kesehatan Nahdlatul Ulama receives USAID grants for HIV and tuberculosis prevention, diagnosis, and treatment. Kyle Knight, of Human Rights Watch's LGBT Rights Program, describes Nahdlatul Ulama as "an extremely influential organization . . . in religious spaces[,] civil society activism, socioeconomic development, and policy-making" whose support for criminalization of same-sex sexuality and a ban on the "promotion" of same-sex sexuality contradicts its "ideology of tolerance and social justice."[58]

As the revelation of health and anti-LGBT advocacy in Indonesia suggests, SOGI/LGBTQ CSOs and alternative media have an important role to play in researching and reporting cases in which US aid is applied—directly or indirectly—to violating the human rights of LGBTQ people. Global programs, including PEPFAR, the Global Development Partnership, and other initiatives, can coexist with human rights violations that compromise or threaten SOGI human rights. In these circumstances, it is necessary for citizens, journalists, and CSOs to publicize human rights abuses and hold the US government responsible for the outcomes of its policies and practices. This is the process of working to make governments accountable for upholding human rights. This process often fails and is never complete, but it's a project we cannot abandon.

In his 2013 "Pride @ State" address, Secretary of State John Kerry described personnel at the State Department as enjoying a "privilege of being here"—both as members of the agency and as US citizens—that also confers a "larger responsibility" for improving the standing of LGBTQ people abroad. Kerry made this connection in the context of a statement that echoed the theme of his predecessor's 2011 human rights speech in Geneva: the fact that some LGBTQ people endure torture and murder for their nonnormative gender or sexuality. Finally, Kerry affirmed his general support for the strategic national value of embracing SOGI human rights and, more specifically, for the GEF announced by Clinton in Geneva. For Kerry, support for LGBT human rights abroad is "the right thing to do. It's also in our country's strategic interest."[59]

I return to this question of congruence between US support for human rights abroad and strategic national interests later. For the moment, I note that such a claim about human rights cannot be taken at face value. This is so not because it can be assumed that avowed support for human rights abroad on the part of government officials is a deception that systematically cloaks less savory goals and motives. Rather, government officials operate in a context in which budgets are limited, US policy forecloses some possible practices, agency officials may disagree about the efficacy and prioritizing of programs and interventions, officials across the US government disagree about the legitimacy of support for SOGI human rights and other foreign policy goals that may—and often do—conflict with and trump human rights goals. However, even if we can't take Kerry's statement as incontrovertible fact, his State Department made a high-profile investment in SOGI human rights when it appointed the first Special Envoy for LGBT Human Rights.

## Special Envoy for LGBTI Human Rights

In February 2015, John Kerry announced the appointment of Randy W. Berry to be the first US Special Envoy for Human Rights of LGBT (later, LGBTI) People, a position he held when Donald Trump entered the White House.[60] The post of Special Envoy is a senior staff position in DRL; the Special Envoy reports to the Assistant Secretary of DRL and coordinates with an assistant and officials in DRL. For some time before the appointment, US-based LGBTQ organizations had collectively lobbied members of Congress and pressed the State Department to appoint a Special Envoy or Representative, whom they believed would focus and enhance the US government's efforts to support SOGI human rights. This activism was evident in the summer of 2014 when LGBTQ activists held a briefing that I attended, "The United States' Role in Generating Debate on LGBT Rights" in the Rayburn House of Representatives Office Building on Capitol Hill.[61] Speakers at the briefing represented Advocates for Youth, IGLHRC (OutRight Action International), and the Human Rights Campaign (HRC), a domestic CSO that only became involved in international SOGI advocacy in 2013.[62]

Speakers and members of the audience, many of whom were US-based activists, voiced support for the appointment of a Special Envoy and for two pieces of legislation that have not received serious attention in Congress. One, the Global Respect Act, would deny entry to the United States to foreign leaders or citizens who violate the human rights of LGBTQ people outside the United States. A more far-reaching law, the International Human Rights Defense Act, would commit the United States to embed LGBTQ human rights in its foreign policy, require the designation of a Special Envoy, and require the United States to develop a global strategy to prevent and respond to discrimination and violence against LGBTQ people abroad.[63] Although these bills stood no chance of passing during Obama's second term, Kerry implemented the portion of the International Human Rights Defense Act within the scope of his authority, creating the new post of Special Envoy and appointing Berry to it.

News of the position and appointment was hailed by many LGBTQ activists and organizations. Mainstream media outlets, including BuzzFeed, the *New York Times, Time, USA Today, US News and World Report*, and the *Washington Post*, picked up the story. In its report, *Politico* dug into the background circumstances in which the position was created and speculated briefly about the prospects for the role if Republicans regained the White House in the 2016 presidential election; the author notes dryly that "requests for comment from leading 2016 GOP presidential hopefuls about whether they would keep the position were ignored, declined or not directly answered."[64] Although it's by no means clear what will become of the position or a commitment to SOGI human rights, Berry remained at his post in the early months of the Trump administration.

However, not all LGBTQ human rights defenders supported the position. For example, soon after Berry was appointed, Nigerian LGBT rights advocate Adebisi Alimi reiterated a frequent concern about the appointment of Special Envoys for geographic regions or issues: that these envoys can function as symbolic substitutes for robust and well-resourced political commitment.[65] Alimi also criticized the appointment of a white man to such a post, pointing out the possibility that the choice could reinforce conceptions of same-sex sexuality as a Western practice at odds with non-Western cultures.[66]

In fact, Berry admits to having been "a bit reluctant" to accept the position when he was first approached about it because of questions about the clarity of the mandate and how well resourced the position would be. Although Kerry wanted a career diplomat for the position, Berry was aware that many State Department officials and activists were ambivalent about the utility of the post. He decided to accept the post for reasons he describes as "very human and very personal": becoming a parent and perceiving the possibility of improving the environment for human rights. Berry believed that the timing was right for the kind of human rights engagement represented by the appointment of a Special Envoy because of positive changes in the status of LGBTQ people in the United States and support across branches of the US government.[67]

An early intervention for Berry was a 2015 tour of more than fifteen nations to introduce himself to foreign leaders in governments and other institutions and promote SOGI human rights. This tour included a visit to Jamaica by Berry and Larson that was documented in an interview and article in the *Jamaica Observer* under the headline "We Came to Listen and Talk, Not to Judge." Berry and Larson discussed meeting with Jamaican policy makers and faith leaders, and they responded to protests organized by church groups that the US officials had come "to force Jamaica to embrace [the] homosexual lifestyle as normal." Referring to the protests, Berry said that he and Larson had

> been very, very careful—as the president (Barack Obama) was during his visit and others—to ensure we are engaging in a spirit of equality within a human rights framework. That

is what we are interested in. We are not at all interested in making judgements, in using any other manner than to seek just an honest dialogue.

Berry and Larson addressed the US embrace of SOGI human rights as a process and a "framework" for US policy that could provide grounds for "conversation" and "dialogue" between Jamaican communities and the United States. Emphasizing that US commitments regarding SOGI human rights have changed over time, Berry noted that "we're speaking very clearly to our friends about where US policy is, understanding that we have also come into this space after a long struggle and to see how we can be a positive partner."[68]

Grassroots activists also have traveled to Washington to meet with Berry and discuss problems they encounter when advocating for SOGI human rights in their own nations. For example, in February 2016, activists from two LGBTQ CSOs in the Central Asian Republic of Kyrgyzstan met with Berry at the State Department. Aizhan Kadralieva (of Labrys Kyrgyzstan) and Ruslan Kim (of Kyrgyz Indigo) "highlighted . . . examples of anti-LGBT violence and discrimination" in Kyrgyzstan and discussed their concerns about a "gay propaganda" bill introduced in the legislature in 2014 and modeled on a similar Russian law that went into effect in 2013.[69] The most recent State Department Country Report for conditions in the Kyrgyz Republic in 2015 suggests a dire human rights situation for many groups across multiple social and political sites. The report's executive summary cites "police-driven extortion of sexual and ethnic minority groups" as well as "discrimination and violence against women, persons with disabilities, ethnic and religious minorities, and persons based on their sexual orientation or gender identity." Under the particular category "Acts of Violence, Discrimination, and Other Abuses Based on Sexual Orientation and Gender Identity," the litany of human rights violations include physical and verbal abuse, loss of livelihood, public outing of LGBTQ people, extortion, police brutality, and denunciation by political figures. The report specifically addresses the vulnerability of lesbians and WSW to forced marriage and "corrective rape."[70]

The office of the Special Envoy did not include subject matter expert staff until spring 2016, when DRL Program Officer Jesse Bernstein became a Senior Advisor in Berry's office. Bernstein assists the Special Envoy in developing and coordinating policy for SOGI human rights assistance, and one ongoing goal of the Special Envoy's office is to strengthen and advance regional leadership on SOGI human rights. For example, Berry, Bernstein, and Davis traveled to Australia in late 2016 for meetings held alongside the Pacific LGBTI Youth Forum. In a press release, the State Department described these meetings as related to

> stepping up [the agency's] efforts in the Indo-Pacific region to combat discrimination and violence against LGBTI people, coordinate how [the agency] provide[s] targeted funding for LGBTI communities and improve [the agency's] outreach to civil society organizations, which play a vital role in driving change.[71]

Bernstein and Berry agree that the appointment of a Special Envoy for LGBTI human rights has made a significant difference in raising the profile of SOGI human rights and publicizing the needs of LGBTQ people as a marginalized group. For Berry, the position of Special Envoy generates opportunities for private, senior-level meetings with government officials around the world in which honest discussions of LGBTI human rights can take place. Complementing such diplomacy are other forms of international attention to LGBT human rights such as the creation of the Equal Rights Coalition in Uruguay and the appointment of a UN Independent Expert on Sexual Orientation and Gender Identity—both of which occurred in 2016.

Although the office of the Special Envoy for LGBTI Human Rights has not been eliminated, the outlook for human rights policy in the Trump administration isn't clear. Also unknown are answers to specific questions about US support for SOGI human rights: whether (or to what extent and in what ways) the administration will commit the United States to international SOGI assistance and advocacy. In late 2016, I attended the ILGA world conference in Bangkok, Thailand, in part to observe some international LGBTQ reactions to the US presidential election. In Bangkok, worry about the future of funding and assistance for SOGI human rights was palpable. Nobody could predict how the election of America's "post-truth" president might reshape and possibly disrupt the US commitment to SOGI human rights abroad, but a number of participants speculated and tendered perspectives and strategies to deal with possible global consequences. It was clear that human rights advocates, grantees and implementing partners of the US State Department, and other donors were anything but indifferent to the consequence of the election for US human rights assistance.

## SOGI Human Rights Skepticism

Like so many other labels, concepts, and categories of political life, "human rights" is a contested idea between the political left and right in the United States, as well as among constituencies in these broad ideological camps. Often identified with the political left in the global North, it is also accurate to say that human rights has skeptics on the left and proponents on the right. In recent years, the Christian right has turned more attention and resources to resisting SOGI rights outside the United States and any actions and rhetoric that indicate the US government affirms the rights and well-being of LGBTQ people.

The most obvious ideological group in the United States to oppose LGBT civil rights at home and US government intervention on behalf of LGBT human rights abroad is conservatives. Some oppose virtually all forms of foreign assistance as purposes for which taxpayer funds should not be used. The resolve, if not the numbers, of such US citizens no doubt has been bolstered in recent years by the near collapse of the global economy and the rise of the Tea Party movement.[72] However, I focus on the objections of an overlapping constituency within and outside the Tea Party: the Christian conservative movement also known as the Christian right.

Christian conservatives and organizations that advocate Christian conservative social and policy positions oppose the eradication of stigma related to LGBTQ identity, same-sex sexuality, and nonnormative gender as well as the inclusion of such people, identities, and issues in the category of human rights. Although they actively work against US government support for LGBTQ people and human rights, their orientation toward human rights is complicated by support for religious freedom and rights, including the right to discriminate against LGBTQ people. In chapter 4, I unpack the beliefs, activism, and predicaments associated with the US Christian right's struggles against SOGI human rights and against the US government's advocacy of those human rights.

Chapter 4

# No Human Right to Sodomy

*Christian Conservative Opposition to SOGI Human Rights*

### The "External" Critique of SOGI Human Rights

The conservative critique of SOGI human rights and of the US government as a champion of those rights is "external" to the LGBTQ movement in the sense that it doesn't originate in a concern for the well-being of those who engage in same-sex sexual relations and/or exhibit a nonnormative gender identity. The Christian conservative movement is the most consistent and persistent opponent of LGBTQ civil rights in the United States. In addition to resisting the normalization of same-sex relations and the erosion of stigma against same-sex sexuality and nonnormative gender identities, the Christian right opposes policies and social practices that incorporate LGBT people into institutions, organizations, and professions from which they previously have been excluded, including teaching, marriage, military service, Scouting, parenthood, and the clergy.

In recent decades, the Christian right has encountered what appears to be an intractable problem with its anti-LGBTQ politics in the United States: a gradual but unmistakable rise in support for inclusion and equal treatment for LGBTQ people. The worry that LGBT-friendly public policies stimulate social and political backlash against LGBT people has long been common among LGBTQ people and activists in the US. However, political scientists Benjamin Bishin, Thomas J. Hayes, Matthew Incantalupo, and Charles Anthony Smith demonstrate that what has been read as backlash is another phenomenon: the intensification of "existing negative opinion" as anti-LGBT elites mobilize their constituencies to oppose challenges to bias and discrimination.[1] Even this intensification of anti-LGBTQ politics may be difficult to activate in the future, however. Not only are many younger Christian conservatives more LGBT-affirming than their elders, some Christian conservatives have come to gradually occupy a position of "structured ambivalence" toward same-sex sexuality and the LGBTQ people they encounter in social settings.[2]

Some groups and leaders of the Christian right have responded to LGBT-affirming attitude changes by resigning themselves to moral defeat, but most insist that Christian conservatives will ultimately prevail. Since the 1990s, many organizations, leaders, and activists responded to an increasingly challenging domestic cultural environment by moving some of their attention and operations to arenas outside the United States that hold more promise for implacable antagonism to LGBTQ rights. In some parts of the world, these US-based anti-LGBTQ missionaries have become recognized as "experts" on the problem of LGBT people and the dire consequences their existence poses for the specific communities and the nations in which they reside.

I take the title phrase of this chapter, "no human right to sodomy," from a 2014 essay by anti-LGBTQ pastor and attorney Scott Lively, who has played a prominent role in inciting bias and hostility to LGBTQ people, particularly in Russia and Uganda. In his essay, Lively positively assesses official Russian policy against same-sex sexuality and LGBTQ people and asserts that Russia will soon emerge as "the greatest defender of true human rights" among nations.[3] LGBTQ Americans who were adults in the 1980s may also hear echoes of a similar phrase from the majority opinion in the 1986 Supreme Court case of *Bowers v. Hardwick.* Writing for the majority, Justice Byron White stated that the US Constitution does not confer "a fundamental right to engage in homosexual sodomy."[4] Indeed, the phrase, or one like it, can be found in many contexts of conservative opinion.

To understand the nature of the Christian right's opposition to US government engagement in programs and policies to defend the human rights of LGBTQ people abroad, it's necessary to address the movement's orientation toward LGBTQ rights and its simultaneous repudiation and embrace of human rights under certain conditions. Hence, I begin with the Christian right's struggle against LGBTQ civil rights and social recognition in the United States.

International Christian conservative activism against LGBT people, same-sex sexuality, and nonnormative gender identity has required alliance formation and the constant development of new rhetorics and practices. When it comes to Christian conservative rhetoric and activism against LGBTQ human rights and the US government's affirmation of those rights, the Christian right movement relies on ministers and churches, political information networks, legal advocacy, domestic and international coalitions, missionary activism, and multilateral advocacy. The US Christian right has been active for many years in the international arena, most notably through its advocacy on behalf of antifeminist and anti-LGBTQ "family values." As Doris Buss and Didi Herman show in *Globalizing Family Values*, in its advocacy at the United Nations, the Christian right—their term is Christian Right UN or CRUN—"views global space as controlled by a number of anti-Christian forces" and "embraces the international realm as a space for conservative social change."[5]

Anti-LGBTQ human rights advocacy also relies on multiple forms of domestic anti-LGBTQ rhetoric that informs and primes Christian conservative constituencies to embrace particular conceptions of human rights and SOGI human rights. Most Christian conservatives are probably not well informed about the specific forms Christian right advocacy takes in international networks and institutions, but they do know that a great global struggle between good and evil is afoot and that conservative believers are engaged on every front. A theme that unites diverse forms of Christian conservative anti-LGBTQ politics and rhetoric across national borders is that religious liberty—described as a natural right, a human right, or both—and SOGI human rights exist in a mutually exclusive, zero-sum relation to each other.

Even more intriguing are two rhetorical, political, and pedagogical shifts in Christian conservative discourse on LGBTQ/SOGI human rights abroad that have been produced as Christian conservative elites and organizations grapple with rising support for SOGI human rights and the public exposure of violations of these rights. The first shift is the appropriation and reframing of the left-progressive charge that the United States engages in imperialism when the government engages in human rights discourse or interventions outside the nation's borders. The second follows logically from the first or is at least logically consistent with it: making common cause with people abroad who reject SOGI human rights and framing these beleaguered foreign allies as victims of US power who have a right to their traditional beliefs and practices. An historical irony of this new interest of the Christian right in the harms enacted by US imperialism is the role of Christian missionaries in displacing indigenous religious beliefs and functioning as Western colonial emissaries. This history is effectively erased in a context of contemporary alliances between the United States and indigenous anti-LGBTQ actors.

I argue that the Christian right's rhetorical support for anti-SOGI cultures and policies enacts a cultural relativism that we don't expect to find on the Christian right, one that fits uneasily with most other dimensions of Christian conservative politics and theology. Unfortunately for the Christian right movement, many of the same ally states that stand firm in their cultural commitment to stigmatizing and punishing LGBTQ people also discriminate against religious minorities. This overlap between anti-SOGI and religiously discriminatory states and societies exposes and complicates the Christian right's defense of local cultures and denunciation of cultural imperialism.

Although the Christian right movement's primary political activism is domestic, it has been engaged for many years in global cultural activism on many fronts, including against LGBTQ/SOGI rights and security. In the 1990s, evangelical Christian missionaries flocked to Russia and Eastern Europe in the wake of the collapse of the Soviet Union to proselytize and build institutions.[6] In the 2000s, Christian missionary groups delivered health services and abstinence-only sex education funded by George W. Bush's PEPFAR in poor African nations.[7] Anti-LGBT Christian conservatives have achieved authority on cultural issues by cultivating ministers, political leaders, and other moral entrepreneurs from poor, politically unstable, and authoritarian nations as well as providing assistance to people in those countries. Thus, the US Christian right uses assistance to vulnerable people as a means to target other vulnerable people who are gender and sexual minorities.

As we will see in this chapter, anti-LGBT activism in the United States and anti-SOGI activism abroad present different challenges for the Christian right. But understanding US Christian right anti-SOGI advocacy requires examining the domestic context of LGBTQ civil rights struggles and the discourses about gender and sexual minorities produced by US Christian conservative leaders.

## US Anti-LGBT Civil Rights Politics

As categories, "civil" and "human" rights don't refer to two mutually exclusive sets of rights, but the categories reference different sources of rights: civil rights are enshrined in the laws and other public policies of states, and human rights generally have been understood by their proponents to originate in our status as human beings and not to be predicated on ethnic, national, or other statuses that differ among people or groups. In its anti-LGBTQ rhetoric and politics in the United States, the Christian right produces narratives that delegitimize LGBTQ civil rights and mobilize Christian conservatives to oppose those rights. Delegitimizing support for global SOGI human rights in domestic US politics requires different tools. These strategies and rhetorics perform a number of operations: they subject to scrutiny the very idea of "human rights"; they discredit and undermine claims that sexuality and gender identity are grounds for human rights protection; they link support for SOGI human rights to the illegitimate values and agenda of liberals/progressives/LGBTQ people/Democrats/Obama/Hillary Clinton; they praise the resistance of leaders and communities abroad to support for SOGI human rights; and they align themselves with those leaders and communities, celebrating the right and imperative for people to cultivate and live out their anti-LGBTQ values.

In the United States, the post-Stonewall gay liberation movement launched in a sociopolitical context of counterculture and civil rights movements, especially the African American civil rights movement, the women's movement, and the anti–Vietnam War movement. In the late 1960s, same-sex-attracted Americans faced pervasive stigma and discrimination. Even though many weren't open about their sexuality in the 1970s, unprecedented gay and lesbian visibility and mobilization had many effects, including some early public policy victories and the antagonistic political response from a Christian conservative movement that was also mobilizing in the 1970s. As Didi Herman documents in *The Antigay Agenda*, by the late 1960s and 1970s, the Christian magazine *Christianity Today*, which previously had framed same-sex sexuality as a kind of abject identity, began to cast it as "a sin with a movement behind it."[8] Early progay policies such as the 1973 Washington, DC, Human Rights Law that prohibited discrimination against lesbians and gay men and the 1977 Dade County, Florida, gay rights ordinance sparked antigay—later, anti-LGBT—mobilization and resistance.[9] Jyl Josephson demonstrates that this history of sexual regulation and the resistance to the "exclusionary and disciplinary politics" of sexual regulation is manifest in a wide range of public policies.[10]

As many scholars and journalists have detailed, since the 1970s the Christian right and LGBT movements have carefully monitored each other, developing strategies, formulating cultural politics, and advocating policies. The two movements didn't exercise equal power and influence from the 1970s through the 1990s, so they weren't quite the "perfect enemies" of

Chris Bull and John Gallagher's book of the same title.[11] In Tina Fetner's phrase, "the religious right shaped gay activism," and in turn, gay activism shaped the religious right from the 1970s to the present. This relationship between adversaries can be traced through a close examination of social movement frames, rhetorical strategies, media representations, and modes of movement institutionalization that reveal social movement constraints and opportunities.[12] It also can be traced through the policies and litigation strategies pursued by each side.[13]

Although the struggle against LGBT rights and recognition has long historical roots, the current anti-LGBTQ movement in the United States is in important respects also an ambivalent antigovernment movement. When the Tea Party movement began to form after Barack Obama took office in spring 2009, leaders and activists outlined the movement's aspirations in a "public transcript" that celebrated government of the sort that adherents believe prevailed in the founding era: small, nonintrusive, fiscally responsible, and faithful to the Constitution. The less public "hidden transcript" included socially conservative positions on LGBT and reproductive rights, a conservative Christian counterhistory of the United States, elements of Ayn Rand's market fundamentalism, and a sturdy and measurable vein of anti-immigrant xenophobia and antiblack racism.[14] These components of the hidden transcript were not present consistently throughout the movement, but they have been documented by many methods, including survey research. For example, the Pew Research Center finds that Christian conservatives support the Tea Party and Tea Party supporters are conservative on both economic and social issues.[15] Thus, the carefully cultivated public image of the Tea Party as a spontaneous movement of citizens who merely want to re-create the United States' eighteenth-century constitutional order is false.[16]

Partially underwriting the Tea Party by way of its profound influence on the politics of the Christian right in recent decades is the philosophy and theology of Christian Reconstructionism. Julie Ingersoll carefully analyzes the secular and Christian left concern that Reconstructionists and other Christian conservatives influenced by the theology advocate theocracy, showing how Reconstructionism constructs particular tenets— for example, of "politics" and "theocracy"—that conceal the coercion that would be necessary if the United States were to be governed by "biblical law." The aspiration to "restore America as a Christian nation" would not be limited to moral or cultural changes, but would extend to Christian dominion over the government. For Gary North, son-in-law and intellectual heir of Reconstructionist Rousas John Rushdoony, the "restoration" of America would include, for example, "replacing the State Department with missionaries and businessmen."[17] The articulation of this goal in a theology and political ideology that's pervasive on the Christian right suggests how decisively transformed US advocacy for SOGI human rights would be under such a regime.

Human rights have often been understood by their proponents to be grounded in our shared status as human beings. This is not to suggest that human rights scholars, activists, and professionals have agreed about how to conceptualize human rights or even about precisely which rights are fundamental. Where there is agreement, some aspects of that agreement may manifest an overlapping consensus about human rights, such as freedom from violence, that are nearly universally agreed on or for which neutrality or disagreement cannot publicly be expressed as a principle. Support for particular human rights or for the extension of those rights to particular disfavored groups can also change over time, just as support for SOGI human rights has grown in many places since the 1990s. Although it is not a staple of Christian right rhetoric in the United States, the Christian conservative movement has developed positions on human rights that can be activated and disseminated under appropriate circumstances. These circumstances include such "focusing events" as the Obama administration announcing its support for SOGI human rights and Clinton delivering her SOGI human rights speech in Geneva.[18] They can also include less publicized processes in which Christian conservative moral entrepreneurs find themselves at odds with the US government on beliefs and practices related to SOGI human rights abroad.

## The Christian Right's Human Rights

To understand the Christian right movement's orientation toward the idea of SOGI human rights we must investigate the movement's orientation toward the idea and applications of human rights doctrine itself. Judging from the discourse produced by the movement, Christian conservatism is of two minds about human rights—what they are as well as how Christian conservatives should think about them. One perspective is that human rights are specious, a deplorable fiction, and a "human construct" like ideas such as the separation of church and state. The second perspective—partially subscribing to human rights doctrine—is more complex than simple rejection and more likely to be deployed in circumstances in which a pragmatic appeal to human rights may pay off in Christian conservative grassroots enthusiasm and mobilization, successful litigation, and/or support from elected officials.[19] Rather than being mutually exclusive perspectives with their own constituencies, however, these two views of human rights are flexible enough that Christian conservatives can easily subscribe to whichever view is most functional in the context at hand. One way to regard the existence of human rights narratives that aren't completely consistent with each other is in terms of what Mary Jackman calls "ideological baggage": that is, ideas that are "the property of the group" that "gain or lose currency according to their efficacy in meeting the political needs of the moment."[20]

Contributing to this flexibility are key elements of overlap between the two perspectives. The first overlapping element is that the Christian right rejects interpretations of "human rights" that incorporate "second-generation" social and economic rights because such rights are inconsistent with their economic beliefs—especially the beliefs of Christian conservative elites and opinion leaders. Although US Christian conservatives haven't always been economically laissez-faire conservatives, a strong current of prosperity gospel market fundamentalism runs through US history, from "acres of diamonds" to the contemporary conviction that the Bible teaches the superiority of free-market capitalism and the moral wickedness of the welfare state.[21] The second overlapping element is that the movement repudiates applications of human rights doctrine to some particular categories of identity. These include (but are not limited to) nonheterosexual sexual identities and variations of sexual behavior and gender identity that are inconsistent with the ideal of the "natural family"—that is, the model of the family ordained by God that consists of a married husband and wife and their biological children.

In spite of these overlaps, there are important distinctions between the two perspectives on human rights that the Christian right enunciates and holds out to followers. The first perspective is that human rights are a modern construct that undermines God-given natural rights. An example can be found in the Heritage Foundation's Understanding America series of booklets that aim to educate readers about "how the United States' commitment to the universal truths of human equality and the right to self-government—as proclaimed in the Declaration of Independence—requires a vigilant defense of the cause of liberty, both at home and abroad."[22] One booklet in the series is *How Should Americans Think About Human Rights?*, which I received at a Christian conservative Values Voter Summit. The author of the booklet is Kim R. Holmes, a Heritage distinguished fellow and an Assistant Secretary of State for international organization affairs under the Bush administration from 2001 to 2005. As the title suggests, the booklet is dedicated to the pedagogical purpose of explaining the proper perspective on human rights, in this case distinguishing natural rights embraced by the American founders from human rights "manufactured" by more modern social engineers.

The booklet begins with an account of categories of rights that sharply contrasts natural rights with "the thoroughly modern idea of 'human rights.'" While natural rights are "endowed by God" and "do not change over time," human rights "constantly change" and give rise to, for example, a "cottage industry" of "new 'economic and social rights'" formulated and defended by "international bureaucrats." While the natural rights of individuals can be satisfied without "infringing on someone else's rights," human rights require a government so powerful as to "crush the natural rights and liberty of individuals." While natural rights respect individuality, human rights that recognize the risks of harm associated with categories of identity such as sex or gender identity inevitably undermine the humanity of those they aspire to protect: "if your social value is defined by your sex, class, or race, then your intrinsic value as a person is lost." A final anxiety is that human rights treaties among nations erode national sovereignty by subjecting Americans to spurious standards of international human rights.[23] These contrasts between natural and human rights show that for US Christian conservatives, "human rights" is not a benign idea. Rather, a shared international regime of human rights threatens individual human beings and—to the extent the United States espouses and abides by such a regime—the sovereignty and Christian character of the nation.

The second Christian right perspective on human rights doctrine rests on a more selective affirmation of human rights than prevails among liberal Christian and secular human rights organizations and proponents. Examples of this selective affirmation of human rights demonstrate that the Christian right doesn't merely reject the concept and application of human rights. What's more surprising, even for those who are familiar with US Christian conservative movement politics, is that the Christian right is occasionally willing to invoke and employ norms and conventions of international human rights, including international human rights treaties that are generally anathema to conservative elites and activists. Where Christian conservatives differ from other adherents to an international regime of human rights is in their consistent opposition to defining social and economic rights as human rights and in their interpretation of what kinds of identities and forms of harm provoke human rights protection. For the Christian right, freedom of religious belief and practice and protection for people who are menaced on account of their faith justify recourse to human rights.

There are many examples of the US Christian right's activism on behalf of a natural and human right to religious freedom in the international arena. Consider one example that has received relatively little attention outside the movement: the freedom to homeschool children. A case of the right to homeschool that has become a cause célèbre among Christian conservatives is the Romeike family of Bissengen, Germany. In 2006, evangelical Christians Uwe and Hannelore Romeike, residents of the German state of Baden-Württemberg, began to homeschool their children in defiance of a law that requires children to attend either public or private school. Confronted with fines and the threat of prosecution, in 2008 the Romeikes brought their children to the United States and settled in Tennessee after an immigration judge granted their request for asylum on the basis of religious persecution. However, the family's tribulation was not over yet. After the Board of Immigration Appeals overturned the initial ruling and the Supreme Court refused to hear their case, Christian conservatives petitioned the White House to permit the family to remain in the United States, and the Romeikes were granted permanent legal status.

In the United States, the Romeikes were championed by the Home School Legal Defense Association (HSLDA), which raised funds for and provided their legal defense and coordinated the messaging strategy for them and other homeschooling families. Michael Farris, HSLDA founder and chairman, and Michael Donnelly, HSLDA director for international affairs, explicitly linked the Romeike family's plight with human rights doctrine. In a 2013 press release that accompanied a petition to the Supreme Court, Farris said that "parents, not the government, decide first how children are educated. *Germany's notorious persecution of families who homeschool violates their own obligations to uphold human rights standards and must end.*"[24] Donnelly defended the Romeikes' claims, in writing and in court, and alluded not to natural law but to the incorporation of human rights principles in international legal instruments:

> As Americans, we enjoy great freedoms guaranteed by our con-
> stitutions and laws. Among these freedoms is the right to direct

the education and upbringing of our children—a fundamental right recognized by the United States Supreme Court in the landmark case *Pierce v. Society of Sisters* and its progeny. This right has not only been recognized by the Supreme Court, *but has also been noted in the constitutions of other countries and in international treaties and declarations.*[25]

In the context of US conservative "fear," "mistrust," and "disillusionment" with the UN and international law, the Christian conservative appeal to "the constitutions of other countries" and "international treaties and declarations" in making the case for the Romeike family is nothing short of remarkable.[26]

Christian conservatives typically eschew citations to foreign or international norms, laws, treaties, and institutions on behalf of human rights claims as violations of US sovereignty and God-ordained US exceptionalism. However, that's when appeals are being made to more liberal or progressive policies or practices. For example, Michael Farris and the HSLDA were pivotal in defeating Senate ratification of the United Nations Convention on the Rights of Persons with Disabilities, which the UN General Assembly adopted in 2006 and Obama signed in 2009. In 2012 and 2014, Christian conservatives mobilized and lobbied against the treaty, arguing that it was likely to "infringe on the rights of parents . . . threaten states' rights and become a legal tool for pro-choice advocates."[27] In the Romeike case, by contrast, Christian conservative homeschooling proponents made pragmatic appeals to human rights they believe both reflect God-given liberty and restate natural rights that precede the establishment of government.

However Christian right organizations and advocates interpret and either deploy or reject human rights, they repudiate discourse that explicitly identifies LGBTQ people as victims of human rights violations or that specifically advocates for their inclusion in human rights protections. To do otherwise would constitute a kind of concession to identities and practices that Christian conservatives abhor. A similar tactic of rejecting explicit references to LGBT people, identity, or behavior emerges with reference to school bullying in the United States. As the phenomenon of bullying began to receive wide public attention in recent years, Christian conservatives acknowledged bullying as a problem but opposed efforts to highlight anti-LGBT bullying and incorporate education about LGBT issues and toleration into school programs. For Christian conservatives, these measures accorded unacceptable legitimacy to LGBT identity as the price of confronting the harm done by bullying.[28] LGBT people can be considered already included in human rights principles such as equality before the law or prohibitions against discrimination without being named specifically as beneficiaries of these protections. Of course, SOGI activists and human rights professionals argue that the prevalence of religious objections to LGBT human rights and religious justifications for discrimination make it necessary to explicitly include sexuality and gender identity in the articulation of human rights.[29]

Christian right and other organizations that engage in mobilization and activism on the basis of opposition to LGBT civil and human rights tend to focus their political rhetoric on domestic issues and threats to religious freedoms and on Christian believers abroad for their audience of US activists. However, Christian right rhetoric about SOGI issues and LGBTQ people takes many forms. If we look closely enough at the messaging of Christian conservative elites and organizations, we can see a variety of frames that shape their views of the zero-sum nature of SOGI and religious human rights. Some rhetoric is explicit, commending nations and leaders that repudiate LGBTQ people, behavior, relationships, and advocacy. Some is more circuitous, commending anti-LGBTQ beliefs and practices of peoples and nations or positively contrasting these nations with the amoral United States or Europe. A third form of rhetoric works through juxtaposition and features distinct denunciations of LGBTQ rights (including the Obama administration's support for LGBTQ and SOGI rights) and the precarious position of religious believers that occupy space in the same broadcasts, speeches, subscriber email alerts, website resource lists, and other communications of Christian right moral entrepreneurs to Christian conservative followers.

The theme of the Obama administration's interest in LGBTQ human rights and putative lack of interest in persecution and human rights violations against Christians was apparent in a variety of forms in Christian right rhetoric throughout Obama's term in office. As Christian conservatives push the Trump administration to reverse Obama-era policies and practices, such messaging continues to be a staple of their rhetoric. A central claim is common: that the Obama administration refused to intercede on behalf of threatened religious minorities or individual Christian believers—indeed, that Obama refused to declare publicly the reality of persecution on the basis of religion. The message these juxtapositions convey is: leftists/unbelievers/Democrats cater to LGBTQ people/gays/homosexuals but do nothing to protect embattled Christians to whom human rights commitments properly belong. However, this framing is fraught with silences and empirical inaccuracies. For example, Bill Clinton signed the International Religious Freedom Act into law in 1998. The State Department appointed its first Ambassador-at-Large (or Special Envoy) for International Religious Freedom and generated the first "Annual State Department Report on International Religious Freedom" in 1999, during the Clinton administration.[30] During Obama's terms in office, the State Department appointed a Special Advisor for Religious Minorities in the Near East and South/Central Asia. Finally, in addition to advocating for SOGI human rights, the DRL also advocates for the religious freedom of endangered religious minorities, including Christians, abroad.

## SOGI versus Religion in Human Rights

As Brooke Ackerly points out, the diffusion of human rights discourse and advocacy is likely to be accompanied by backlash against human rights, and this is certainly true of SOGI human rights.[31] The most direct and explicit way that US Christian conservatives denigrate SOGI human rights is to publicize the anti-LGBTQ beliefs, commitments, and public policies of nations and leaders who represent what they understand to be a biblical position on sexuality and gender identity. For example, Christian conservative leaders, activists, and advocacy organizations have showered Russian President Vladimir Putin and his government with encomia for its anti-LGBTQ laws and social practices. Scott Lively is a coauthor (with Kevin Abrams) of *The Pink Swastika: Homosexuality in the Nazi Party* and president of the antigay nonprofit organization Abiding Truth Ministries. Lively bills himself as "one of the most knowledgeable and articulate opponents of the homosexual agenda in America," and he brought his expertise on the gay agenda to a conference in Kampala, Uganda, just before the Anti-Homosexual Bill was introduced in 2009. Lively boasts about that conference in his online "Report from Uganda," noting with pride the eminence of his audience, which included lawyers, teachers, ministers, and members of the Ugandan legislature. Lively was backed up by two other US experts on the "gay agenda": ex-gay Caleb Lee Brundidge and Don Schmierer. All three have disclaimed responsibility for the bill that quickly followed, though Lively currently is being sued by Sexual Minorities Uganda (SMUG), a Ugandan LGBTI group, for "inciting the persecution of gay men and lesbians."

There are many examples of Christian right encomia to the world's anti-LGBTQ authoritarian leaders. There is, for example, Lively's assertion that Putin's Russia is poised to be "the greatest defender of true human rights among nations." Antiabortion activist Randall Terry notes, "The Russians have it right; we don't evangelize our children into the homosexual lifestyle." The American Family Association offers the rhetorical question: "Which president is the lion of Christianity, the defender of Christian values, the president that's calling his nation back to embracing its identity as a nation founded on Christian values?," answering: "Vladimir Putin, the president of Russia." And Franklin Graham, heir to Billy Graham and president and CEO of two Christian conservative organizations, has this to say on the Russian President's anti-LGBTQ statements and policies:

> In my opinion, Putin is right on these issues. Obviously, he may be wrong about many things, but he has taken a stand to protect his nation's children from the damaging effects of any gay and lesbian agenda. Our president and his attorney general have turned their backs on God and His standards, and many in the Congress are following the administration's lead. This is shameful. The world used to look to America for moral leadership. But those days are long gone.[32]

During the 2016 presidential race, Christian conservatives supported the candidacy of Donald Trump as he spoke approvingly of Putin and continued to support the president as his administration began to be investigated for its ties to Putin and Russia. Christian conservative rhetoric that over many years has contrasted a godless Obama with the anti-LGBT Putin helps explain such a seemingly inexplicable affinity.

Another example of a nation singled out by Christian conservatives for engaging in anti-LGBTQ policies and rhetoric is Uganda, designated along with Rwanda by Saddleback Church's Pastor Rick Warren as a "purpose-driven" nation.[33] Warren's designation laid a foundation for a continent-wide All African Purpose Driven Church Conference originally slated for 2015 but later held in Kigali, Rwanda, in early 2017. Paul Cameron's Family Research Institute, no longer a major player in anti-LGBTQ human rights, explicitly supported Uganda's Anti-Homosexuality Bill, noting that "depending on the severity of the homosexual offense, a fine, prison or even capital punishment is warranted. The most important thing is to make it illegal. . . . Indeed, if Uganda is to learn anything from us, it is to be harsh with those who choose to act on homosexual desires."[34] Donald Wildmon's American Family Association took the position that "Uganda stands with Phil [Robertson of *Duck Dynasty*]. Make homosexuality contrary to public policy. It can be done."[35]

However, not all Christian conservative reporting and pedagogy on the conflict between SOGI human rights and religion is so explicit. Much of it relies on comprehensive ingroup pedagogy to signal affirmation of and affinity with anti-LGBTQ regimes as well as opprobrium to less homophobic regimes and public attitudes to Christian conservative believers. The Family Research Council, the preeminent US Christian conservative research, lobbying, and education organization, produces a great deal of this kind of rhetoric which, because it often doesn't mention LGBTQ or SOGI rights or issues directly, might not be recognized as commentary on SOGI.

For example, in October 2012, Uganda's pious President Museveni delivered a speech in which he publicly repented of his and his nation's sins, dedicated his country to God, and renounced "the Satanic influence" of "the last 50 years of [Uganda's] history." Museveni did not mention homosexuality or the Anti-Homosexuality Bill specifically in the long list of national sins which he called on God to forgive Uganda, but he did name "sexual immorality," and political observers connected the proposed legislation to the subtext of the speech.

The Family Research Council (FRC) responded to Museveni's repentance speech from a variety of social media platforms, including Twitter. On November 26, 2013, FRC dispatched an email alert—daily alerts are captioned "Tony Perkins' Washington Update"—to subscribers titled "During Revival, Media Still Atone Deaf." FRC's communiqués on Museveni and the repentance agenda quoted liberally from Museveni's speech and had two prongs: the first commended Museveni as a Christian national leader. The November 6 FRC alert announced an "inspirational moment for the [Ugandan] nation" and lavished praise on Museveni and his government for proclaiming the kind of "faithfulness" "that will raise Uganda's status as a new power in Africa." The second prong assailed critics of Museveni in coded terms. The FRC noted that Uganda "has stood—often alone—for traditional values, abstinence, and families despite tremendous pressure from the West." A target was the mainstream media in the United States which, having drawn attention to violations of LGBT peoples' human rights in Uganda, was accused of being "so threatened by religion that it refuses to leave another country alone to pursue its own views on sexuality and faith."

What is striking about the construction of the FRC email alert is not only the enthusiastic affirmation of Museveni's insistence on "faithfulness" on matters of "sexuality and faith." It is also that, significantly, the only person quoted besides Museveni is Scott Lively, the anti-LGBTQ activist who is widely known for his prominent role in instructing and lobbying Ugandan elites on the threat posed by LGBTQ people. In "During Revival," Lively testified to the superiority of Museveni's Christian leadership and his goal of governing Uganda according to biblical law. Readers familiar with Christian conservative discourse on SOGI would draw the conclusion that FRC is confirming its support for the highly publicized Anti-Homosexuality Bill and, by extension, for other anti-LGBTQ attitudes and public policies.

However, the FRC is obviously concerned about having its mainstream reputation linked to reprehensible anti-LGBTQ policies and penalties. Days after "During Revival" went out, FRC released a follow-up email alert, "Lyin' Taming over Africa." Referencing its earlier encomium to Museveni, "Lyin' Taming" denied that FRC approved of the death penalty for same-sex sexuality or, as FRC President Tony Perkins asserted in 2010, any "penalty which would have the effect of inhibiting compassionate pastoral, psychological, and medical care and treatment for those who experience same-sex attractions or who engage in homosexual conduct."[36] At least as interesting as FRC's various statements distancing the organization from Uganda's Anti-Homosexuality Bill are its consistent positions opposing "the suggestion that gay and lesbian acts are universal human rights" ("Lyin' Taming") and "sweeping and inaccurate assertions that homosexual conduct is internationally recognized as a fundamental human right" ("FRC Statement on H. Res. 1064").[37]

Finally, anti-SOGI human rights rhetoric that relies on juxtaposition for its effectiveness requires its audience to make the associations they have been tutored to make by the theopolitical discourses that circulate in the Christian right movement. I have collected many examples of such juxtapositions, and here I offer one from the FRC's email alerts delivered to members and contacts who participate in Christian conservative activism. On Monday, February 16, 2015, I received an FRC email alert that contained three separate subheadings. The first, "Libs Come Back for Moore," reported on Alabama Chief Justice Roy Moore—infamous for a controversy over a Ten Commandments monument in the state Judicial Building—instructing probate judges throughout Alabama to defy a federal court order to conduct same-sex marriages. In this section, the issue of same-sex marriage is framed in terms of states' rights and constitutional authority, but the underlying issue is same-sex marriage. The second report, "Balk Like an Egyptian," assails Obama for failing publicly to denounce the Islamic State as a Muslim group targeting Christians for their faith after the murders of twenty-one Egyptian Coptic Christians. The Obama administration did denounce the "cowardly murders," but it didn't do so in terms that satisfied FRC. This is only one example of criticism of the administration for failing or refusing to adequately support people subjected to (Christian) religious persecution abroad and to sound the tocsin about the reality of "Christian genocide in the Middle East."

Finally, in the same alert, there is "Ark. de Triumph! Leaders Fight SOGI Wave." This report focuses on support in the Arkansas legislature for a law (the Conscience Protection Act, a version of which was signed into law in 2015) that would protect business owners from incurring penalties for refusing to serve LGBTQ customers in accordance with their religious faith. It is interesting to note that nowhere in "Ark. de Triumph!" is the abbreviation SOGI explained or the phrase "sexual orientation and gender identity" used. I suspect the deployment of this abbreviation without explanation is a rare lapse in messaging for the FRC because in my years following Christian right rhetoric on LGBTQ people and issues I've never encountered either "SOGI" or "sexual orientation and gender identity." Christian conservative organizations have publicized many terms and symbols of queer life: the rainbow flag, the pink triangle, the term "queer" as an ingroup expression, and various definitions of transgender. But perhaps because it typically is used in international discourse, "SOGI" still has not been integrated into Christian right messaging.

Since the Supreme Court's decisions in *Hollingsworth v. Perry* (2013), *United States v. Windsor* (2013), and *Obergefell v. Hodges* (2015), a robust discourse detailing the zero-sum nature of conflict between SOGI and religious civil and human rights in the United States has become a staple of Christian right discourse. The zero-sum rights discourse wasn't invented in 2013, but the anxiety about—replaced by the reality of—the defeat of California's Proposition 8 and the federal Defense of Marriage Act has intensified rhetoric about Christians' loss of freedom to exercise religion. This rhetoric has been crafted in various ways for consumption by Christian conservatives; some is direct, some is less direct, and some relies on believers to connect the dots between Christian resistance to same-sex marriage or transgender rights, (the left's indifference to) the persecution of Christians abroad, and the persecution of Christians in the United States caused by policies and increasingly positive attitudes toward LGBT civil rights. The inference believers arrive at again and again is this: just like Christians in parlous conditions around the world ("Balk"), US Christians are persecuted on the basis of their faith ("Ark"), and their persecution is at the hands of LGBTQ people and their allies, including but not limited to Obama, Hillary Clinton, and their allies ("Libs").

Over time, the common forms of rhetoric to which believers are constantly exposed across the Christian conservative movement instruct and prime them to understand human rights, religious persecution, LGBTQ/ SOGI civil and human rights, anti-LGBTQ/SOGI national leaders, and Obama administration domestic and foreign policy in ways that shape attitudes and mobilize believers. The finer points of Obama administration support for SOGI human rights abroad usually have been absent from the domestic rhetoric generated by the Christian right for US audiences. Right-wing news organizations collect and report instances of this support in ways that inform and bolster Christian conservative rhetoric and activism on the pro-LGBTQ and anti-Christian priorities of Obama, Clinton, the Democratic Party, and the US left.

Christian conservative media disseminate anti-LGBTQ messaging in and through loosely integrated information networks. These networks operate through sharing and cooperation as well as coordination among participants: prominent elites and personalities, para-church and advocacy organizations, foundations, and policy entrepreneurs. Messaging is disseminated horizontally across news platforms and advocacy organizations and then "down" and among bloggers, activists, subscribers, parishioners, constituents, and television and radio audiences. Through a variety of platforms and media, believers receive Christian conservative news, cultural and political commentary, and even prayers and devotional rhetoric whose contents can be analyzed as political texts.[38] Investigative journalism and research traces funding sources and networks for organizations that produce educational and policy discourses. For example, the National Committee for Responsive Philanthropy produced "Funding the Culture Wars: Philanthropy, Church and State," a report that provides a snapshot of the largest Christian right funders and the share of funding for many Christian conservative organizations.[39] Researchers also illuminate the web of "external institutions"—think tanks, research centers, and foundations—that "develop and promote the Right's key ideas and policies."[40]

Christian conservative elites use a variety of media and rhetorical forms to engage in political pedagogy with conservative believers directly on issues of religious and SOGI human rights and indirectly on a variety of issues that bear on human rights and aspire to construct a Christian conservative consensus on these issues. Some purveyors of (Christian) conservative news and information are well known. These include Focus on the Family, Pat Robertson's *The 700 Club*, the Family Research Council (and its "legislative affiliate," FRC Action), the Heritage Foundation (and its "policy advocacy" arm, Heritage Action), and a burgeoning group of Christian conservative public interest law organizations. The Fox News Channel is a cable and satellite news service founded in 1996 by Australian media entrepreneur Rupert Murdoch and, until he was deposed by sexual harassment allegations, headed by Republican political consultant and strategist Roger Ailes. Despite its slogans—"Fair and Balanced" and "We Report. You Decide"—scholars who study Fox News and its viewers conclude that Fox is better understood as "the loudest voice in conservative media."[41] Besides Fox News, other secular sources of information and political commentary on which Christian conservatives rely for news and information include the conservative newspaper the *Washington Times*, *Townhall.com*, *NewsMax*, and *Breitbart News*. The importance of media organizations, news aggregators, blogs, and other platforms for the Christian right movement can be observed in the work of high-profile and less-well known groups that constitute the Christian right. Even small groups and projects that are relatively unknown outside the Christian conservative movement rely on a variety of conservative media and sources for the raw material of the rhetoric that primes movement activists and believers on the important issues of the day.[42]

Christian right organizations tend to focus their rhetoric to US Christian conservatives on domestic issues, yet many of the same groups that engage in US-based anti-LGBTQ advocacy monitor signs of pro-LGBTQ US government interventions in US spheres of influence. Journalists and other sources who report for conservative, anti-LGBT organizations commonly explain that the Obama administration initiated a commitment by the US government to SOGI human rights and then inform readers about specific programs and policies that express the commitment. Some reporting is distinctly ideological and polemical. However, a common journalistic device in these reports is to cite and quote as critics of SOGI human rights programs and policies not domestic US Christian conservatives but officials, prominent individuals, or other citizens of nations that reject SOGI human rights. Anti-SOGI reporting of this kind is not necessarily coordinated across news and partisan organizations. Nevertheless, the putatively objective reportage that relies on foreign moral objections to nonnormative gender and sexuality is extremely useful for the rhetorical and pedagogical purposes of Christian conservative organizations that fight multifront conflicts against LGBTQ/SOGI rights in the United States and abroad.

Such a framing is evident in reporting on the Obama administration's 2011 SOGI presidential memorandum. The *Christian Post* described the directive as "a memorandum to world nations controversially claiming that the fight for LGBT rights was part of the United States' commitment to international human rights" and noted that "the clear objective of using taxpayer funds to support LGBT communities abroad is sure to anger conservatives at home, as well as conservative governments abroad; Obama is already facing criticism for the announcement of the initiative."[43]

In contrast to Fox News, the *National Review*, and the *Washington Times*, Cybercast News Service News (CNSNews.com) is a relatively obscure source for conservative news and commentary. CNSNews—whose motto is "The Right News. Right Now"—was founded in 1998 as the Conservative News Service by pro-life and anti-LGBT activist L. Brent Bozell III.[44] In 1987, Bozell also founded the Media Research Center, the "largest media watchdog organization in America," to identify liberal media bias and "create a media culture in America where truth and liberty flourish."[45] Bozell's reputation in the Christian right movement is such that he was the honored guest at the annual Faith, Family, and Freedom gala and recipient of the Vision and Leadership Award at the FRC-sponsored 2015 Values Voter Summit in Washington, DC. A division of the Media Research Center and a nonprofit 501 (c)(3) organization, CNSNews.com was set up as:

> an alternative news source that would cover stories that are subject to the bias of omission and report on other news subject to bias by commission. CNSNews.com endeavors to fairly present all legitimate sides of a story and debunk popular, albeit incorrect, myths about cultural and policy issues.[46]

However, even if CNSNews isn't a household name for conservative news, it is one of many outlets and venues through which right-wing news content and perspectives are produced and delivered to the fiscally and socially conservative activists and supporters of the Christian right.

In June 2013, in an article titled "State Department to Spend $450,000 Protecting Transgenders Overseas," CNSNews reported that DRL had earmarked "$450,000 in taxpayer dollars" for a grant dedicated to "protecting transgender persons from violence and combating impunity."[47] Author and CNSNews senior editor Melanie Hunter based her reporting on the announcement of the grant on the US government website Grants.gov.[48] CNSNews has also reported on State Department changes in policies regarding transgender US citizens and passports. It has generated LGBTQ-related news reports that have been picked up by Tea Party movement organs and thus disseminated throughout the overlapping political movements with which the Tea Party shares members.[49]

In summer 2013, an article titled "No Gay Diplomats: U.S. and British Promotion of LGBT Rights Sparks Backlash" explored "stepped-up efforts" by the US and UK governments to "promote homosexual rights abroad." The efforts included public statements, diplomacy, support for international SOGI human rights policies, and the appointment of openly gay ambassadors. In characterizing these efforts to promote SOGI human rights as "risking a backlash in conservative countries, where critics say the West is trying to impose norms that clash with local tradition, religion and culture," the author uses a particular frame to define the problem for conservative readers.[50] This is the frame of the United States threatening and committing cultural imperialism against peoples and nations that are simultaneously less powerful and more moral than the Goliath with whom they disagree on SOGI human rights.

## The Travels of Cultural Imperialism

That the United States or other Western nations or actors may, deliberately or not, engage in imperialism through human rights interventions is a central concern of a wide range of scholars and human rights professionals. Efforts to properly identify and circumvent Western dominance, coercion, and some forms of influence are common subjects at meetings of SOGI human rights advocates. Today, however, the US left *and* the

Christian conservative right find the category of imperialism fruitful for delineating the source and content of pernicious Western influence and coercion, as well as the elimination of distinct cultural traditions and practices. Indeed, among the many concepts and categories that in recent years have migrated from the political left to the right is this denunciation of cultural imperialism. It's just that now, on the right, imperialism is understood to be at play in US efforts to challenge policies, attitudes, and acts that stigmatize and punish gender and sexual minorities.

For the Christian right, a US government that includes SOGI human rights as one prong of its foreign policy and advocates for the human rights of LGBTQ people is engaging in cultural imperialism.[51] One goal of such an indictment is to delegitimize rights discourses and advocacy that run counter to Christian conservative goals and beliefs. Another is to reinforce and influence anti-LGBTQ discourse, policies, and social practices by building alliances with people and organizations abroad to stem, and if possible reverse, a global movement for SOGI human rights.

A longtime purveyor of the indictment of cultural imperialism is the World Congress of Families (WCF), a low-profile Christian right organization that's based in the United States but performs most of its work abroad. The WCF is headquartered at the Howard Center for Family, Religion, and Society, a research center in Illinois that "provides a base for [Christian Right] global activists."[52] The WCF isn't an independent entity but a product—perhaps even a brand—of the Howard Center. Since 1997, the Howard Center/WCF has had a prominent role in organizing a series of global World Congresses of Families—most in foreign locations—including congresses in Prague (1997), Geneva (1999); Mexico City (2003); Warsaw (2007); Amsterdam (2009); Madrid (2012); Sydney (2013); Tbilisi, Georgia (2016); and Budapest (2017). In addition to its networks and projects abroad, the WCF is part of a dense and cooperative web of organizations with anti-LGBTQ commitments within the United States. In 2015, the Human Rights Campaign issued reports intended to expose WCF as a Christian conservative organization with anti-LGBTQ and other political objectives and relationships with similar US groups.[53] In "A Call for Civil Dialogue and Constructive Engagement," WCF responded to HRC and the Southern Poverty Law Center:

> **HRC Accusation:** "WCF is an organization with strong ties to American religious and conservative groups—including Focus on the Family, Alliance Defending Freedom, American Fam-

ily Association and Family Research Council—and religious groups—such as The Church of Jesus Christ of Latter-day Saints and the Knights of Columbus."

**The Truth:** Guilty as charged. Though the WCF is not a religious organization, and has no religious affiliation, it is honored to partner with these exemplary, pro-family and religion-based organizations, as well as with secular organizations and individuals involved in sustaining the natural family.[54]

For a number of years, the WCF and its congresses have deployed rhetoric charging the US/Western governments and advocacy organizations with cultural imperialism for interfering with anti-LGBT conservative beliefs and cultural traditions. At the 2009 World Congress of Families in Amsterdam, the Director of International Government Affairs for the US group Focus on the Family accused Western nations of practicing "neo-cultural imperialism" in "developing nations" that "affirm[s] abortion, [and] devalues the natural family and traditional marriage." In its reporting on this congress, the Catholic News Agency highlighted this indictment of imperialism—made by a US-based participant—in the article "Speakers at World Conference of Families Decry Anti-Family 'Cultural Imperialism." Quotes by non-US participants suggest that such a critique of the United States or West is well received by cultural conservatives from the global South.

> The King of Ghana, Drolor Basso Adamley I, [sic] was among the panelists. He stated that the developing world can make a significant contribution in promoting the natural family and has "a great deal to teach the West."[55]
> Another panelist, Christine Vollmer of the Latin American Alliance for the Family, concurred and said that the underdeveloped world is beginning to teach "humanity" to the developed world.[56]

In contexts such as WCF conferences, solidarity between Christian conservatives from developed and developing countries is achieved partly through shared denunciations of Western immorality and cultural contrasts between iniquity and moral virtue. US Christian conservatives understand and depict themselves not as Westerners engaging in their own form of imperialism but as Christians engaging in "fellowship" with believers abroad.[57] As Christopher Stroop reports, the 2017 World Congress of Families in Budapest provided many opportunities for Christian conservative Russians and Americans to "network within the right-wing international" against LGBTQ human rights.[58]

Like the World Congress of Families, Family Watch International (FWI) is a US-based organization, isn't a household name in the United States, and engages in anti-LGBT advocacy in multinational venues. FWI also deploys the frame of "cultural imperialism" that resonates globally with many people from poorer and postcolonial nations to undermine US government and CSO support for SOGI human rights. FWI's short film, *Cultural Imperialism: The Sexual Rights Agenda*, makes the case that the Western agenda of sexual rights that constitutes cultural imperialism in developing countries is gay rights and that the HIV/AIDS epidemic in these countries is a direct consequence of the gay sexual rights agenda.[59] The film juxtaposes interviews with African children orphaned by AIDS with images of predominantly white LGBTQ people, for example, at public Pride events in the West, but the film never mentions heterosexual transmission and what has been called the "heterosexual HIV epidemic" in sub-Saharan Africa. Public health researchers have long known that women in this region bear the brunt of HIV/AIDS mortality and that risk for contracting HIV increases for women with marriage (especially, but not only, early marriage), gender-based violence, and women's low socioeconomic status.[60]

As I argue in *Sin, Sex, and Democracy: Antigay Rhetoric and the Christian Right* and *Tough Love: Sexuality, Compassion, and the Christian Right*, Christian conservative moral entrepreneurs carefully craft anti-LGBTQ political and therapeutic rhetorics and differentiate those for ingroup and public audiences within the United States.[61] In the case of the "cultural imperialism" frame, the indictment has been crafted to appeal to and resonate with audiences outside the United States, especially people in nations whose histories and present circumstances have been shaped by colonial rule. Thus, it was directed first to believers and potential allies abroad. Only in recent years has it begun to be used within the United States as an additional frame for US Christian conservatives to denounce interventions concerning reproductive rights and SOGI human rights.

An example of the charge of cultural imperialism directed to US Christian conservatives about the US government over SOGI human rights occurred on June 3, 2015. That day, Chapman University law professor John Eastman delivered a policy lecture on "Cultural Imperialism and the Obama Administration" at FRC headquarters in Washington. The FRC had advertised the event in this way to its members and subscribers:

> The Obama administration has engaged in an aggressive effort to force recipients of American foreign aid to accept the President's pro-homosexual agenda. This has gone even to the point of demanding that African nations change their laws against same-sex intimacy and those barring same-sex marriage or risk losing U.S. assistance and even American military support in fighting terrorist organizations.[62]

On the same day the FRC hosted its lecture on US pro-LGBT cultural imperialism, emails with the subject line "Stop Cultural Imperialism" began to appear in the inboxes of State Department officials. The source of the email template is a relatively new and unknown conservative group, CitizenGO, that defines its objectives in this way: "CitizenGO is community of active citizens who work together, using online petitions and action alerts as a resource, to defend and promote *life, family, and liberty*. We work to ensure that those in power respect human dignity and individuals' rights."[63] The CitizenGO website does not acknowledge any irony in pledging support for human dignity and individuals' rights while mobilizing supporters to oppose the "radical sexual agenda" of LGBT human rights the US government is using to "coloniz[e] the developing world with their sexual revolution." The organization's website helpfully provides the following template for supporters to write to the State Department—to protest State Department support for LGBTQ human rights and demand that the position of Special Envoy for LGBT Human Rights be terminated. Here is the letter template in its entirety:

> Dear Secretary of State Kerry and Asst. Secretary Malinowski,
>
> I am deeply concerned by the creation of a Special Envoy for the Human Rights of LGBT Persons. I support human rights for *all* human beings, but this is a politicized act of cultural imperialism that forces secular Western values and morality on developing nations, particularly in Africa, Asia, and the Carribean [*sic*].
>
> The creation of this envoy position and Mr. Randy Berry's international travel on behalf of the United States government

in this capacity deprecates American interests abroad by damaging relations with nations in these regions.

The United States should not impose its radical beliefs on sexual morality upon the rest of the world, or use its diplomacy to advance a particular sexual agenda. This is ideological colonization and cultural imperialism.

I demand that the State Department revoke the position of "Special Envoy for LGBT Rights" and recall Mr. Berry from his assignment.

Sincerely,

[Your Name][64]

Given the rhetoric of the letter template and the accompanying website text, it's no surprise that Brian Brown, Founder and President of the National Organization for Marriage, is a member of CitizenGO's board of trustees. But the goals and personnel of this international activist platform also testify to the transnationalizing of culture wars in a time when US Christian conservatives have less confidence of winning on LGBT issues in the United States than they have ever had. I assume it's no coincidence that FRC hosted a lecture on US imperialism toward anti-LGBTQ states and cultures on the same day CitizenGo launched its letter-writing campaign. Indeed, with regard to coordination among anti-LGBTQ activists and organizations, CitizenGO staffed an information booth at the FRC-sponsored 2015 Values Voter Summit in Washington, DC. At that booth, I obtained brochures about the organization and how to participate in its activities, as well as a mini-lip balm branded with the CitizenGO logo.

Given the leveraging of "imperialism" by Christian conservatives and anti-SOGI human rights figures outside the United States, we might ask how SOGI human rights advocates react to the charge. At the Conference to Advance the Human Rights of and Promote Inclusive Development for LGBTI Persons in Washington, DC, in 2014, an African journalist and activist addressed this issue directly. He quoted a 2014 speech by Uganda's President Museveni in which the president excoriated the West's "attempt at social imperialism to impose social values" and concluded, "if that's cultural imperialism or social imperialism, then I'm a social imperialist." The activist then argued that the increasing homophobia confronted by many LGBTQ people and activists was the result of a "new global environment" in which—"in a world of diminishing borders"—such issues could no longer be deferred or silenced. He also pointed out that it was "extraordinary" that such a meeting was being held by the United States even though the nation continues to be riven with conflicts over LGBTQ civil rights and SOGI human rights.[65]

## Christian Conservatism as Cultural Relativism

Not only Western states but also Christian missions have been closely identified with imperial projects. European and North American missionaries have been involved in propagating Christianity or evangelizing for particular sects or traditions in colonized or formerly colonized nations and regions.[66] This history of Christian missionary projects exposes an important difference between the Christian conservative groups, ideologies, and moral entrepreneurs I discussed in this chapter and most Christian missionaries who came before them. Christian missionaries traditionally have understood themselves as transferring culture, knowledge, skills, goods, hierarchies of authority, modes of worship, and/or the means of salvation to members of poorer, less privileged, or less Christianized peoples. By contrast, anti-SOGI missionaries are in the business of affirming the superiority of the cultures, convictions, and practices of those with whom they minister. As SOGI human rights–respecting norms and policies have spread to parts of the world where they previously didn't exist, including the United States, Christian conservative missionaries "forum shop for locales where human rights norms are more poorly developed."[67] Christian conservatives thus bolster SOGI human rights resistance abroad and praise resistance to SOGI human rights norm diffusion as moral and Christian.

Christian conservatives selectively embrace and simultaneously deny human rights doctrine, depending on whether the human rights in question involve freedom to believe and practice religious—especially Christian—faith, or freedom with regard to nonnormative gender or sexual identities or practices. Taking both this selective appropriation of human rights doctrine and the aim of anti-SOGI Christian missionaries into account, it's clear that the Christian conservative movement now has to negotiate discourses that are fundamentally contradictory: within the United States, a discourse that stands unapologetically against cultural relativism (and for religious liberty) and, abroad, a discourse that stands unapologetically for cultural relativism, at least where it comes to SOGI human rights.

However, it's also worthwhile to carefully consider the kind of cultural relativism the Christian right champions in sites where LGBTQ and same-sex-attracted people are vulnerable to human rights violations. As long as there has been a field of human rights, there have been debates over universalism versus relativism, and such debates over theory and practices continue. At one pole in these debates is an absolute—perhaps ideal type—human rights universalism: "the view that all values, including human rights, are entirely universal, in no way subject to modification in light of cultural or historical differences." At the other pole is radical relativism. Political scientist Jack Donnelly argues that these absolute positions are undesirable for different reasons; however, between the two lies a spectrum of possible relativisms he collects into categories of "strong" and "weak."[68]

Donnelly defines his own position as one of "relative universality," a form of "weak relativism" that pairs a defense of universal human rights with "space for national, regional, cultural particularity and other forms of diversity and relativity." In terms of Donnelly's taxonomy, it appears that the anti-SOGI Christian right embraces "substantive cultural relativism"—a "normative doctrine that demands respect for cultural differences."[69] However, on the Christian right we don't see a general respect for the beliefs of other cultures so much as an attraction to parts of the world where the movement has cultural credibility that can be used to reinforce and intensify beliefs that quickly are being disqualified as bias in the United States.

I suggest we distinguish this version of culturally relativist belief system from other versions of cultural relativism and call it *projective cultural relativism*, a practice of projecting one's own already settled beliefs onto other cultural contexts and then cultivating and demanding respect for those beliefs as indigenous cultural products. Such a framing doesn't require that the beliefs in question are entirely alien to the context in which they are being reinforced and cultivated. It means merely that the outsider missionaries or movements have a preexisting set of beliefs and attitudes that it is their goal to teach, encourage, and promote, usually in poorer or less politically stable countries than their own. An excellent depiction of this process between US Christian conservative missionaries and Ugandan people and elites is Roger Ross Williams's *God Loves Uganda*.[70] One feature of projective cultural relativism is easy to predict:

if societies that now reject nonnormative gender and sexuality as antithetical to traditional morality were to become more accepting, tolerant, or even indifferent to such identities and practices, it's unlikely that the anti-SOGI human rights Christian right would accede to the changes and defend them on grounds of cultural authenticity.

Ironically, cultural relativisms are more often identified with the political left, against whom the criticism of "moral relativism" is commonly leveled by voices on the political right. However, SOGI human rights is an occasion for the Christian right to embrace a concern with cultural difference, at least to the extent that it enables the movement to designate as virtuous and authentic those societies and cultures that deny human rights protections to LGBTQ people, incite social disapprobation against them, and encourage the use of public policy to prosecute them.

As a movement, the Christian right deploys projective cultural relativism to undermine and repudiate SOGI human rights. However, the commitment to stand in solidarity with states and peoples that oppose SOGI rights has a side effect that may not be evident much of the time in the Christian right's anti-LGBT rhetoric: many nations that defend discrimination against gender and sexual minorities also discriminate against religious minorities. This conflict between the anti-SOGI human rights and pro–religious freedom commitments of the Christian right was obvious in May 2016 at the UN summit dedicated to Uniting Nations for a Family Friendly World, held at UN headquarters in New York City.[71] Reporting on the conference for People for the American Way, Peter Montgomery observes that the Group of Friends of the Family, a twenty-five-member organization of UN member states launched by Belarus, Egypt, and Qatar in 2015 includes many members identified by the US Commission on International Religious Freedom as grave violators of religious freedom.[72] Thus, many of the very states that US Christian conservatives praise as virtuous and valiant resisters against Western LGBTQ/SOGI human rights simultaneously violate the one natural/human right Christian conservative leaders and organizations recognize and defend.

The mere fact that US Christian conservatives express alarm about cultural imperialism and embrace a kind of cultural relativism doesn't mean that these conservatives are "radical" or thoroughgoing cultural relativists "who see culture . . . as the source of all values."[73] Given their commitment to a natural (human) right to religious faith and practice—especially, sometimes exclusively, for Christians—they cannot commit to such a principle. Recognizing how and why the Christian right practices projective cultural relativism can help advance our understanding of what the Christian right is doing when it exports "America's culture wars" around the world.[74] It can help us see the culture wars subtext in the charge of imperialism that Christian conservatives are likely to continue to use to leverage foreign support for anti-SOGI practices and policies.

The Christian conservative movement and its worldview have not remained the same since the movement was constituted in the 1970s. As US politics has changed, Christian conservatism has faced new challenges and developed new organizations, tactics, strategies, rhetorics, and networks. However, the Christian right is not just what it once was: a movement whose operations were primarily concentrated in the United States and targeting attitude and cultural change, public policy, and the election of biblical leaders. Today it is a global movement that vigorously opposes SOGI human rights and exports its opposition, activists, and resources to influence religious doctrines, social norms, and civil laws wherever its representatives can attain a cultural and political foothold.

The Christian right doesn't merely reject the concept and commitments associated with human rights; the movement's leaders and organizations rhetorically and politically circumscribe the appropriate boundaries of human rights and the forms of identity to which human rights principles and commitments should apply. In this, the Christian right's orientation toward human rights is like the movement's orientation toward compassion for people who exhibit a same-sex sexual orientation or who engage in same-sex relations. At different times and in different contexts, the movement may either repudiate compassion and human rights entirely or carefully circumscribe the contexts and conditions under which either should be invoked to attract proponents, influence the culture, undermine pro-LGBTQ attitudes, and advance political advocacy in favor of the movement's understanding of biblical principles. This means that in key respects, the rhetorical processes by which the boundary between proper objects of human rights principles and protections are created and maintained are similar to the processes by which proper objects of compassion are marked as deserving of compassion rather than punishment.[75]

These US moral entrepreneurs also identify and cultivate religious, intellectual, and political authorities abroad, especially in nations that are poor, unstable, or authoritarian. Historically, it has been the case that US and Western intellectuals and political activists on the left have aligned themselves with people in developing nations and become coproducers with postcolonial peoples of discourses on the meaning and consequences of western imperialism. Now, however, "political homophobia" is exported by churches, missionaries, faith-based "experts," and advocacy organizations. Thus, the conservative version of cultural imperialism is seeded and cultivated in poor nations by Western (especially US) Christian conservatives and by indigenous authorities whose interests are served by homophobia and transphobia. In an article on US and UN advocacy for SOGI human rights, the *National Review* makes this point by directly addressing people around the world who are bullied by the United States over SOGI: if "your culture doesn't align with . . . progressive ideology on abortion and homosexuality," "the United States, buttressed by its liberal European allies[,] will exert imperial power to suppress and supplant your country's traditional cultural values."[76] Some poorer nations explicitly reject Christian right anti-LGBTQ ministries, but these nations remain in the minority.[77]

In Chapter 5, I turn from Christian conservative to critical humanist opposition to US government advocacy for SOGI human rights. One way to distinguish the two forms of opposition is a matter of emphasis. Christian conservative moral entrepreneurs vociferously oppose SOGI human rights and US government advocacy for these human rights. Critical humanists express deep skepticism that shades into opposition to the US government engaging in SOGI human rights advocacy. I won't suggest that these forms of opposition are the same, but as I showed in Chapter 2, there are significant similarities that bear close inspection. In their own ways, these sides aspire to have their understandings influence US attitudes, policies, and acts as well as resistance to US attitudes, policies, and acts. Christian conservative opposition to SOGI human rights exacts a terrible human toll around the world. But academics' convictions about human rights assistance can also harm vulnerable people abroad if these convictions put political beliefs before careful empiricism.

# Chapter 5

# Dispensing Human Rights?

## Critical Humanists and SOGI Human Rights

### The "Internal" Critique of SOGI Human Rights

In contrast to the Christian conservative critique of SOGI human rights, the humanist critique of US government human rights interventions abroad is "internal" in the sense that it originates with scholars who generally are well disposed toward gender and sexual minorities. This is to say that critical humanists tend to be concerned about the well-being of those who engage in same-sex sexual relations or exhibit a nonnormative gender identity even if their scope of interest and concern is not limited to members of these groups. At the same time, many of these scholars strongly repudiate purported universalisms, including assertions of universal human rights that challenge or trump cultural beliefs and practices, or that in their view reflect the imposition of standards held by elites in the global North. One human rights skeptic is Gayatri Chakravorty Spivak, Columbia University Professor of English and comparative literature, who characterizes human rights interventions pejoratively as "the dispens[ing of] Human Rights."[1]

I begin this chapter by briefly outlining an error common in critical humanist analyses of government and policy: a tendency to misunderstand and oversimplify "the state," which is to say how the US government and federal system are structured and how they function. This oversimplification matters for many reasons, including because it licenses the use of some particular site of government action—such as military force or immigration discourse and policies—to stand for all possible government acts. Next I illustrate my concern with the intellectual implications and political consequences of analyses of and commentaries on the US government produced by critical humanist scholars by offering two case studies. The first is a cautionary tale I call "when critique goes bad." The scholar in this story is Ward Churchill who, at the time of the September 11, 2001, terror attacks, was a professor of ethnic studies at the University of Colorado at Boulder. In the immediate aftermath of September 11, he composed and published an essay, "Sometimes People Push Back: On the Justice of Roosting Chickens," but he achieved notoriety only in 2005 when commentator Bill O'Reilly brought Churchill and his essay to the attention of Fox News viewers. I focus on Churchill's account of official state acts and their consequences for two reasons. First, the essay was widely publicized and came to represent progressive academic critique of US government intervention and the unintended consequences of such intervention. Second, the response of academics to this controversy implicated many in Churchill's polemic.

My second case study is of some of the claims and deficiencies in a concept and theory of SOGI human rights that has captivated many scholars and students of sexuality. This is Jasbir Puar's concept/theory of homonationalism from her 2007 book, *Terrorist Assemblages: Homonationalism in Queer Times*. Now a central text in many corners of the humanities, and especially in the interdisciplinary fields of women's/gender, ethnic, and sexuality studies, *Terrorist Assemblages* is the most influential critique of US and other Western interventions that support (or ostensibly support) the civil or human rights of LGBTQ people. Because homonationalism is widely taken to be the most insightful analysis of sexuality and gender politics in national and transnational contexts, no account of LGBTQ politics can now be written without coming to terms with it.

Finally, because I regard the problems with much critical humanist political critique as structural, I reflect briefly on epistemological and methodological dimensions of the kinds of analyses I criticize. These structural problems begin with, but are not exhausted by, uninformed assumptions regarding the structure and nature of the state.

## The Problem of the State

A persistent problem with critical humanist political critiques of US intervention, including the role of official government actors in disseminating human rights discourse and engaging in human rights interventions, is a simplistic conceptualization of the state. In an interview, author Paul Berman addresses the ubiquity on the progressive left of two assumptions:

that "what the U.S. does is always, simply, by definition, imperialist"; and that the US state acts as a single unit with predictable effects.

> In this analysis one views the U.S. as very nearly a single unit . . . and everything that the US does must have very nearly a single quality—imperialistic and oppressive. . . . The United States, like any society, consists of thousands of different currents which go this way and that way, and the actions of the US—both of private individuals and the state—can likewise go this way or that, with many different effects.[2]

But what if we separate "private individuals" and nongovernmental entities from this commentary and concentrate only on the state? Even with regard to the federal government, and not the other levels of our federal system, the state is large, complex, and fragmented, and no single national ideology or set of national interests has prescribed government goals or acts in the present or over the course of US history.

In "Homonationalism, State Rationalities, and Sex Contradictions," Paisley Currah takes on this kind of misunderstanding and "naturalizing" of the state common in queer theory, and I argue that this critique also applies to a great deal of humanist scholarship that relies on other theoretical paradigms. The main points of Currah's critique are first, that the state is understood and depicted as "far more monolithic than it is," and second, that "a unity of intention" is consistently attributed to "state actors." As a foundation for scholarship on sexuality and gender, he argues that such a perspective

> naturalize[s] the state, and attach[es] certain properties to "it"—a totalizing logic, an ordered hierarchy, a comprehensive rationality, a unity of purpose and execution. [The perspective] assume[s] the executive, as a single branch, produces non-contradictory policy outcomes. . . . [It] assume[s] that the actual policy outcomes are always intended. [It] assume[s] a universalist rationality—good or bad—to "the" state's actions.[3]

There is even a subgenre of literature in US politics and policy that investigates and analyzes the outcomes of fragmentation in domestic bureaucratic policy making. These cases demonstrate that many (including contradictory) motivations can drive policy making in specific arenas but also that different agents and agencies of the US government, engaged in rule making and oversight in the same policy arena, can pursue and produce diverse—and sometimes contradictory—outcomes.[4]

As Currah points out, misunderstanding "the state" in these ways has far-reaching consequences: "fetishizing a generalized idea of the state—the conceptual state—obscures what is actually happening in the local, micro, particular sites where public authority is being exercised." The example he points to is diverse government sex classification criteria, which

> often reflect different state projects. . . . What seem to be
> contradictions in sex definition—across jurisdictions, between
> agencies, and at different times—are simply the consequences
> of the fact that 'the state' is not a singular entity but multiple,
> does not do one thing, but many, is not produced through
> one process, but many.[5]

Indeed, much of what the US government does, domestically and internationally, is executed by and through government bureaucracies and over two million civil servants who work in them. For philosopher Judith Butler, these officials are "petty sovereigns" who make "discretionary decisions . . . within governmentality":

> These are petty sovereigns, unknowing, to a degree, about what
> work they do, but performing their acts unilaterally and with
> enormous consequence. Their acts are clearly *conditioned*, but
> their acts are judgments that are *unconditional* in the sense that
> they are final, not subject to review, and not subject to appeal.[6]

In this view, there is no need to gather information about, for example, human rights policies and their implementation by the United States and other governments. Deploying a theoretical device such as "petty sovereigns" also makes it unnecessary to investigate structural and interpersonal dynamics commonly found in bureaucratic organizations, the processes by which policy agendas are developed and executed, or "iron triangles" in policy making—all dimensions of bureaucratic organization that bear on how the federal government operates with regard to particular issues and domains of decision making.

There is another, related problem with conceptualizing "the state" and its neoliberal, imperialist, or oppressive character and acts that Currah gestures toward: that critical humanist scholarship on politics often represents the state not only as monolithic but also as adept in carrying out its agenda. In this view of the US government as global hegemon, there is little room for ordinary inefficiency, accidents, groupthink, clientitis, conflicting objectives, multiplicative efforts, institutional/bureaucratic inertia, and unexpected side effects. One source of illumination on this point is literature in political psychology and international relations that speaks to a general shared psychological tendency to overestimate an adversary's efficacy, a tendency that can undermine the quality of decision and policy making. On matters of foreign policy, scholars find, for example, a common "causal inference": the "tendency to overestimate the degree to which the behavior of others is planned and centralized."[7] This fantasy of motivation and efficacy easily can lead to "the tendency to regard one's enemy as more rational and centralized than he is and the tendency to overestimate rather than underestimate him."[8] Of course, this is only an identifiable pattern of thought, not a lead-pipe certainty. But the analysis helps make sense of both the remarkable degree of homogeneity that characterizes critical humanist scholarship on US government acts and interventions and the lack of interest in empiricism obvious in much of the scholarship produced by humanists on "the state."

## When Critique Goes Bad

In the weeks after September 11, there were many contenders for an intellectual explanation of the cause or at least the precipitating factors of the attacks on New York City and Washington, DC. A shorthand version of the Christian right's explanation was offered by television evangelists Jerry Falwell and Pat Robertson, who attributed the attacks to God's wrath toward the United States for its tolerance of diverse forms of immorality, including sexual immorality. As I documented in *Sin, Sex, and Democracy*, although Falwell and Robertson were the most visible Christian conservative proponents of the argument for collective national guilt, they certainly were not alone. The explanation for why God "continues to lift the curtain and allow the enemies of America to give us probably what we deserve" was already deeply embedded in Christian conservatives' perspectives on the United States, sinful disobedience, and eschatology. Many Christian right moral entrepreneurs offered versions of the explanation.[9]

For many critical humanists, the actual (if not proximate) cause of the attacks was equally self-evident: blowback from US acts and policies that have killed, maimed, and dispossessed innocent people abroad. Different scholars have offered versions of this kind of explanation, many of which identify specific US foreign policies or acts of state that constitute US government racism, imperialism, war crimes, or genocide. Of these indictments, the one that received most public attention was Ward Churchill's "Sometimes People Push Back." The passage of the essay that most inflamed his critics was one in which Churchill dubbed those who worked in the World Trade Center and became casualties in it "little Eichmanns" who bore remote responsibility for US war crimes committed on behalf of "America's global financial empire." The full passage contains Churchill's indictment and a glimpse of the style of what his defenders later characterized as his "scholarly argumentation."

> As for those in the World Trade Center . . . Well, really, let's get a grip here, shall we? True enough, they were civilians of a sort. But innocent? Gimme a break. They formed a technocratic corps at the very heart of America's global financial empire—the "mighty engine of profit" to which the military dimension of U.S. policy has always been enslaved—and they did so both willingly and knowingly. Recourse to "ignorance"—a derivative, after all, of the word "ignore"—counts as less than an excuse among this relatively well-educated elite. To the extent that any of them were unaware of the costs and consequences to others of what they were involved in—and in many cases excelling at—it was because of their absolute refusal to see. More likely, it was because they were too busy braying, incessantly and self-importantly, into their cell phones, arranging power lunches and stock transactions, each of which translated, conveniently out of sight, mind and smelling distance, into the starved and rotting flesh of infants. If there was a better, more effective, or in fact any other way of visiting some penalty befitting their participation upon the little Eichmanns inhabiting the sterile sanctuary of the twin towers, I'd really be interested in hearing about it.[10]

Once the essay was publicized, the University of Colorado at Boulder came under pressure from conservatives to undertake a review of Churchill's scholarship, and many academics rallied to his defense. A product of the controversy was "An Open Letter from Concerned Academics" that ultimately attracted the support of hundreds of Churchill's academic colleagues from universities across the country. Like many of their colleagues, the "concerned academics" saw in the controversy and the subsequent inquiry into Churchill's published work the opening of another front in the long-running struggle between left-leaning academics and their conservative critics. This reading accounts for the direness of the signatories' warning, coupled as it is with a qualification about the caliber of the work being defended:

> To be clear: the issues here have nothing to do with the quality of Ward Churchill's scholarship or his professional credentials. However one views his choice of words or specific arguments, he is being put in the dock solely for his radical critique of U.S. history and present-day policy in the wake of the events of September 11, 2001. Apparently, 9/11 is now the third rail of American intellectual life: to critically probe into its causes and to interrogate the international role of the United States is treated as heresy; those inquiring can be denied forums, careers, and even personal safety. And now Churchill's persecutors have gone further, repeatedly ridiculing his scholarly argumentation that the United States committed genocide against the indigenous people of this continent, and that the FBI systematically attempted to disrupt and destroy the movements and leaders of the 1960s. Rather than debate or disprove such theses, Churchill's attackers attempt to render them beyond the pale of respectable discourse. Through all this, new ground rules are being established: *any* criticism or even questioning of the institutional foundations of the United States, or of the motives and interests behind its policies, will be treated as essentially treasonous. Left unopposed, this trajectory will lead to a situation of uncontested indoctrination enforced by the state. . . .

> It would be hard to overstate the serious nature of what has already happened, let alone what it would mean should the Regents fire Churchill. If this assault on academe succeeds, the

consequences for American society as a whole will be nothing
short of disastrous.[11]

To be clear: the scholars who expressed support for Churchill's freedom
of speech and academic position were not expressing confidence in the
quality of his scholarly perspective as it was revealed in "Some People Push
Back," and for good reason. The essay is sardonic and provocative, but
intellectually it is embarrassing and indefensible. There are many threats
to higher education—including but not exclusively threats to tenure and
academic freedom—but a change in the status of Churchill's academic
employment was not such a threat. Churchill's academic defenders were
wrong: the consequences of his firing for "American society as a whole"
fell far short of disastrous.

What is unfortunate is that so many scholars were provoked into
defending Churchill because of the campaign waged against him by right-
wing media personalities. But the story doesn't end there. In defending
Churchill from charges of plagiarism and falsification of evidence, the
Colorado Conference of the American Association of University Professors likened him to televangelist Pat Robertson, who they point out made
an argument much like Churchill's about September 11. The professors
indignantly note that in spite of the similarities between Churchill's
polemic and Robertson's, "Pat Robertson's career and reputation were
not destroyed."[12] Thus, the members of the Colorado Conference of the
AAUP defended Churchill by arguing—correctly, in more ways than they
acknowledged—that in his essay Churchill had performed an analysis like
that of noted right-wing conspiracy theorist Pat Robertson, for whom the
Masons, the Illuminati, and the Trilateral Commission are central actors in
the consolidation of an evil New World Order that will culminate in the
Second Coming of Jesus.[13] Clearly, it did not occur to Churchill's defenders
that Robertson had made his living fabricating and disseminating claims
of transhistorical Satanic plots. Nor did it occur to them that as a scholar,
Churchill should be held to a higher standard.

Of course, Churchill's case for the justice of roosting chickens is a
polemic rather than a formal piece of academic scholarship. However, in
his essay, Churchill makes truth claims that can be subjected to analysis,
including his claim about the motivation that drove a group of Saudi
members of al Qaeda to skyjack the four airplanes. Churchill argues that
the skyjackers were motivated by a desire for retribution for the deaths of
Iraqi children as a result of the US economic sanctions imposed in 1990

after Iraq's invasion of Kuwait. And he agrees that those who died in the World Trade Center received a "penalty befitting their participation" in the deaths of these Iraqi children. However, he failed—or refused—to consider that the skyjacking and murders might have been motivated by a particular shared political ideology, or by one of a set of closely related ideologies, rather than merely a very specific desire for retribution. Indeed, since the 1990s, many scholars have examined the roots, ideology, organizing, demographics, and consequences—including violence against Muslims—of Wahhabism and Salafism, the contemporary Islamic extremist movements with which violent extremists have affiliated. This literature is large and, as far as I can tell, is virtually ignored by critical humanist scholars who write on topics related to violent Islamic extremism. If such extremism exists as a phenomenon and cannot be reduced solely to justifiable outrage, it's necessary for scholars who write about political violence to take existing research from history and the social sciences into account in formulating our analyses. A geopolitical reality of such violence is that the United States and other Western nations are not the only targets of such attacks. In addition to state violence from the United States and its allies, apostate Muslims in the Middle East and elsewhere are frequent targets of deadly religiously motivated extremism.[14] By refusing to take into account realities of violence that don't fit our template for righteous rage against the United States and the West, US academics may well effectively abandon vulnerable Muslims in their struggles against violent extremism.

Thankfully, most academics are not Ward Churchill, but he set an extremely low bar for political arguments, and he was defended—not censured or ignored—by many of his colleagues. The alternative to Churchill's "radical" "interrogat[ion] of the international role of the United States" is not unconditional support for the US government or confidence in the essential virtue of its acts and policies. Rather, it is the same posture of skepticism and intellectual curiosity we bring to the study of other topics, combined with the willingness to collect and analyze evidence and the prudence to exercise caution in making cases and generalizations.

The politicized exposure of Ward Churchill's essay and the subsequent spectacle surrounding it and him don't bear directly on government SOGI human rights interventions abroad. But to the extent that assumptions and assertions like this are taken as fact—and Churchill understood as a martyred truth-teller—such a spectacle isn't just a distraction. The convictions that undergird Churchill's polemic on US government practices abroad may be correct, partially correct, or entirely incorrect, but their facticity is an empirical question that challenges scholars in different disciplines. No matter how passionately they are held, particular critical convictions regarding the motivations and outcomes of US discourse and acts cannot be taken as fact in particular cases.

## What about Homonationalism?

The genealogy of homonationalism runs from homophobia through heteronormativity and homonormativity to homonationalism and beyond—most recently to homoprotectionism, transhomonationalism, and homotransnationalism.[15] The concept and theory of homonationalism rests on two broad claims. First is the claim that arguments for LGBT rights grounded in post–September 11 US citizenship are parasitic on and intensify exclusions, especially exclusions of racialized Arab/Muslim, African American, and Latino/a others. Second is that regimes—including but not limited to the US government—actively and strategically enact and advertise a pro-LGBT facade and stage pro-LGBT progressiveness to camouflage racist, repressive, and reactionary politics and to recruit LGBTQ people into colluding with and championing these politics.

With regard to the first claim, many readers on the political left will disapprove of white middle-class lesbians, gay men, and bisexuals making rights claims when many others—citizens of color, documented and undocumented immigrants, noncombatant casualties of US military force—are profiled, marginalized, deported, or disproportionately prosecuted. Nonetheless, it is a truism that even though rights aren't zero sum—protection of my human rights doesn't preclude protection of someone else's human rights—all rights claims and all assertions of identity are exclusionary in some sense. When members of a particular group are identified—or identify themselves—as at risk of having fundamental rights violated, activists and policy makers may craft social and political discourses and public policies to address those risks and the situatedness of that group.

Indeed, this is the logic behind the Black Lives Matter movement: not, as critics have insinuated, to assert that *only* black lives matter but to demand an end to "antiblack racism" and state violence against African Americans.[16] Thus, in the process of articulating and addressing a particular rights claim, these discourses and policies include some rights claims, violations, and remedies and exclude others. In the United States, although many LGBTQ people are white, male, well educated, or economically privileged, many are not. In addition, under current political arrangements, LGBTQ people of color benefit directly and measurably as a group from rights to marriage and equality in other family policies.[17] Any theory that doesn't account for the existence of LGBTQ people of color as political claimants fails to take race and other forms of identity into account and thus virtually assures that analyses of policies and political practices will be partial.

The second claim that for Puar confirms homonationalism consists of the strategic enactments of a pro-LGBT facade: state actors deploying "progressive" policies in the area of LGBTQ rights as the basis of a comparison, usually to highlight the bias against LGBTQ people in Arab societies and among Muslims and/or people of color more generally. What Puar points to here as proof of homonational racism is, first, overdrawn as a phenomenon and, second, an ordinary and mundane dimension of practical politics, which is to say it's trivially true. This phenomenon is taking credit for popular policies and social transformations that one's party or ideological group might have opposed and then deploying those policies and shifts to the advantage of oneself or one's party, nation, or ideology.

Consider an example that has nothing to do with LGBTQ issues. In September 2015, Senator Marco Rubio took the stage at the annual Values Voter Summit to speak to the hundreds of Christian conservative activists assembled at the Omni Shoreham Hotel in Washington, DC about issues of religious freedom and economic well-being. In the course of his speech, Rubio praised the Family and Medical Leave Act (FMLA), signed into law by President Bill Clinton, as a way for family members to be able to take care of each other. Rubio even suggested that FMLA wasn't sufficient to meet the needs of families, though he quickly noted that the solution to the problem of caregiving should be a "free enterprise" solution rather than one mandated by the government. He offered tax policy as a way for the government to induce businesses to offer paid family leave, a solution that would in fact require government action and policy making.[18]

Given intense conservative and Republican opposition to FMLA, which mandated twelve weeks of unpaid leave for particular family events in certain sectors of the economy, it might seem strange that Rubio would speak of it as though his fellow conservatives supported the policy. Not only did conservatives not support FMLA at the time of its passage, it was intensely opposed by the Chamber of Commerce and a majority of Republican members of Congress. It was a "threat," "Europeanization," and, of course, "socialism." Indeed, "future Speaker of the House of

Representatives, John Boehner (R-OH) complained that the legislation would 'be the demise of some [businesses].' 'And as that occurs,' he continued, 'the light of freedom will grow dimmer.' "[19]

Policies are regularly opposed by parties and movements; however, once such policies are implemented, and especially when they prove popular or successful, the incentive structure changes, and policy makers adjust their behavior and political rhetoric to try to achieve new objectives. Policy makers revise political rhetoric to take credit for outcomes they opposed to accomplish some other end, rehabilitate their reputation, or "center" themselves and their policies, an argument to which I return later.[20] Elected officials and national representatives rarely will pass up an opportunity to compare themselves, their party, or their country favorably to other, contending individuals, parties, or countries.

The term that has come to be applied to this phenomenon when it concerns LGBT civil or human rights is "pinkwashing," a subset of homonationalism. Among critical humanists, pinkwashing has become a favored interpretation to explain a variety of state actions and political narratives related to disjunctions between ostensibly progressive LGBT social life and public policies on one hand, and racism, militarism, exclusion, or economic depredation on the other. The concept of pinkwashing is most identified with author and activist Sarah Schulman. Schulman argues that Israel has deliberately deployed a message of Israeli progressivism with regard to sexuality to "rebrand" the nation and deflect attention from human rights violations perpetrated by the state against Palestinians in Israel and in occupied territories.[21] But the indictment of pinkwashing is highly portable, and it's rhetorically invoked as an explanation whenever political figures call—or are perceived to call—on LGBTQ people and their allies to ally themselves with a nation, a party, a political candidate, or some abstraction such as freedom or democracy. Too often elided by the charge of pinkwashing are two questions. The first question that must be investigated is the accuracy of the claim or comparison in every particular context for which it's invoked. In the enterprise of interpreting political rhetoric, the difference between truth and falsehood matters. Second, scholars who interpret political rhetoric must consider as much as possible a range of likely explanations for the rhetoric being deployed.

A search might begin, for example, by taking into account domestic political cleavages among contending policy entrepreneurs and constituencies, the ways ideological constituencies use such comparisons to advance their interests, and the extent to which these rhetorics fail or succeed. For example, Israel's relations with its neighbors are characterized by deep enmity and distrust, and Israel's military actions have isolated it from other peoples in the Middle East and throughout the world. However, Israel also has deep domestic cleavages between secular and ultra-Orthodox Jews regarding the appropriate status and membership of gender and sexual minorities. Thus, national figures deploying a progressive public narrative about SOGI makes sense as a tactic for solidifying domestic political gains and creating leverage for future gains. Similar kinds of debates in the United States between social liberals and social conservatives over civil unions, same-sex marriage, employment nondiscrimination, and public restrooms are easy to identify.[22] The phenomenon of pivoting from condemnation to support regularly occurs across social and political domains. Unfortunately, the concept of homonationalism has, for many readers, effectively rendered this phenomenon as one that specifically implicates LGBTQ attitudes, people, and policies in racism against Muslims and people of color. We can and should interpret the meanings and effects of such rhetorics without identifying LGBTQ and SOGI-related applications as particularly culpable and deplorable.

There are some academic critiques of homonationalism, and scattered critiques of foundational assumptions of homonationalism have appeared in a variety of venues. In addition to Paisley Currah's essay, "Homonationalism, State Rationalities, and Sex Contradictions," there is Terry Goldie's "Queering the Problem," a largely positive review of Terrorist Assemblages;[23] and Jason Ritchie's "Pinkwashing, Homonationalism, and Israel-Palestine: The Conceits of Queer Theory and the Politics of the Ordinary."[24] More devastating to homonationalism than the authors acknowledge are Aleardo Zanghellini's "Are Gay Rights Islamophobic? A Critique of Some Uses of the Concept of Homonationalism in Activism and Academia" and Michael Bosia and Meredith Weiss's "Political Homophobia in Comparative Perspective," which introduces their volume, Global Homophobia.[25]

Combining these disparate critiques of homonationalism produces a catalog of significant criticisms:

1. That as an explanation, homonationalism evinces a misunderstanding and misrepresentation of "the state" (Currah).

2. That in adumbrating and applying homonationalism, proponents, including Puar, engage in factual distortion to make their facts fit a favored interpretation (Zanghellini).

3. That the use of homonationalism is marked systematically by "denial and strategic silences," that is, the lack of interest in or dismissal of alternative explanations (Zanghellini). A particularly key "strategic silence" is the silence of Puar (and other theorists of homonationalism) on the religious motivations and justifications people give for embracing and acting on homo- and transphobia (Goldie).

4. That homonationalism is a case of "presupposed paranoid structuralism" or, in simpler terms, confirmation bias (Zanghellini).

5. That in considering the situation of same-sex-attracted people in majority-Islamic societies, Puar reifies Muslims' efforts to reconcile faith with sexuality as a form of cultural identity that always already repudiates (Western) human rights (Zanghellini).

6. That homonationalism oversimplifies racism and "tolerance" of homosexuals instead of requiring that these phenomena be evaluated in their social and political contexts (Ritchie).

7. that as an explanation, homonationalism confuses causes with effects (Bosia and Weiss).[26]

I find all of these criticisms valid, and in what follows I respond briefly to some key claims and examples in a way that suggests the extraordinarily wide scope of the theory and concept of homonationalism as well as its flaws.

A meaningful "silence" in *Terrorist Assemblages* is Puar's reliance on a phenomenon that's been widely noted and analyzed in the politics of outgroups. In *The Boundaries of Blackness: AIDS and the Breakdown of Black Politics*, political theorist Cathy Cohen uses the concept of "secondary marginalization" to investigate the phenomenon of "power relationships within marginal communities." Particularly of interest to Cohen is the phenomenon in which "the most vulnerable and stigmatized" people in outgroups may be targeted for "blame and punishment" by more normative outgroup members.[27] Although Puar cites Cohen, Cohen's analysis of secondary marginalization doesn't appear in *Terrorist Assemblages*.[28] Instead, Puar writes as though she has discovered the inter- and intragroup relations Cohen explicates and that these relations are specific to a US and global effort to enlist gay support for the War on Terror. By contrast, Bosia and Weiss cite Cohen's secondary marginalization and explicitly note the salience of Cohen's analysis in revealing the limitations of homonationalism as an explanation that links post–September 11 racism and xenophobia to LGBTQ civil rights claiming.[29]

In recent years, a controversial political goal of LGBT movements, not just in the United States but in Europe and Latin America, has been legalizing same-sex marriage, a goal that's been realized in more than twenty countries. Queer theorists and some other critical humanists in the academy have repudiated same-sex marriage as conservative and normalizing, but Puar and those inspired by her analysis move beyond this disagreement between those who support marriage equality for whatever legal, social, political, or personal reasons and those who reject it. Puar implicates the policy and practice of same-sex marriage, as well as those who support it politically and those who marry a same-sex partner, in state ideologies of racism. She writes, for example, that support for same-sex marriage and the desire to get married after the Supreme Court decision in *Lawrence v. Texas* "is fueled by conscious and unconscious yearnings to reinstate the privileges of whiteness, in fact, white Americanness."[30]

However, if we interrogate this implication, we find that there are alternative explanations for support for same-sex marriage that rely less on a singular, comprehensive characterization of "the state" or people who support marriage equality and that take account of complex historical processes of states, policies, and cultural formations. One of these explanations is Angelia Wilson's analysis of European "lesbian- and gay-friendly" social policies. Wilson closely analyzes the evolution of policies that have incorporated same-sex families into "the political economy of care" in the United Kingdom and multiple European states. What she finds is a set of national cases that differ from one another but share certain features, including a post–World War II consensus in favor of universal social welfare services; "mixed economies of care" in which government and faith-based and voluntary institutions cooperate in distinctive ways in different nations to provide care for citizens; a "care crunch," or contraction of resources necessary to deliver care; and the incorporation of same-sex families into marriage and responsible citizenship in part on the basis of caregiving that relieves overburdened public and private welfare providers. Wilson is critical of the conceptions of policy "friendliness" and citizenship that emerge from this analysis, but her careful empiricism is an antidote to Puar's totalizing equation of same-sex marriage with xenophobic racism.[31]

Throughout *Terrorist Assemblages*, Puar makes a variety of unfounded claims and assumptions that, as far as I know, critics have not responded to directly. She suggests, for example, that rising support in the United States for LGBTQ civil rights is a post–September 11 phenomenon, and this timing seems to irrefutably implicate ostensibly progressive attitudes and policies in racism against Muslims and people of color. However, Puar is factually wrong on the trends of rising support for LGBTQ rights which, as many social scientists have demonstrated, began well before 2001 in countries where pro-LGBTQ attitudes are most advanced today.[32]

Second, Puar consistently positions mass murderers of civilians (such as suicide bombers and those who aspire to commit mass murder) only as rational "politically motivated" actors.[33] She has no interest in the vast literatures in psychology, sociology, political science, and other disciplines about religious motivations and justifications of acts such as the murder of noncombatants. By contrast, when she addresses the motivations and feelings associated with "the bonding ritual of the carnival of [US-sanctioned] torture—discussing it, producing it, getting turned on by it, recording it, disseminating the proof of it, gossiping about it," she confidently interprets the practices as "the ultimate performance of patriotism."[34] As I read this passage, there is no position that US citizens of any ethnic or racial heritage can take—including the position of relying on, for example, photos of torture at Abu Ghraib to demand an end to official practices of torture—that doesn't implicate us all in the "carnival of torture" that constitutes "the ultimate performance of patriotism."[35]

Another dubious claim for which Puar adduces no evidence is that "the state"—or, the US government throughout its history—has refrained from banning displays of visible signs of religious belief to create the opportunity for "the watching and the assaulting of these different bodies."[36] This interpretation assumes the existence of a transhistorical goal of the US state to mark (at least certain categories of) religious believers for extralegal violence. This is a conviction, but it isn't an argument with evidence to support it. What is striking and should be obvious to any scholar who reads Puar's analysis is her extraordinary reliance on insinuation as a mode of argument, especially to make connections between phenomena or adduce their underlying meaning and motivation. Also striking are the moments in the analysis when she states or suggests that she is not interested in discerning the truth or falsity of a claim that will underlie or justify her argument.[37]

A complete rejoinder to *Terrorist Assemblages* would have to address too many topics, literatures, and facts to fit into a short space. Among these would be the following: the routine phenomenon of secondary marginalization in outgroups vying for political rights and recognition; the well-documented "rally 'round the flag" effect identified by political scientists when the United States is attacked or uses military force;[38] the pre– and post–September 11 continuity of LGBT electoral behavior;[39] the multiple problems with identifying support for same-sex marriage as correlated with racism, including a comparison of the demographics of groups who have led acceptance of same-sex marriage with demographics of implicit and explicit racism;[40] and many more.[41] A complete analysis of *Terrorist Assemblages* and a reassessment of its claims and interpretations also would have to try to sort out, in a way that Puar doesn't, a distinction between acts (of state or of other social agents) that intentionally operate to induct LGBTQ people into nationalism and support for the War on Terror and effects that, while not deliberate, may accomplish these or other, completely different ends. It's clear from her analysis that Puar doesn't recognize the task of investigating such distinctions to be a core dimension of responsible scholarship.

There are, of course, alternatives to Puar's analysis, and I'll offer one here that I believe has more potential for helping us understand what may be happening politically when right-wing political figures make overtures to LGBT people. In *New Right Discourses on Race and Sexuality*, Anna Marie Smith theorizes the strategy by which the "intolerant," who "always misrecognize themselves as 'tolerant,' " "center" themselves and their discourses by deploying an "imaginary promise of inclusion." Even more apropos is Smith's article, "Why Did Armey Apologize? Hegemony, Homophobia, and the Religious Right," which focuses on Representative Richard Armey's 1995 antigay slur against Representative Barney Frank. Armey referred to the openly gay Frank as "Barney Fag" and later apologized for the slur. Smith begins her analysis by refuting the explanation for the apology preferred by the Log Cabin Republicans: that Armey and other Republicans were appealing to "the gay vote," which could go to the Republican Party if the party recognized gays as "a political force Republicans must finally reckon with." So why, according to Smith, did Armey apologize? Her conclusion is that the progay rhetoric is addressed to "an imaginary lesbian and gay audience" to "center the extremism of the Republicans. The apology is aimed, first and foremost, not at gay voters but at homophobic Republicans. It does not appeal to an already constituted interest group; it reconstructs the homophobic popular bloc." In short, Smith argues that a central feature of contemporary right-wing political discourse is the conservative appropriation of "such key signifiers as 'freedom,' 'equality,' 'democracy,' and 'tolerance of difference' " by engaging in discourse that allows them to position themselves as "the real defenders of liberal democracy."[42]

Why is such an analysis useful in rethinking homonationalism? One reason is the timing of the event that Smith analyzes, which took place before 2001. This timing demonstrates that conservative overtures to LGBT people aren't just a function of the racism and US imperialism unleashed and justified by the War on Terror. Second, central to her analysis is Smith's account of how conservatives "center" their racial and sexual politics by making appeals to and about members of race, gender, and sexual outgroups that target right-wing constituencies—not outgroups. Third, Smith's careful critique of the naive reading of conservative outreach to LGBT people—that such appeals are intended to seduce LGBT people who aren't already supporters of right-wing politics and induct them into racist nationalism—also applies to Puar's naive reading of political discourse. Finally, Smith's interpretation of progay conservative discourse neither stigmatizes LGBTQ civil or human rights–claiming as racist and imperialist nor requires scholars and activists to repudiate these rights as implicitly racist and imperialist.

Although there are alternatives to Puar's analysis, there is no single alternative account of racism, imperialism, US domestic and foreign policy, civil rights, US political behavior, and LGBTQ politics. Part of the allure of homonationalism is that it knits together a group of phenomena, not only in the United States but quite literally everywhere we look, and connects what appear to be disparate rhetorics, policies, beliefs, impulses, and effects into an ideological package that accords with the political convictions of a significant subset of critical humanist scholars and students. The process of finding better—that is, more robust and empirically sound—explanations for the wide set of phenomena Puar introduces as either examples or proof of homonationalism cannot be done by constructing an alternative explanation. In the end, what does Puar's concept of homonationalism and its application to a wide variety of social and political phenomena contribute to our understanding of US government advocacy for SOGI human rights? Unfortunately, the answer is: very little. The concept of homonationalism gives us little purchase on the topic at hand because it is a deeply flawed theoretical rendering of what essentially are a set of unrelated empirical phenomena. Put another way, it's an answer to empirical questions that's fraught with what psychologists call "motivated reasoning."[43] Taken together, the criticisms of

homonationalism are devastating; nevertheless, the currency of homonationalism as a foundational assumption and a perspicacious explanation,
especially for critical humanist scholars writing about race and sexuality
in US domestic or foreign policy, remains high.

## On Critique Running Out of Steam

In the course of researching and writing this chapter, I asked myself whether
the critical humanist worldview I discuss here is enough of a problem to
set criticisms of it alongside human rights objections of the conservative
right. I think it is, and one piece of evidence is that in some cases high-
profile scholars who have contributed to the worldview have thought it
necessary to air their culpability in propounding arguments whose flaws
they didn't foresee and whose political uses have migrated easily from left
to right. Consider the situation of Bruno Latour, an eminent scholar of
philosophy of science. In 2003, Latour delivered a Stanford Presidential
Lecture at Stanford University, subsequently published in *Critical Inquiry*,
titled, "Why Has Critique Run Out of Steam? From Matters of Fact to
Matters of Concern." Latour suggests that the problem he identifies with
humanist critique is associated with its migration from the political left to
the political right, but he also confesses that this migration has exposed
weaknesses in the project of progressive critique. Posed as a counterfactual, Latour speculates that if humanist critique has in fact found itself
at home on the political right,

> the danger would no longer be coming from an excessive
> confidence in ideological arguments posturing as matters of
> fact—as we have learned to combat so efficiently in the past—but
> from an excessive *distrust* of good matters of fact disguised as
> bad ideological biases! While we spent years trying to detect
> the real prejudices hidden behind the appearance of objective
> statements, do we now have to reveal the real objective and
> incontrovertible facts hidden behind the *illusion* of prejudices?
> And yet entire Ph.D. programs are still running to make sure
> that good American kids are learning the hard way that facts
> are made up . . . while dangerous extremists are using the very
> same argument of social construction to destroy hard-won
> evidence that could save our lives.[44]

Quoting a passage from Latour's mea culpa in 2011's "The Science Wars Redux," Michael Bérubé responds to Latour's tormented statement "why can't I simply say that the argument [about the existence of anthropogenic climate change] is closed for good?" with "Why, indeed?"

Like Latour, Bérubé reassesses the implications of a subset of critical modes of argument and conclusions in a context in which "attacks on 'objective knowledge' that were once the province of the left have been taken up by the right." A result is that "the climate-change deniers and the young-Earth creationists are coming after the natural scientists" and "using some of the very arguments developed by an academic left that thought it was speaking only to people of like mind." Bérubé expresses the hope that "perhaps humanists are beginning to realize that there is a project even more vital than that of the relentless critique of everything existing, a project to which they can contribute as much as any scientist—the project of making the world a more humane and livable place."[45] Although my concerns point in a different direction, I agree with Latour's and Bérubé's second thoughts.

In his lecture, Latour notes the similarities between right- and left-wing modes of critique and the provenance of those modes on the critical humanist left as "weapons smuggled through a fuzzy border to the wrong party." Nonetheless, he states categorically that "conspiracy theories" of the sort retailed by the political right—examples include that September 11 was an inside job and that mass shootings have been fabricated by the government as an excuse to impose gun control—"are an absurd deformation of our own arguments."[46] With all due respect for Latour's trust in the integrity of humanist critique, homonationalism doesn't vindicate this hope.

It's not only that the claims and arguments associated with homonationalism aren't falsifiable—much theory in humanist disciplines and subfields isn't directly falsifiable. Rather, it's that the form of so many political claims and arguments and the presumption of truth with which they are presented vitiate the criterion of falsifiability by rendering it unnecessary, suspect, or politically reactionary. Homonationalism in now routinely deployed to problematize and repudiate rights claims by LGBTQ US citizens as implicitly nationalistic and racist. But this very conviction and the theory in which it's nested create a problem for this literature that isn't a challenge for other kinds of human rights scholarship: how can or should we understand and characterize the SOGI human rights claims deployed by non-US citizens who use such claims to appeal for human rights protections denied them in their own countries?

If we follow the logic of the kind of critical humanist case against human rights I've outlined, we will guess that human rights–claiming on the part of indigenous people in situations of human rights jeopardy may be stigmatized; indeed, that is a conclusion some scholars reach. Gayatri Spivak describes "human rights advocates in the countries of the South," as "some of the best products of high colonialism, descendants of the colonial middle class."[47] In his popular and widely cited critique of what he calls "the Gay International," Joseph Massad dismisses advocates of LGBT rights in the "Arab world" as "the upper classes and the increasingly Westernized middle classes." These "native informants," who have "adopted a Western identity" are implicated in the Western LGBT human rights "campaign to incite discourse on homosexuality in the Arab world." What Massad means by "incitement to discourse" is speech and action that has the effect of "attracting . . . antigay Islamist and nationalist reactions"; that is, LGBT human rights advocacy and the human rights demands of "native informants" are responsible for inciting violence against LGBT people, MSM, and WSW.[48]

Such accounts of SOGI human rights claims-making in the global South surely aren't meant to affirm solidarity with indigenous human rights advocates. Nor are such perspectives uncontested among scholars, including those who would identify as Third World feminists. Philosopher Uma Narayan, who so identifies, has addressed questions about who has standing to criticize cultures, legal regimens, and traditions, and the ways colonial histories complicate the process and provenance of critique. Although she acknowledges many complexities in taking up these questions, Narayan directly challenges the use of "Westernization" as a way to dismiss the criticisms of scholars and others who address themselves to inequities and injustices in cultures with which they identify. Nevertheless, Western students continue to learn from prominent humanist scholars that the perspectives of people in the global South who criticize aspects of their cultures "are suspiciously tainted and problematic because of [their] 'Westernization.'" How did it come to be the case that prominent critical humanists routinely impugn civil and human rights claims, including those related to discrimination and violence against LGBTQ people, sometimes even when they are articulated by cultural "insiders"?[49] We will find some clues to these political convictions in epistemological and methodological assumptions that are common among progressive critical humanists.

## Knowing What We Know

Critical humanists don't usually conceive of their research designs in these terms, but I find it useful to approach this body of research from the perspective of both deductive and inductive reasoning. The humanist critique I'm concerned with can be read as deductive in that it begins with a hypothesis-like assumption that, while not stated explicitly as a hypothesis, is a generalization that guides the research. In the scholarship I have considered and criticized, that hypothesis may be taken as something like the following statement or some key portion thereof: *when the US government engages in international (SOGI) human rights discourse, such discourse ineluctably buttresses US sexual exceptionalism and US imperialism.*[50] Examples of US government actions are presented and interpreted as supporting the hypothesis-assumption, which is to say that they demonstrate a categorical conclusion that links US government interventions (including but not limited to human rights) with harm (including but not limited to from US imperialism and pernicious assertions of exceptionalism).

Alternatively, we can consider this body of theory to be constructed inductively, even if not systematically so. That is to say, scholars sometimes choose one or more instances of US government action and conclude from studying these instances that when the US government engages in international (SOGI) human rights discourse, such discourse ineluctably buttresses US sexual exceptionalism and US imperialism. The problem with this approach, especially as a way of settling the question of human rights intervention or conditionality, is one pointed out by David Hume in *An Enquiry Concerning Human Understanding* as the "problem of induction." As Mary Hawkesworth puts it in her historical and philosophical survey of epistemology, Hume shows that "it is not possible to have sufficient empirical evidence to conclusively prove any inductive generalization" because to be true the "generalization would have to hold for all past, present, and future cases."[51] In other words, we simply don't know—indeed, can't know—what critical humanist scholars often state as incontrovertible fact.

The problem I identify isn't that critical humanists incorrectly analyze and draw conclusions about the political phenomena on which they focus, though scholars in different disciplines and using different modes of analysis often would and do come to different conclusions about these phenomena. Instead, the problem is that, having completed their analysis and being familiar with many similar analyses that begin with similar assumptions and result in similar conclusions, there is little possibility that the scholar—or her students or readers—will draw any other conclusion than the categorical one that seems to follow inexorably from what we timelessly "know" about the US government or "state." The state is a neoliberal, imperialistic hegemon whose agents are skilled in ruses that manipulate our hopes and fears and in pretexts that turn our naive yet high-minded desires to render aid against the vulnerable and to the benefit of the United States or its elites.

The continuum of political ideas in many self-defined critical, progressive disciplines is shorter than the continuum evident in political discourse outside the university and skews left. Indeed, this critical humanist continuum runs approximately from a European-style center-left to a left that's regularly identified approvingly in classrooms and scholarship as "radical." Whatever position we take on the ideological continuum of the humanities, real consequences follow from the relative absence of countervailing perspectives in an insular world of humanist scholarship and the relative lack of interest of many of these scholars in empirical research produced in the social sciences.

Critical humanists who inscribe the political project I criticize here contrast their own radical/progressive commitments, arguments, and conclusions with other scholars, including those who name the object of their work as LGBT politics or identities. The commitments, arguments, and conclusions of these less radical scholars and activists—a group in which I have no choice but to include myself—are cast as merely liberal. This is to say, they are assimilationist, larger-piece-of-the-pie seeking, aligned with and complicit in forces of domination, and implicitly white (racist) and neoliberal. In other words, conservative, even if not so in terms the US conservative movement would recognize. Indeed, far from being one depiction among many, this contrast is conventional wisdom across many nontraditional disciplines as well as in some subfields of traditional disciplines.

There are no doubt many ways to account for this political difference between the radical politics of critical humanists and the less radical politics of those who either embrace a liberal political identity or are cast pejoratively as liberals. One is that critical humanists over time have evolved standards for scholarship of playfulness, performativity, irony, and radical politics that often displace dull logic, empiricism, and close attentiveness to relevant academic literatures and counterevidence. Whether explicit or implicit, standards and conventions for what counts as scholarship on politics create an incentive and reward system—to which graduate students are carefully attuned—that equates scholarship with wit, charisma, adherence to radical ideology, and an affinity for intellectual and political boundary pushing. What results from such a system of incentive and reward is scholarship that has less to do with political fact-finding, analysis, and the inclusion of relevant research and interpretations than it has to do with affirming a critical humanist "thought style."[52]

In his critique of homonationalism, Aleardo Zanghellini calls the form of analysis that produces homonationalism as an explanation "pre-supposed paranoid structuralism."[53] This methodological critique exposes the casuistry of arguments and theories that suffer from "sweeping and groundless claim[s]" as well as "turn[ing] a possible, if apparently unlikely, reading . . . into an assumed truth." Given the thoroughness of his critique of the key concept of homonationalism, Zanghellini is modest in subtitling his article "A Critique of Some Uses of the Concept of Homonationalism in Activism and Academia." Although his critique is valid, I don't think it is adequate to see the problems he identifies merely as methodologi-cal, as though the scholars in question would correct these problems if only they came to see the methodological error of their ways. Rather, such arguments are a symptom of another problem: political views and commitments that set the terms of scholarship by prescribing what is legitimately "thinkable" because it constitutes an appropriately radical position, argument, or question and, conversely, what is "unthinkable."

## Human Rights and the Unthinkable

Most contemporary political theorists are critics of liberalism as a phi-losophy and critics of actually existing liberal democracies, including the United States. An overlapping yet also distinct set of critical humanists holds the individualism and rights orientation of liberalism to be particu-larly fertile and dangerous ground for the production and maintenance of despised and oppressed outgroups. So, for example, in *Liberalism at its Limits: Crime and Terror in the Latin American Cultural Text*, Ileana Rodríguez, a distinguished professor emeritus of literatures and cultures of Latin America, writes that the purpose of her book is "to demonstrate the aporetic and politically untenable position of a particular philosophy of freedom [liberalism] whose only condition of possibility is the eradication of difference through the politics of indiscriminate force."[54] The problem is that Rodríguez understands all political theories and practices that have arisen historically in the global North as "liberal," and this category mistake renders much of her analysis of an identity between liberalism and imperialism ineffectual.

Similarly, in an interview about her book, *The Empire of Love: Toward a Theory of Intimacy, Genealogy and Carnality*, Elizabeth Povinelli, professor of anthropology and gender studies, is asked: Why did you choose love and intimacy as the place from which to discern liberal processes of legitimation? Povinelli responds:

> When liberals experience themselves as facing an instance of a so-called morally repugnant form of life, they insist that not all forms of life should be allowed to exist—or to be given the dignity of public reason. Too much difference is said to lie outside reasonable disagreement. . . . This is an irresolvable limit internal to liberalism's account of itself. In *Cunning*, I was interested in how recognition projects this internal liberal tension between public reason and moral sense onto the subject of recognition and says to her, "You figure out how to be different enough so we can feel you are not me, but not so different that I am forced to annihilate you and thereby fracture the foundation of my exceptionalism."[55]

As I and many other theorists have argued, this depiction of difference inciting idealization of one's own group and hostility and destructiveness toward other groups is a matter of what we might—at the risk of essentializing—understand as a common element of group psychology across groups, societies, and polities that must be carefully investigated empirically.[56] By contrast, interpreting destructive identitarianism exclusively as a problem of the philosophy and practice of liberalism has the predictable effect of attenuating support for civil and human rights, championed as they are at least partly under the banner of liberal respect for individuals. This is how Puar comes to argue of the freedom individuals have in the United States to don visible signs of religious identity—a freedom that has been tested in courts and continues to evolve in policy and practice—as a precursor to "the watching and assaulting of these different bodies." In such a worldview, we can know without a shadow of doubt that what appears to be respect for the civil or human rights of individuals is incontrovertibly yet another form of oppression.

A real-world product of a critical humanist identification of liberal politics with the need and desire to eradicate "morally repugnant forms of life" is a deep intellectual and moral skepticism about any possible role of the United States in funding, designing, and supporting human rights interventions abroad. A generous reading of the claims and conclusions of this scholarship is that the intentions, power, resources, and forms of conditionality the West brings to such advocacy cannot but be harmful and oppressive to those the United States and West purport to assist. However, much of this scholarship rests on definitive claims/conclusions about the cynical motivations and harmful purposes of US human rights advocacy that rest on a staunch belief in the invariable and predictable nature of official US government perfidy.

Implicit in this worldview of what I'm calling "critical humanism" and what Richard Rorty calls the "cultural left" is the belief that "the nation-state is obsolete." As Rorty argues,

> the trouble with this claim is that the government of our nation-state will be, for the foreseeable future, the only agent capable of making any real difference in the amount of selfishness and sadism.
>
> It is no comfort to those in danger of being immiserated by globalization [or violations of human rights] to be told that, since national governments are now irrelevant, we must think up a replacement for such governments.[57]

In his response to the cultural left he criticizes, Rorty maintains that even if poststructuralist theorists are "largely right" in their critiques of "Enlightenment rationalism," their ideas "should not be taken as guides to political deliberation." Replacing "old-fashioned reformist" liberalism with radical, subversive, abstract theorizing, and the political conclusions critical humanists inevitably draw from it, fails to serve human security and human rights.[58]

A wide range of human rights scholars are concerned with problems for democracy that I address in more detail in the afterword, including questions of transparency, cultural impositions and conditions of assistance, the need to support democracies and democratic institutions, and the risks of authoritarian repression. Many of these scholars are not naive about many questions that are central to human rights, among them the need to protect human pluralism and protect endangered individuals from the depredations of powerful groups and the risks and possible harms associated with state interventions. Today, many contemporary human rights scholars emphasize the social construction of human rights and the need to approach human rights in ways that don't rely on philosophical foundations or cultural essentialisms. There are many varieties of such arguments, but consider two: framing human rights as political demands and attending to the performative dimensions of human rights claims. Michael Goodhart argues for the need to think nonfoundationally about human rights or, in other words, to eschew a continued search for an underlying philosophical grounding. Goodhart argues that there's no human rights discourse that compels all persons by its irrefutable logic because human rights make sense only in the context of certain sets of values.[59] Applying such an argument for nonfoundationalism to SOGI human rights, Anthony Tirado Chase invokes the people most in danger of being harmed by anti-SOGI movements and notes their "unprecedented mobilisations" around demands for human rights.[60]

A second kind of nonfoundational perspective focuses attention on the performative dimension of human rights. Karen Zivi has argued that human rights claims are brought into existence through repetition in different kinds of cultural and institutional contexts rather than being recognized as a set of preexisting moral truths. Hence, Zivi argues that

> when we treat rights claiming as a political and social practice that is performative—generative of identities, political subjectivities, communities, even national identities. As such, we cannot dismiss the arguments we find objectionable on intellectual grounds alone. Nor can or should we abstract the arguments we admire from the practices in which they are embedded.[61]

Neither of these nonfoundational perspectives requires preemptively proscribing Western state advocacy on behalf of SOGI human rights. Indeed, both perspectives encourage close attentiveness to the empirics of the contexts in which human rights claiming and advocacy take place. An example of this scholarship is Phillip Ayoub's *When States Come Out*, which carefully reconstructs processes of norm diffusion and norm reception in the transnational LGBT human rights movement and the mobilization and significance of "norm entrepreneurs" who influence the pace and shape of SOGI attitude change.[62]

A cogent argument in favor of SOGI human rights assistance is that victims of homophobia abroad may need to count on the support of more empowered outsiders. In human rights literature, scholars have observed and theorized a "boomerang pattern" to human rights advocacy in which citizens who have no effective voice for self-advocating appeal to transnational networks of "international allies [that] bring pressure on its government to change its domestic practices."[63] Marc Epprecht addresses both this transnational dynamic and the danger that can accompany transnational interventions:

> Africa's tiny lgbti and msm groups, with their often similarly vulnerable allies in civil society and ministries of health, are never on their own going to be able to move entrenched politicians or charismatic religious leaders. Additional pressure will need to come from friends on the international scene. Because of the high potential for backlash, donors will need to be careful that such interventions do not increase the exposure of sexual rights groups to further victimization.[64]

In *Global Homophobia*, Michael J. Bosia and Meredith L. Weiss adopt a wide global perspective on this question of nonindigenous support for SOGI human rights, concluding their essay with a strong statement regarding radical academic critiques of Western state action against anti-LGBT "political homophobia." Confirming that western pro-LGBTQ rights discourse and intervention are commonly understood as "quasi-imperialist, and hence . . . reprehensible," Bosia and Weiss forcefully push back against the conclusion that Western human rights interventions constitute the biggest problem LGBTQ people abroad must face.

> That reading ignores both the fact that political homophobia is so often substantially imported—borrowed by segments within those countries with power to condemn rather than an authentic local impulse—and the reality that without basic rights to dignity, livelihood, and self-realization, local activists may be powerless to contest political homophobia independently, absent "boomerang" activism from abroad.[65]

Such an observation and interpretation directly challenges deeply entrenched understandings of the nature of assistance relations between international human rights communities and marginalized groups.[66]

One issue that's raised by the kind of juxtaposition I offer in this book between the Christian conservative right and the critical humanist left is the question: what do "we"—that is, all those who would like to see respect for rights, democracy, economic justice, and human flourishing expanded and protected—think and do about systematic group-based human rights violations, such as those based on actual or perceived SOGI? I don't have the answer to this question, but my career in the US academy has left me confident that humanist critiques of US hypocrisy and cultural imperialism can't confront the challenges these human rights violations pose. To confront these challenges we need less political coherence and conviction and more curiosity.

## On Blaming America First

Questions about what membership in a wealthy and powerful Western nation requires are a crucial variable in vehement disagreements over US government policies and interventions abroad and within the United States. In evaluating the motivations, meaning and effects of US government interventions abroad, critical humanists factor into their conclusions their knowledge of US government responsibility for a long series of well-documented foreign "adventures," from declared wars and other military interventions to myriad forms of covert operations, unilateralism, duress directed against foreign regimes, and quid pro quos with foreign regimes. For their part, conservatives declare that academics "blame America first." However, abstracted from the historical record of US intervention, this charge isn't enlightening because it fails to explain the basis for a progressive worldview of skepticism toward the record of US national interests and acts.

The slogan "blame America first" also ignores the compelling ethical requirement to ruthlessly submit our "own" beliefs and practices to scrutiny. At its best, the willingness of critical humanists to condemn their own government's harm-doing is a species of ethical self-scrutiny. For this question of refusing to ignore or justify the harm to others committed by one's group, I find it useful to look to the political thought of Hannah Arendt. The theme of holding one's group responsible for harm to others was central to the controversy between Arendt and her critics over *Eichmann in Jerusalem*. Perhaps because of the personal and intellectual stakes of that controversy, Arendt returned to the theme many times in the years that followed. In 1964, soon after the publication of *Eichmann*, Günter Gaus interviewed Arendt and asked her if human beings don't "need commitment to a group, a commitment that can then to a certain extent be called love." Arendt answered with an emphatic "No," and then explained that "in the first place, belonging to a group is a natural condition. You belong to some sort of group when you are born, always." Later in the interview, she returned to the problem of partiality toward one's group and the ethical necessity of holding one's own responsible for harm: "If someone is not capable of this impartiality because he pretends to love his people so much that he pays flattering homage to them all the time—well, then there's nothing to be done. I do not believe that people like that are patriots."[67] Critical humanists who do research on imperialism and US policy would agree.

It makes more sense to amend the charge that critical humanists "blame America first" by noting that much writing about politics in the humanities take US—and, by extension, Western/colonial—guilt and ulterior motives as a foregone conclusion rather than a conclusion arrived at in every particular case through careful assessment of evidence. When scholarship is produced in this way, progressive convictions can thwart progressive political goals by exposing as racist, imperialistic, or hypocritical programs and policies on which vulnerable people rely for protection or resources.

It's a problem that scholars who fit a conservative profile of "the blame America first crowd" often apply a blanket heuristic to all possible cases of action by any US government actor that's consistent with historical knowledge of US government aggressions and duplicities. This is how we get from a declarative historical statement—such as "the US government has engaged/engages in imperialism, defined by features A, B, C and effects X, Y, Z in nation/region Q"—to a declarative statement and prediction such as "when the US government engages in international (SOGI) human rights discourse, such discourse ineluctably buttresses US sexual exceptionalism and US imperialism." Depending on one's convictions, the latter statement may constitute good politics. But it doesn't constitute good scholarship.

# Afterword

## Reflections on SOGI Human Rights and Democracy

### Opposing SOGI from the Right and Left

In the United States, there's an array of positions on government support for SOGI human rights that roughly can be traced from left-progressive skepticism through center-left support to right-conservative opposition. There are similarities and differences between the conservative and progressive cases against US government interventions on behalf of SOGI human rights abroad. One similarity is that both right and left arguments reject the idea of a fixed or essential gay/same-sex attracted or transgender identity, although they do so for different reasons. For the Christian right, denying gender or sexual minority identity is necessary to secure the appropriately gendered heterosexuality of God's plan for human sexuality, the natural family, and the nature of all persons. Among critical humanists, many reject these fixed identities not because they rely on the foundations of heterosexual human nature but from an equally foundational skepticism about fixed or immutable identities.[1]

A second similarity is that those in both ideological positions network with groups outside the United States that share their perspectives, effectively incorporating allies to a position that has political and philosophical—and for the Christian right, theological—implications. For the Christian conservative movement, some of these collaborations are with natural allies as, for example, when conservative US Episcopal congregations placed themselves under the spiritual leadership of an antigay Nigerian Anglican archbishop rather than yield to their denomination's 2003 consecration of a gay bishop, Gene Robinson. Other collaborations constitute what Francis Schaeffer, adopting a term of military strategy, called co-belligerence, a doctrine that has been crucial to Protestant evangelical cooperation with conservative Catholics, Mormons, Muslims, and other believers. For Schaeffer, "a co-belligerent is a person with whom I do not agree on all sorts of vital issues, but who, for whatever reasons of their own, is on the same side in a fight for some specific issue of public justice."[2] At the same time, perhaps because of opposition to or disinterest in national and transnational political institutions, the critical humanism I've criticized doesn't represent a robust network of allies in existing US political institutions.

Of course, the differences between the cases against US government intervention on behalf of LGBTQ people abroad illustrates the divergence of political ideology between the two and highlights elements of ironic convergence when the subject turns to official US support for SOGI human rights. First, in the brief time frame of a generation, members of the Christian right movement have seen their ideology with regard to LGBTQ civil rights and SOGI human rights go from being virtually unquestioned common sense to being perceived by majorities in the United States and some other parts of the world as an ideology of bigotry and intolerance. The tenets of queer, poststructuralist, and postcolonial theories are not as widely disseminated and embraced by political constituencies as Christian social conservatism once was and still is. However, in the humanities and among humanist scholars in social science disciplines, all have gone, as one scholar has written of queer theory, "from being . . . radical outsider ideology[ies] to orthodoxy."[3]

A second difference between Christian right and critical humanist opposition to SOGI human rights advocacy is that critical humanists are well disposed toward the proliferation of queer bodies, gender identities, and sexual pleasures, if not the fixed categories that for them threaten to contain and regulate nonnormative gender and sexuality. Of course, Christian conservatives are not well disposed toward queerness, whether it is manifested through the nonidentitarian pursuit and display of polymorphic sexual pleasures or through the political embrace of identity categories and the formation of relationships that may imply to observers some more or less fixed nonnormative SOGI.

Third, although the Christian right and critical humanists are suspicious of US government interventions on behalf—or, for the academics, ostensibly on behalf—of gender and sexual minorities abroad, these groups impute quite different motivations for such interventions. Regardless of whether LGBTQ-friendly official rhetoric or public policies occur in a domestic US context or originate in government efforts to assist LGBTQ people elsewhere, Christian conservatives understand such rhetoric and policies as undermining Christian morality. At worst they are deliberate acts of moral sabotage, and at best they are ill-advised attempts at inclusion and moral neutrality that nonetheless are inconsistent with God's laws. Critical humanists often have disagreed with the particular goals of domestic US LGBT activists, including same-sex marriage and military inclusion, not because they were too radical an attack on morality but because they were too timid, conservative, and normalizing. As for US government rhetoric and programs on behalf of LGBTQ people abroad, critical humanists understand SOGI interventions as the cultivation of democratic and human rights pretexts for imperialist and neoliberal goals and outcomes. Hence, high levels of skepticism and even opposition to such interventions make sense as applications of anti-imperialist and anti-neoliberal political commitment.

Finally, the Christian right is not in principle always opposed to the human rights paradigm for some groups, especially those persecuted for their religious beliefs or practices. Of these groups, of course, embattled Christian minorities attract the most attention, rhetoric, resources, and engagement. The debate among US conservatives after terror attacks in Paris in 2015 about how to exclude Syrian Muslims from the United States or perhaps accept only Christian immigrants fleeing wars in the Middle East is one example. Compared to persecuted Christian minorities and individuals, people persecuted for same-sex sexuality or stigmatized gender identity easily can be represented by Christian conservatives as same-sex marriage advocates consistently have been in the United States: as activists whose (ab)use of a civil rights or human rights paradigm masks the true goals of undermining both Christian faith and the legitimate principles on which invocations of human dignity and equality should be premised. By contrast, critical humanists tend to extend a principled skepticism about universalizing paradigms to other identity groups and categories. This skepticism has challenged the coherence of ascriptive forms of identity, such as gender and race, as well as the universal morality and applicability of rights-based approaches to empowering citizens and ameliorating harm. In the particular case of US government programs to support SOGI human rights abroad, the values of the socially conservative right and the humanist left could hardly diverge more. But the two sides share an uneasy accord in a conception of the federal government as a hegemon that imposes alien and pernicious cultures on poorer and weaker peoples.

Of the two brands of opposition to US government SOGI human rights advocacy, the Christian conservative side can most fruitfully be engaged politically. US citizens who support SOGI and other kinds of human rights discourse or interventions can use conventional and unconventional political mechanisms to advocate, instruct, lobby, and vote. By contrast, responding to the opposition of critical humanists is an intellectual challenge. Critical humanists tend to commit themselves to being transparent about their political beliefs in their scholarship and teaching, at least partly so that these beliefs don't form the kind of unreflective background and foundation these scholars have been trained to perceive in research in traditional disciplines.[4] In practice, however, scholars' political beliefs can be—and often are—"baked into" their work so thoroughly that the analysis of any cultural or political phenomenon is coextensive with their belief system and that of the larger thought community with which they identify. When an analysis is indistinguishable from a scholar's political commitments, it's easy to fail—even refuse—to consider counterdescriptions or counterarguments that would challenge one's political worldview or identity.

The Christian conservative case against US intervention on behalf of SOGI human rights is framed differently for different audiences, but undergirding it is moral opposition to nonnormative sexualities and forms of gender identity and expression. For Christian conservatives, toleration in the form of egalitarian applications of law and political policy should not coexist with personal intolerance and abhorrence. The failure of nations, especially the United States, to stigmatize and punish sexual and gender disobedience to God courts divine destruction. As to analyzing the Christian right's values and political goals, the perspective I have held consistently is that my jobs as a scholar are first, to be as fair as possible in understanding and representing those values and goals to others, and second, to carefully and thoroughly analyze the context and consequences of their attitudes and political projects. As for the critical humanists' case against US government interventions on behalf of SOGI human rights, I share many (though not all) of their political values and goals. From a scholarly perspective, however, I find too many arguments and conclusions about politics that are produced by critical humanist scholars to demonstrate some of the same characteristics "we" humanists and social scientists have criticized in the work of others. First and foremost is the tendency to reproduce the assumptions of a thought collective packaged as unassailable—if not "objective"—scholarship.

From whatever perspectives and with whatever analytical tools we engage with SOGI human rights interventions of the US government, such interventions raise broader questions about the theory and practice of democracy. As I suggested in discussing fundamental questions that animate scholarship in human rights in the introduction, there are many such questions and implications. The questions about and criticisms of human rights discourse and interventions that issue from progressive humanists intersect with those of other human rights scholars, but the two sets of questions aren't the same. Therefore, I briefly take up four human rights criticisms that can be found in critical humanist discourse or are strongly implied by critiques of US government intervention. Indeed, some critics would take one or more of these perceived deficiencies of state intervention to definitively call into question a role for the US government in SOGI human rights advocacy. Because I have addressed the criticisms elsewhere in this book, I do not include charges of hypocrisy and imperialism leveled, as I noted in Chapter 2, at Hillary Clinton's 2011 Geneva speech.

## SOGI Human Rights and Problems for Democracy

The first question raised by SOGI human rights advocacy is transparency, an issue that becomes salient when government officials don't disclose detailed, specific information regarding, for example, the forms and recipients of US government human rights assistance. A second question sometimes raised by humanist critics of US government interventions with and on behalf of gender and sexual minorities is that the terms of government assistance, or the inequalities that prevail between the United States and poorer nations, may impose a particular, usually Western, framework or understanding of sexual or gendered identity on recipients of human rights aid.[5] Third, there is a conviction that the agendas and priorities of LGBTQ movements tend to be imposed from the top down, rather than being developed and effectuated from the grass roots up and that this domination of interests of money and power inevitably thwarts and poisons indigenous democracy. Finally, humanist critics argue that Western human rights interventions can strengthen violent authoritarian states, institutions, and tools of domination as external demands for human rights protections provide leverage, and possibly resources, to these states and authorities. I regard these as valuable questions to raise regarding SOGI and other forms of human rights interventions, and I address each briefly in turn.

## On Evading Human Rights Transparency

Democratic theorists generally embrace the proposition that government transparency with regard to official acts and communications is crucial to an informed, deliberative, and participatory citizenry.[6] Scholars and other political commentators have reflected on and debated the institutional conditions for transparency, the modes of classification and communication that best inform citizens and electorates, and the circumstances that may require difficult judgments about what kinds of information may or even should be withheld to serve some important purpose.[7] Transparency has been understood as a good in and of itself as well as a necessary (though not a sufficient) condition for holding policy makers and other government officials accountable.[8] A lack of transparency on human rights programming and interventions may dispose scholars and citizens to assume the worst about the motives, efficacy, and consequences of these interventions.

LGBTQ activists have called for information that would permit them to gauge the scale and efficacy of programs such as the Global Equality Fund (GEF). One of these is longtime AIDS and LGBT activist Michael Petrelis, who has documented his attempts to elicit information about the GEF and his criticism of the Department of State's failure to provide detailed information about the GEF and its grantees. In his blog, the Petrelis Files, he offers readers a request that he sent to the State Department:

> I wish to learn about the transparency of the Global Equality Fund and need to know where I can find a list of all donors, amounts contributed, expenses, and grants made to LGBT groups since the fund's inception. Where do I obtain this info on the web? Looking around the State Department site and various government and independent watchdog sites, has not turned up a financial accounting for the public and taxpayers. As both a global gay advocate and transparency activist, I very much wish to see documentation about the money that has flowed in and out of the fund.

On the GEF website, Petrelis found the names of "two analysts," Robert Haynie and Jesse Bernstein; in response to the inquiry he sent them, Petrelis received a "bland reply" that didn't supply the information he was seeking:

> Thank you for your email. The Global Equality Fund provides an important platform for like-minded governments and other

partners to stand together in support of LGBT persons and their universal human rights. For further information, please find attached a fact sheet.

To underscore the inadequacy of this response, Petrelis makes a classic case for transparency from public officials who oversee and administer the GEF. He emphasizes that "the question before us is how do we follow the money and learn who verifies that the contributions are reaching their intended beneficiaries." Petrelis shares the frustration of many citizens and activists who have tried unsuccessfully to extract information from their government to hold policy makers and other public officials accountable when he writes that "the GEF has to engage in respectful dialogue with transparency advocates and immediately release a financial accounting to the public."[9]

As the circumstances of the ASOGIHRO conferences suggest, in the arena of human rights, an unresolved conflict can prevail between legitimate demands for transparency and the value of protecting members of endangered groups. Even before conferees assembled for the 2015 meeting, we were reminded of the grave conditions in which many LGBTQ individuals and activists live and work. An ASOGIHRO leader emailed participants traveling to the conference with instructions not to inform anyone of the existence or purpose of the meeting once we arrived in the host country. Organizers arranged transportation from locations in a nearby city to the undisclosed location where the conference would be held. In situations where lives are endangered, US officials sometimes sacrifice transparency to shield those whose human rights are imperiled. One way to characterize this peril is to say that in the case of SOGI human rights violations, people face double jeopardy: LGBTQ people and human rights defenders may suffer persecution for *being* LGBTQ or an advocate for LGBTQ people, and they may suffer suspicion and persecution for cooperating—or being perceived to cooperate—with US government cultural imperialism or in Western moral degeneracy generally. "It is bad enough to be denounced as a *pédé* ('faggot'). But it hurts to be labelled as a zombie or whore to the West as well."[10]

As I noted in Chapter 3, DRL receives an exemption from the US government's marking policy for its human rights programming. As a consequence, human rights defenders and organizations aren't required to "brand" products of US government assistance and thus effectively come out of the closet as implementing partners or grantees. In turn, the State Department doesn't divulge detailed information about the funds and recipients of the GEF and other forms of assistance without permission from grantees. Several US officials I spoke to noted that Western LGBTQ activists can always seek information directly from local LGBTQ advocates and organizations about their sources of assistance. These officials also referred to a DRL survey intended to enable grantees to give or withhold consent for DRL to reveal local LGBTQ activists' assistance relationship with the United States to actors outside the US government. US officials who referred to the survey attested that most grantees surveyed either did not consent to the exposure of this information or requested that DRL seek permission each time this information was requested.[11]

An alternative to complete transparency on human rights assistance is for US officials to release aggregate data that do not compromise the identity or security of grantees who are members of marginalized groups. Such a report recently has been published by Funders for LGBTQ Issues and Astraea's Global Philanthropy Project (GPP), which focuses its work on LGBTI human rights donors, endeavoring to increase funding and to "enhance [donors'] effectiveness as grantmakers."[12] In 2016, private and public funders, including the United States and other nation members of the GEF, cooperated with the GPP to provide general information on funds dedicated to and disbursed for projects that support LGBTI human rights worldwide. The "2013–2014 Global Resources Report: Government and Philanthropic Support for Lesbian, Gay, Bisexual, Transgender, and Intersex Communities," is the "first comprehensive report of its kind on all foundation and government funding for LGBTI issues." The report lists US dollar figures for US government contributions in 2013–14 and for pooled GEF funding from member countries. It breaks out recipients of LGBTI human rights funding by region, an approach that doesn't identify recipient groups or even countries where outside funding for LGBTQI groups and individuals would be culturally or legally proscribed.[13]

Of course, the fact that the Department of State or other foreign affairs actors in the US government and officials in other governments abroad refuse demands for transparency when it comes to the human rights of marginalized populations doesn't mean that members of vulnerable groups are being well served or are benefiting from the shield of secrecy. As we know, government secrecy can hide many things, including incompetence, official criminality, avarice and self-aggrandizement, and violations of civil or human rights. Without transparency, citizens are deprived of the opportunity to understand and participate in the operations of governing. On the other side of the equation, US officials involved in human rights assistance tell grantees that they are committed to grantees' safety and security.

## On Imposing Western Gender or Sexual Identities

Second, critics of Western hegemony worry that a Western or US understanding of relatively fixed LGBT identities almost certainly produces a normalizing effect on local, non-Western human rights advocates and on gender and sexual minorities. It isn't necessarily the case that this normalizing is a deliberate goal of those who design and execute programs and, rather than being imposed explicitly, may be an effect of the terms of assistance or other dimensions of the operations of programs that aren't visible to Western officials. For critics, the consequence of the power imbalance between Western/US government officials and local, indigenous human rights advocates who seek resources is likely to be a de facto requirement that LGBTQ, MSM, or WSW foreign citizens make themselves recognizable as (potential) victims to gain access to resources or forms of protection. Such legibility would consist of identifying as gay, lesbian, bisexual, or transgender rather than in some more indigenously authentic way and conforming to the terms of these Western identities.[14] This anxiety about the imposition of forms of identity or identification is a subset of larger worries about Western cultural imperialism that are central to many personal worldviews, theoretical systems, and practical political programs.

For these critics, the ASOGIHRO conferences provide an informative example of the operation of US government outreach to those whose human rights are imperiled on the basis of sexuality or gender identity/expression. The conferences are organized by an indigenous LGBTQ organization on behalf of a consortium of African groups, and the US representatives and other funders who attend are guests of the conference organizers. Thus, donors, including US officials, are in no position to pressure recipients either to present themselves or identify in ways that would satisfy Western expectations of LGBTQ identity or to screen possible recipients for their adherence to particular sexual or gender identifications that fit a model preferred by or familiar to Western or US elites.

There is little doubt that categories of gender and sexual identity have migrated from Western to non-Western societies throughout the twentieth century and continue to do so. What remains to debate are the reasons for this migration and its possible consequences. A common explanation—indeed, the most common in critical humanist scholarship on politics—is one that makes sense of many cultural, economic, and political phenomena: imperialism that imposes or regulates identity and leaves people from the global South no position from which to resist domination implicit in identity categories. However, there are other explanations for this particular phenomenon besides—or in addition to—cultural imposition and imperialism, three of which are: (1) the operation of "functional human rights universality"; (2) practices of cultural hybridity and mestiza identity, along with the code switching that may accompany such hybridity; and (3) the deliberate political embrace of identities as a form of resistance against dehumanizing discourse seeded by Western anti-LGBT Christian conservatives.

The first alternative or supplementary explanation for the migration of concepts and configuration of sexuality and gender from North to South is what Jack Donnelly calls "functional human rights universality." Donnelly extrapolates this functional universality from the transnational similarities of threats to human rights and argues that under such conditions we would expect to "find widespread active endorsement of internationally recognized human rights." As he points out, it's not only elites that appeal to these human rights but also grassroots "movements for social justice and of political opposition."[15] Donnelly's position constitutes a direct challenge to the arguments of scholars such as Spivak and Massad that undercut the human rights claims of indigenous citizens by calling into question the cultural authenticity of the claimants.

A second likely explanation for the use of gender and sexual categories that first appeared in the West is cultural hybridity, which entails borrowing between cultures, and the adoptions, interpenetrations, resistances to power, and novel transformations that can result. Cultural sharing and hybridity have been understood to be unavoidable consequences of processes of globalization that persistently alter cultural referents and identities as people participate in and/or resist cultural changes.[16] Even so, hybrid or borderland identity is often represented in disciplines such as women's and gender studies as a means of conveying culture, exercising cultural authority, and constructing novel forms of identifications and knowledge.[17]

A third alternative explanation for the use of these categories is that identity categories that originate in the West may be embraced by others as a deliberate response to anti-LGBTQ discourses. Meredith Weiss and Michael Bosia use the terms "anticipatory" or "preemptive homophobia" to analyze the widespread formation of anti-LGBTQ movements in parts of the world where pro-LGBTQ movements and activism are nascent or nonexistent. They unsettle the common worry that Western LGBTQ activists and states import and impose Western categories of sexual identity on gender and sexual minorities in the non-Western world by pointing out that "in many cases, it is the homophobes who import a model of same-sex intimacy in terms of Western concepts of LGBT community." Or, as Weiss puts it, "the [homophobic] response often comes before the call."[18] Because anti-LGBTQ beliefs and activism employ "a Western sexual binary," that binary "structures reactive organizing among sexual minorities through identities that draw from the Western binary."[19] This dynamic in which oppression is met by a defense that mirrors the terms of group-based harm is consistent with Hannah Arendt's often-quoted principle of resistance to "defamation and persecution": the principle "that one can resist only in terms of the identity that is under attack."[20] "If one is attacked as a Jew, one must defend oneself as a Jew. Not as a German, not as a world-citizen, not as an upholder of the Rights of Man, or whatever."[21]

Yet the belief that all possible forms of US government influence, human rights interventions, and diplomatic discourse automatically constitute imperialism has become a critical humanist version of "anticipatory" or "preemptive anti-imperialism." This anticipatory anti-imperialism doesn't necessarily rely on empirical evidence in every case but springs from deep conviction about the nature and effects of transnational relations under conditions of inequality. Similarly, it's common for the key question of whether the outcomes being asserted result from official motives and/or possible indigenous effects to be elided, just as Jasbir Puar ignores the distinction in *Terrorist Assemblages*.

Indigenous organizations may face some of the same challenges and questions with regard to matching identities with forms of aid as governments or international CSOs that provide human rights assistance. If so, the ways these groups confront similar challenges can help inform observers about processes by which assistance flows from human rights funders to grantees. Embedded in a 2012 interview with Wanja Muguongo, the executive director of UHAI—The East African Sexual Health Right Initiative (UHAI-EASHRI), is an illuminating exchange. Muguongo is asked: "You are an LGBTI and SW [sex worker] grant making organisation. How do you prove that applicants are truly LGBTI or sex workers?" In her response, Muguongo outlines an internal process to which her organization adheres:

The application process allows organisations to self-identify as LGBTI and/ or sex worker. UHAI-EASHRI's funding is made through a peer reviewed process with a Peer Grants Committee (PGC) whose members are nominated from the LGBTI and SW communities. The PGC forms part of the due diligence mechanisms that we use to verify the existence of applicant groups, but we also use our networks. Groups may also include in their application an endorsement from a known group or one that is well established. Likewise, before a grant is disbursed, we visit groups, sit with them, talk to them and that way we are able to establish facts.[22]

The empirical question of whether or under what conditions the US government acts or actors impose particular conceptions or terms related to gender and sexuality on people around the world can be investigated in part by gathering information about the ways US government SOGI human rights programs are designed and administered. In the case of the GEF, as well as other initiatives that are not related to immigration and asylum, US agencies and representatives do not screen individual recipients of human rights resources and assistance for particular configurations of identity. Indeed, immigration is a singular policy arena with distinctive rules rather than an exemplar of US government human rights practices.[23] Instead of establishing particular configurations of LGBTQ identity, organizations—often groups in country and close to those who are served by initiatives like the GEF—serve imperiled individuals and groups without regard for the nuances of how such individuals (or groups) identify themselves or the terms they use to do so.[24]

ASOGIHRO, and the other groups whose members attended the 2015 conference or provided materials there, self-consciously employed identifiers such as LGBT, LGBTI, MSM, WSW, transgender, transwoman, and transman to identify themselves and the objects of their activism.[25] I observed nothing at ASOGIHRO to suggest that activists understood these categories of sexual and gender identity to have been imposed on them by outsiders. My observations are consistent with Sami Zeidan's suggestion that universalized "gay terminology" can "have a locally liberatory function"; enable the "develop[ment] of more local, indigenous terms"; and stimulate the "recover[y] of older, precolonial histories and traditions."[26] At ASOGIHRO, activists who spoke publicly about their identities in conference sessions documented and repudiated the conceptions of identity that they were clear had been imposed on them: powerful homophobic attributions aimed at them in their own social contexts that have cross-cultural appeal and often have been deliberately sown by Western colonial rule and/or anti-LGBTQ Christian conservatives. Groups or individuals sometimes use different kinds of identifiers to signal their own culturally embedded understandings of gender or sexuality. However, we must still seek evidence to support the claim that different naming practices and diverse conceptions of identity jeopardize the ability of people to work with the United States for SOGI human rights.

## On US Human Rights Assistance Undermining Democracy

A third concern of critical humanist proponents of democracy about funding and assistance relationships between the US government and local, in-country LGBTQ organizations is that as a global hegemon, the United States undermines democracies by using its funding and other forms of leverage to impose its will and interests on communities and to degrade their capacity for grassroots activism and democratic decision making. This concern about the coercive effects of large disparities in power and leverage is reasonable for advocates of democracy and community determination to hold. Questions about the effects for democratic self-determination of assistance relationships characterized by large disparities of power are common in human rights literature. Hence, gathering as much evidence as possible about these assistance relationships and their effects on activists and citizens in poorer and less empowered contexts is essential. Assistance relationships under conditions of imbalanced power may have pernicious effects on vulnerable populations, but are these effects unavoidable?

Here again, the ASOGIHRO, its now long-standing relationship with DRL and DRL's implementing partners, and its activist conferences shed valuable light on processes of negotiation through which LGBTQ activist agendas and programs are developed, funded, and executed. At the ASOGIHRO conferences and many similar venues throughout the world, US government officials and grassroots human rights advocates meet or renew their acquaintance, share information about the challenges confronting activists, and discuss the exigencies activists bring to the table and how their needs and work fit into existing assistance programs. In the 2015 session of the ASOGIHRO conference, "We Don't Know the Answers," one of two applause lines was Patricia Davis's plea to the assembled activists to "help me help you" by working with DRL officials to report not only immediate "outputs" associated with assistance but also longer term "outcomes" that could justify aid and contribute to internal State Department accountability for continued assistance.[27]

It's easy to say that CSOs and governments that offer human rights assistance to people in other countries should listen to the voices of the people whose needs and interests they serve, as well they should. Indeed, every US government official I spoke to gave this principle of listening to and following the lead of local LGBTQ activists as the first principle of SOGI human rights assistance. But even if US officials follow this principle, such a practice doesn't resolve situations in which indigenous advocates disagree. In December 2015, the New York Times published an article titled "U.S. Support of Gay Rights in Africa May Have Done More Harm than Good." In the article, Norimitsu Onishi quotes several African LGBTQ people and activists who contend that US support for SOGI human rights has instigated "blowback" from anti-LGBTQ communities that endangers African gender and sexual minorities.

Tom Malinowski, assistant Secretary of State for DRL, responded quickly to the article and its depiction of the effects of official US advocacy for SOGI human rights. More significant, however, was the disagreement with the premise that US support for LGBT human rights has done more harm than good expressed by African LGBT activists: Frank Mugisha, executive director of Sexual Minorities Uganda, and Kikonyogo Kivumbi, elected representative of key affected populations for the Uganda Health Policy Board of the Global Fund. Mugisha asserts that in Uganda, the US government "follows our lead before taking action on our behalf" and notes that "there will always be backlash to activism." In his reply, Kivumbi cites Obama-era modifications to PEPFAR as one example of the United States serving LGBTI communities in African nations. Then, using a discourse of national sovereignty, he calls on African states to govern their people in ways that are consistent with international human rights obligations and articulates the right of the United States to defend human rights and human dignity.[28]

A perspective on Western human rights assistance that is consistent with Mugisha's and Kivumbi's statements is presented by Ludmilla Alexeeva, chair of the Moscow Helsinki Group, the oldest human rights CSO operating in Russia. In a recent article, Alexeeva briefly summarizes the closing of Russian society under Vladimir Putin; the methods by which assistance from Western donor organizations, such as the National Endowment for Democracy and the Soros Foundations, has been foreclosed; and the punitive policies that endanger Russian civil society activists who may receive assistance from the West. Alexeeva describes herself as continuing to have "hope" that the dismantling of civil society and the persecution of activists can be reversed. She pleads with donors for patience and continued focus on human rights failures in her country: "If I were to meet today with all the Western donors who have invested in human rights in Russia, I would praise them for the confidence they had in us 25 years ago, at the hopeful beginning, and plead with them not to abandon their Russian partners now that the going has gotten tough."[29]

What of funding as a means of exercising power over poorer states or peoples? In assistance relationships, does the party who pays the piper invariably call the tune? Very often, yes, but again: this is an empirical question. For example, we might expect that providing assistance, including funds, to organizations or even weaker states always or almost always immunizes the funder of responsibility for harms against recipients. However, even though this kind of immunizing often takes place, such an outcome isn't inevitable. Consider a study produced in 2013 by Physicians for Human Rights, "Securing Afghanistan's Past: Human Identification Needs Assessment and Gap Analysis." For the project that culminated in the report, international and Afghan scientists and investigators collaborated to locate mass graves in Afghanistan and identify human remains and to enhance technological, procedural, medical, scientific, and legal capacities with regard to identifications, repatriation of remains, and the collecting and preserving of evidence from war/crime scenes. The project, funded by the State Department's DRL, includes an account of a mass grave in northern Afghanistan believed by many Afghans to contain the bodies of Taliban prisoners who surrendered to and were executed by US and Afghan Northern Alliance troops. Physicians for Human Rights appealed to the United Nations and the government of Afghanistan for the site to be preserved for further disinterment and study. The report notes that instead, "sections of the mass grave site were dug up and removed, as observed by eyewitnesses and confirmed by satellite photographs," and no investigation has been conducted.[30]

Because the DRL-funded "Securing Afghanistan's Past" reported a possible US war crime, it can be understood as a counterexample of what can easily be taken as a law-like generalization that requires little empirical corroboration. Certainly, such a counterexample doesn't disprove a hypothesis that funding relations between unequally situated entities are rife with the potential for directed outcomes that favor the more powerful party. But counterexamples don't have to disprove such a hypothesis; they merely have to underscore the importance of seeking out corroborating evidence and being willing to entertain and account for the existence of counterexamples.

Scholars and activists who are proponents of LGBTQ rights sometimes argue that over time, LGBTQ activism has become less democratic and grassroots and more driven by the interests and goals of funders to the detriment of grassroots activists and citizens.[31] Given such concerns, it makes sense that SOGI human rights interventions involving the State Department and LGBTQI/human rights organizations abroad would draw close scrutiny. Based on my observations at events such as the 2014 "Conference to Advance the Human Rights of and Inclusive Development for LGBTI Persons" and the 2015 ASOGIHRO conference, I would say that at least some of these interventions are devised and executed neither from the top down nor from the bottom up. Both of these metaphors fail to capture the complexity of the negotiations that produce the human rights agenda and the particular projects to which the funding and assistance of the US government, other governments, and CSOs are applied at a particular moment. Neither do these metaphors adequately account for the complex set of conditions for human rights advocacy that prevail at any particular time. These conditions include exogenous factors (such as presidential administrations; foreign policy events; and executive branch agency rules, norms, and agendas) that influence configurations of policy, programming, networks, and forms of solidarity. Instead, the landscape of US participation in international SOGI human rights programming and advocacy can be conceptualized as constructed through ongoing negotiation among human rights advocates and groups.

### On Strengthening Authoritarianism and Facilitating Violence

Finally, critics of US government human rights interventions worry that human rights interventions strengthen the hand of violent states, or their indigenous police or military, to the detriment of vulnerable citizens.[32] Something like this concern animates a great deal of critical humanist scholarship that is self-consciously antimilitarist and -imperialist, including Dean Spade and Craig Willse's "Sex, Gender, and War in an Age of Multicultural Imperialism." Spade and Willse link the case against (and politics surrounding) Chelsea Manning, the sexual abuse charge leveled against Julian Assange, and Hillary Clinton's 2011 LGBT human rights speech, arguing that all three are products and tools of "U.S. neoliberal war and imperialism." However, the article isn't just an indictment of the many forms of politics, including human rights politics, that serve neoliberal imperialism. It's consistent in rejecting the universalizing of human rights and any participation of the United States in protecting—or purporting to protect—those human rights.[33]

Applying their argument to the domestic United States, Spade and Willse incorporate the example of intimate violence against women to make their case, and their consideration of the issue is informative. For Spade and Willse, the figure of the rape victim in need of governmental protection and redress is mobilized conveniently by apparatuses that are actually significant perpetrators of racialized gender violence. Not only is the figure of the rape victim "mobilized conveniently" by a human rights-abusing state, criminal justice responses to violence against women are the work of "carceral feminists" who discount activist and citizen "strategies" to address violence against women and LGBTQ people in ways "that do not rely on police and courts."[34] The critique here, as it is in other cases in this literature, is not about how to make police, courts, the military, and other institutions function as well, fairly, and humanely as they can in an imperfect and uncertain world, but to imagine a world in which these institutions no longer need to exist.

Such an inquiry about human rights intervention, police powers, and repression raises many questions for researchers, policy makers, and citizens to consider, including whether alternatives to intervention or conditionality would be likely to be more or less effective in diminishing marginalized people's exposure to violence. In other words, it's possible that, depending on the circumstances, human rights interventions might be less harmful to citizens than whatever status quo of human rights jeopardy prevails. A debate of just this sort began in 1944 over the possibility of Allied military forces bombing the gas chambers of Auschwitz-Birkenau or the train tracks that lead to the camp. Proponents of the tactic acknowledged that prisoners would be likely to die in bombing raids, but they believed that more lives might be saved if it were possible to disable the death camp. The idea was vetoed by US military officials and was never attempted.[35]

Like other concerns about Western human rights criticisms and interventions in or about non-Western states, the critique of rights-abusing institutions requires data gathering that, as much as possible, confirms a link between human rights interventions—rhetorical, diplomatic, economic, or other—and increased violence and impunity of police or other groups formally or informally endowed with police power to use force against citizens. The problem is that arguments like Spade and Willse's explicitly reject reform agendas as patriotic, carceral, neoliberal, and homonational-ist. Unlike Spade and Willse, I'm not persuaded that citizen approaches to ending violence against vulnerable groups alone are likely to eradicate these threats. I am particularly skeptical about citizen activism as an antidote to violence when violence against disfavored vulnerable minority groups is organized, pervasive, and state-sanctioned.

## Final Reflections

I have been present on many occasions when fellow academics, whom I take to be committed to the well-being and flourishing of people around the world, have spoken with disdain of the idea that the US government or its representatives "rescue" "third-world" people from their own cultures or legal regimes or from the tender mercies of their fellow citizens. For these critical humanists, the very idea is ludicrous and dangerous, and the fact that anyone could entertain such a position constitutes a damning political and intellectual indictment on such a person. Every educated person knows that through slavery, colonialism, imperialism, economic exploitation, regime manipulation, covert surveillance, military destruction, and many other forms of oppression, the United States or the West (the United States or North America plus Europe) has been at the forefront of every form of damage done to the developing world and its people. Indeed, as scholars and journalists have documented, and continue to document, this has often been the case. Nor has the capacity of scholars and others to expose these realities been extinguished, in spite of the best efforts of anti-intellectual conservatives. Contrary to the fears of many supporters of academic freedom, scholars and other intellectuals who criticize the US government, corporate power, and various official forms and sources of oppression have not yet been silenced. Mostly such intellectuals meet an even more disempowering fate: like Cassandra, they are ignored.

Throughout US history, many journalists, scholars, and other citizens have documented and disseminated information about US and other Western abuses of human rights. The question of whether policies, programs, and interventions of the US government abroad have helped or harmed (or both) those who are their intended recipients is an empirical question. Although theoretical investments and political principles may guide research, such questions cannot—and should not—be answered solely with recourse to theory or political principles. My argument here is that the empirical question of the motivations and outcomes of US government human rights or other interventions cannot be settled in advance by the proper application of progressive principles, philosophy, or even judicious recourse to history, as important as such recourse is. Indeed, even as we consult our own convictions about these questions regarding motivations and outcomes of interventions, it is appropriate that we teach our students to consider the possibility of alternative explanations and to scrutinize information or inputs that may not immediately confirm our convictions. What should challenge us as scholars is the volume of information that must be collected and properly analyzed to understand the motivations behind and the consequences of particular policies, programs, and interventions, whether rhetorical, diplomatic, economic, or military. Much of this kind of research is done. But too little of it breaches academic firewalls that separate theoretical and empirical social science from scholarship on politics in the humanities disciplines and in some humanist subfields of the social sciences.

I have posed a thought question to myself in the course of this research that I think is important for critical humanists who are committed to exposing and exploring the troubling history in which we are implicated by virtue of being citizens of the United States and constituents of the broader wealthy, postindustrial West to consider: is it possible for agents of the US government to devise programs and interventions that, when implemented, improve the conditions and life chances of some people in the global South/developing world?

Why is this an important question? One reason is that the United States remains a powerful nation-state whose institutions, leaders, and actions still command both "hard" and "soft" power around the world.[36] Not only this: many people around the world continue to look to agents and agencies of the US government to publicize their plights, defend their human rights, and pressure their governments for greater political freedom or justice. Many foreign citizens who look to the United States for assistance may be deceived about the will or capacity of US officials to render aid. But the existence of these petitioners constitutes a challenge for critical humanists who might be skeptical about the very existence of such people.

In the late summer of 2001, mere weeks before the September 11 terror attacks, I was invited to attend a meeting and reception at one

of the congressional office buildings on Capitol Hill for a delegation of
women visiting Washington, DC, from the Eastern European nation of
Belarus. Formerly a republic of the Soviet Union, in 2001 Belarus was
governed by President Alexander Lukashenko, who remains in control of
that nation in 2018. In the months before August 2001, the Lukashenko
government targeted journalists and political adversaries to intimidate
politically active citizens and eliminate political opponents and sources of
information about the regime in the run-up to a national election.[37] Some
of the visiting women were widows when they arrived in DC, though they
hadn't been apprised of that fact. They came to Washington to educate
members of Congress about the deteriorated human rights situation in
Belarus, to entreat them to publicize the cases of the missing Belarusians to
European allies, and to keep diplomatic pressure on the regime to respect
human rights and resolve the cases of regime opponents. The Belarusian
election in September 2001 was marked by widespread corruption and
election irregularities, and a full accounting of the atrocities and the status
of victims has not yet been performed. Just a few years after this meeting, Secretary of State Condoleezza Rice placed Lukashenko's dictatorial
government on a State Department list of "outposts of tyranny" alongside
Burma, Cuba, Iran, and North Korea.

The congressional meeting with the Belarusian women was my first
direct experience with citizens of other countries reaching out to US
policy makers and other government officials for protection from their
own governments or from the brutality of dominant or militarized groups
in their own nations. The women did not travel to Washington to seek
redress of grievances against the United States or because the United States
was waging war or occupation in their country. Nor were they hoping
through their activism to avert some harmful outcome to themselves or
their communities that they feared would result from official or covert
actions of the US government. Instead, they came to the United States
to publicize their plight and to petition for US government assistance or
intervention.

From the "evil empire" to the "axis of evil" to "outposts of tyranny,"
the slogans of conservative US government officials who seek to sharply
contrast American (Christian, capitalist) virtue against foreign evil are an
easy target for progressive scorn. The Manichean division of good and evil
they are deployed to stabilize reinforces the deep ignorance of Americans
about US responsibility for the consequences of wars—hot, cold, proxy,
and dirty—as well as a wide range of other actions and failures to act.

Although many of these cases no doubt go undocumented and therefore may be lost to history, many are documented and publicized by a wide range of scholars and journalists.

It would be naive in the extreme for any scholar who hopes to understand the intersection between the complex picture of LGBTQ people's well-being and the US government's commitments as a simple one in which human rights considerations trump all other interests. I cannot imagine any scholar assuming or believing that for agents and agencies of the US government the protection of SOGI human rights is such a primary concern that other economic, political, and military goals have been or will be subordinated to that protection. Fortunately, no student of SOGI human rights has to believe such a farfetched scenario. Instead, we can examine the evidence of US government involvement in programs for sexual and gender minorities in light of our own commitments—whatever they may be—to the well-being and human rights of gender and sexual minorities. And we can judge those programs, and our own political ideas and theoretical terms, accordingly.

Even those of us who are committed to the well-being of sexual and gender minorities or those whose gender and sexuality put them at risk in their communities and nations are likely to disagree about what those conditions of threat ask of our government and of us as citizens of the West. Even if we disagree about what to do, and even if we agree that interventions can go terribly wrong, the solution is not to proactively proscribe US government interventions on behalf of human rights abroad. Instead, we should listen to the voices of those who solicit and are recipients of interventions. We should use this knowledge and these relationships to develop and advance political theories, political institutions, and international human rights.

# Appendix A

*Barack Obama, Presidential Memorandum—International Initiatives to Advance the Human Rights of Lesbian, Gay, Bisexual, and Transgender Persons*

MEMORANDUM FOR THE HEADS OF EXECUTIVE
DEPARTMENTS AND AGENCIES

SUBJECT: International Initiatives to Advance the Human Rights of Lesbian, Gay, Bisexual, and Transgender Persons

The struggle to end discrimination against lesbian, gay, bisexual, and transgender (LGBT) persons is a global challenge, and one that is central to the United States commitment to promoting human rights. I am deeply concerned by the violence and discrimination targeting LGBT persons around the world whether it is passing laws that criminalize LGBT status, beating citizens simply for joining peaceful LGBT pride celebrations, or killing men, women, and children for their perceived sexual orientation. That is why I declared before heads of state gathered at the United Nations, "no country should deny people their rights because of who they love, which is why we must stand up for the rights of gays and lesbians everywhere." Under my Administration, agencies engaged abroad have already begun taking action to promote the fundamental human rights of LGBT persons everywhere. Our deep commitment to advancing the human rights of all people is strengthened when we as the United States bring our tools to bear to vigorously advance this goal.

By this memorandum I am directing all agencies engaged abroad to ensure that U.S. diplomacy and foreign assistance promote and protect the human rights of LGBT persons. Specifically, I direct the following actions, consistent with applicable law:

Section 1. Combating Criminalization of LGBT Status or Conduct Abroad. Agencies engaged abroad are directed to strengthen existing efforts to effectively combat the criminalization by foreign governments of LGBT status or conduct and to expand efforts to combat discrimination, homophobia, and intolerance on the basis of LGBT status or conduct.

Sec. 2. Protecting Vulnerable LGBT Refugees and Asylum Seekers. Those LGBT persons who seek refuge from violence and persecution face daunting challenges. In order to improve protection for LGBT refugees and asylum seekers at all stages of displacement, the Departments of State and Homeland Security shall enhance their ongoing efforts to ensure that LGBT refugees and asylum seekers have equal access to protection and assistance, particularly in countries of first asylum. In addition, the Departments of State, Justice, and Homeland Security shall ensure appropriate training is in place so that relevant Federal Government personnel and key partners can effectively address the protection of LGBT refugees and asylum seekers, including by providing to them adequate assistance and ensuring that the Federal Government has the ability to identify and expedite resettlement of highly vulnerable persons with urgent protection needs.

Sec. 3. Foreign Assistance to Protect Human Rights and Advance Nondiscrimination. Agencies involved with foreign aid, assistance, and development shall enhance their ongoing efforts to ensure regular Federal Government engagement with governments, citizens, civil society, and the private sector in order to build respect for the human rights of LGBT persons.

Sec. 4. Swift and Meaningful U.S. Responses to Human Rights Abuses of LGBT Persons Abroad. The Department of State shall lead a standing group, with appropriate interagency representation, to help ensure the Federal Government's swift and meaningful response to serious incidents that threaten the human rights of LGBT persons abroad.

Sec. 5. Engaging International Organizations in the Fight Against LGBT Discrimination. Multilateral fora and international organizations are key vehicles to promote respect for the human rights of LGBT persons and to bring global attention to LGBT issues. Building on the State Department's leadership in this area, agencies engaged abroad should strengthen the work they have begun and initiate additional efforts in these multilateral fora and organizations to: counter discrimination on the basis of LGBT status; broaden the number of countries willing to support and defend LGBT issues in the multilateral arena; strengthen the role of civil society advocates on behalf of LGBT issues within and through multilateral fora; and strengthen the policies and programming of multilateral institutions on LGBT issues.

Sec. 6. Reporting on Progress. All agencies engaged abroad shall prepare a report within 180 days of the date of this memorandum, and annually thereafter, on their progress toward advancing these initiatives. All such agencies shall submit their reports to the Department of State, which will compile a report on the Federal Government's progress in advancing these initiatives for transmittal to the President.

Sec. 7. Definitions. (a) For the purposes of this memorandum, agencies engaged abroad include the Departments of State, the Treasury, Defense, Justice, Agriculture, Commerce, Health and Human Services, and Homeland Security, the United States Agency for International Development (USAID), the Millennium Challenge Corporation, the Export Import Bank, the United States Trade Representative, and such other agencies as the President may designate.

(b) For the purposes of this memorandum, agencies involved with foreign aid, assistance, and development include the Departments of State, the Treasury, Defense, Justice, Health and Human Services, and Homeland Security, the USAID, the Millennium Challenge Corporation, the Export Import Bank, the United States Trade Representative, and such other agencies as the President may designate.

This memorandum is not intended to, and does not, create any right or benefit, substantive or procedural, enforceable at law or in equity by any party against the United States, its departments, agencies, or entities, its officers, employees, or agents, or any other person. The Secretary of State is hereby authorized and directed to publish this memorandum in the Federal Register.

BARACK OBAMA

# Appendix B

## Hillary Clinton, Remarks in Recognition of International Human Rights Day

[Part One]

[1] Good evening, and let me express my deep honor and pleasure at being here. I want to thank Director General Tokayev and Ms. Wyden along with other ministers, ambassadors, excellencies, and UN partners. This weekend, we will celebrate Human Rights Day, the anniversary of one of the great accomplishments of the last century.

[2] Beginning in 1947, delegates from six continents devoted themselves to drafting a declaration that would enshrine the fundamental rights and freedoms of people everywhere. In the aftermath of World War II, many nations pressed for a statement of this kind to help ensure that we would prevent future atrocities and protect the inherent humanity and dignity of all people. And so the delegates went to work. They discussed, they wrote, they revisited, revised, rewrote, for thousands of hours. And they incorporated suggestions and revisions from governments, organizations, and individuals around the world.

[3] At three o'clock in the morning on December 10th, 1948, after nearly two years of drafting and one last long night of debate, the president of the UN General Assembly called for a vote on the final text. Forty-eight nations voted in favor; eight abstained; none dissented. And the Universal Declaration of

Human Rights was adopted. It proclaims a simple, powerful idea: All human beings are born free and equal in dignity and rights. And with the declaration, it was made clear that rights are not conferred by government; they are the birthright of all people. It does not matter what country we live in, who our leaders are, or even who we are. Because we are human, we therefore have rights. And because we have rights, governments are bound to protect them.

[4] In the 63 years since the declaration was adopted, many nations have made great progress in making human rights a human reality. Step by step, barriers that once prevented people from enjoying the full measure of liberty, the full experience of dignity, and the full benefits of humanity have fallen away. In many places, racist laws have been repealed, legal and social practices that relegated women to second-class status have been abolished, the ability of religious minorities to practice their faith freely has been secured.

[5] In most cases, this progress was not easily won. People fought and organized and campaigned in public squares and private spaces to change not only laws, but hearts and minds. And thanks to that work of generations, for millions of individuals whose lives were once narrowed by injustice, they are now able to live more freely and to participate more fully in the political, economic, and social lives of their communities.

[Part Two]

[6] Now, there is still, as you all know, much more to be done to secure that commitment, that reality, and progress for all people. Today, I want to talk about the work we have left to do to protect one group of people whose human rights are still denied in too many parts of the world today. In many ways, they are an invisible minority. They are arrested, beaten, terrorized, even executed. Many are treated with contempt and violence by their fellow citizens while authorities empowered to protect them look the other way or, too often, even join in the abuse. They are denied opportunities to work and learn,

driven from their homes and countries, and forced to suppress or deny who they are to protect themselves from harm.

[7] I am talking about gay, lesbian, bisexual, and transgender people, human beings born free and given[,] bestowed equality and dignity, who have a right to claim that, which is now one of the remaining human rights challenges of our time. I speak about this subject knowing that my own country's record on human rights for gay people is far from perfect. Until 2003, it was still a crime in parts of our country. Many LGBT Americans have endured violence and harassment in their own lives, and for some, including many young people, bullying and exclusion are daily experiences. So we, like all nations, have more work to do to protect human rights at home.

[8] Now, raising this issue, I know, is sensitive for many people and that the obstacles standing in the way of protecting the human rights of LGBT people rest on deeply held personal, political, cultural, and religious beliefs. So I come here before you with respect, understanding, and humility. Even though progress on this front is not easy, we cannot delay acting. So in that spirit, I want to talk about the difficult and important issues we must address together to reach a global consensus that recognizes the human rights of LGBT citizens everywhere.

[9] The first issue goes to the heart of the matter. Some have suggested that gay rights and human rights are separate and distinct; but, in fact, they are one and the same. Now, of course, 60 years ago, the governments that drafted and passed the Universal Declaration of Human Rights were not thinking about how it applied to the LGBT community. They also weren't thinking about how it applied to indigenous people or children or people with disabilities or other marginalized groups. Yet in the past 60 years, we have come to recognize that members of these groups are entitled to the full measure of dignity and rights, because, like all people, they share a common humanity.

[10] This recognition did not occur all at once. It evolved over time. And as it did, we understood that we were honoring

rights that people always had, rather than creating new or
special rights for them. Like being a woman, like being a racial,
religious, tribal, or ethnic minority, being LGBT does not make
you less human. And that is why gay rights are human rights,
and human rights are gay rights.

[11] It is violation of human rights when people are beaten or
killed because of their sexual orientation, or because they do
not conform to cultural norms about how men and women
should look or behave. It is a violation of human rights when
governments declare it illegal to be gay, or allow those who
harm gay people to go unpunished. It is a violation of human
rights when lesbian or transgendered women are subjected to
so-called corrective rape, or forcibly subjected to hormone
treatments, or when people are murdered after public calls
for violence toward gays, or when they are forced to flee their
nations and seek asylum in other lands to save their lives.
And it is a violation of human rights when life-saving care
is withheld from people because they are gay, or equal access
to justice is denied to people because they are gay, or public
spaces are out of bounds to people because they are gay. No
matter what we look like, where we come from, or who we
are, we are all equally entitled to our human rights and dignity.

[12] The second issue is a question of whether homosexuality
arises from a particular part of the world. Some seem to believe
it is a Western phenomenon, and therefore people outside
the West have grounds to reject it. Well, in reality, gay people
are born into and belong to every society in the world. They
are all ages, all races, all faiths; they are doctors and teachers,
farmers and bankers, soldiers and athletes; and whether we
know it, or whether we acknowledge it, they are our family,
our friends, and our neighbors.

[13] Being gay is not a Western invention; it is a human reality.
And protecting the human rights of all people, gay or straight,
is not something that only Western governments do. South
Africa's constitution, written in the aftermath of Apartheid,

protects the equality of all citizens, including gay people. In Colombia and Argentina, the rights of gays are also legally protected. In Nepal, the supreme court has ruled that equal rights apply to LGBT citizens. The Government of Mongolia has committed to pursue new legislation that will tackle anti-gay discrimination.

[14] Now, some worry that protecting the human rights of the LGBT community is a luxury that only wealthy nations can afford. But in fact, in all countries, there are costs to not protecting these rights, in both gay and straight lives lost to disease and violence, and the silencing of voices and views that would strengthen communities, in ideas never pursued by entrepreneurs who happen to be gay. Costs are incurred whenever any group is treated as lesser or the other, whether they are women, racial, or religious minorities, or the LGBT. Former President Mogae of Botswana pointed out recently that for as long as LGBT people are kept in the shadows, there cannot be an effective public health program to tackle HIV and AIDS. Well, that holds true for other challenges as well.

[15] The third, and perhaps most challenging, issue arises when people cite religious or cultural values as a reason to violate or not to protect the human rights of LGBT citizens. This is not unlike the justification offered for violent practices towards women like honor killings, widow burning, or female genital mutilation. Some people still defend those practices as part of a cultural tradition. But violence toward women isn't cultural; it's criminal. Likewise with slavery, what was once justified as sanctioned by God is now properly reviled as an unconscionable violation of human rights.

[16] In each of these cases, we came to learn that no practice or tradition trumps the human rights that belong to all of us. And this holds true for inflicting violence on LGBT people, criminalizing their status or behavior, expelling them from their families and communities, or tacitly or explicitly accepting their killing.

[17] Of course, it bears noting that rarely are cultural and religious traditions and teachings actually in conflict with the protection of human rights. Indeed, our religion and our culture are sources of compassion and inspiration toward our fellow human beings. It was not only those who've justified slavery who leaned on religion, it was also those who sought to abolish it. And let us keep in mind that our commitments to protect the freedom of religion and to defend the dignity of LGBT people emanate from a common source. For many of us, religious belief and practice is a vital source of meaning and identity, and fundamental to who we are as people. And likewise, for most of us, the bonds of love and family that we forge are also vital sources of meaning and identity. And caring for others is an expression of what it means to be fully human. It is because the human experience is universal that human rights are universal and cut across all religions and cultures.

[18] The fourth issue is what history teaches us about how we make progress towards rights for all. Progress starts with honest discussion. Now, there are some who say and believe that all gay people are pedophiles, that homosexuality is a disease that can be caught or cured, or that gays recruit others to become gay. Well, these notions are simply not true. They are also unlikely to disappear if those who promote or accept them are dismissed out of hand rather than invited to share their fears and concerns. No one has ever abandoned a belief because he was forced to do so.

[Part Three]

[19] Universal human rights include freedom of expression and freedom of belief, even if our words or beliefs denigrate the humanity of others. Yet, while we are each free to believe whatever we choose, we cannot do whatever we choose, not in a world where we protect the human rights of all.

[20] Reaching understanding of these issues takes more than speech. It does take a conversation. In fact, it takes a constellation of conversations in places big and small. And it takes

a willingness to see stark differences in belief as a reason to begin the conversation, not to avoid it.

[21] But progress comes from changes in laws. In many places, including my own country, legal protections have preceded, not followed, broader recognition of rights. Laws have a teaching effect. Laws that discriminate validate other kinds of discrimination. Laws that require equal protections reinforce the moral imperative of equality. And practically speaking, it is often the case that laws must change before fears about change dissipate.

[22] Many in my country thought that President Truman was making a grave error when he ordered the racial desegregation of our military. They argued that it would undermine unit cohesion. And it wasn't until he went ahead and did it that we saw how it strengthened our social fabric in ways even the supporters of the policy could not foresee. Likewise, some worried in my country that the repeal of "Don't Ask, Don't Tell" would have a negative effect on our armed forces. Now, the Marine Corps Commandant, who was one of the strongest voices against the repeal, says that his concerns were unfounded and that the Marines have embraced the change.

[23] Finally, progress comes from being willing to walk a mile in someone else's shoes. We need to ask ourselves, "How would it feel if it were a crime to love the person I love? How would it feel to be discriminated against for something about myself that I cannot change?" This challenge applies to all of us as we reflect upon deeply held beliefs, as we work to embrace tolerance and respect for the dignity of all persons, and as we engage humbly with those with whom we disagree in the hope of creating greater understanding.

[24] A fifth and final question is how we do our part to bring the world to embrace human rights for all people including LGBT people. Yes, LGBT people must help lead this effort, as so many of you are. Their knowledge and experiences are invaluable and their courage inspirational. We know the names of brave LGBT activists who have literally given their

lives for this cause, and there are many more whose names we will never know. But often those who are denied rights are least empowered to bring about the changes they seek. Acting alone, minorities can never achieve the majorities necessary for political change.

[25] So when any part of humanity is sidelined, the rest of us cannot sit on the sidelines. Every time a barrier to progress has fallen, it has taken a cooperative effort from those on both sides of the barrier. In the fight for women's rights, the support of men remains crucial. The fight for racial equality has relied on contributions from people of all races. Combating Islamaphobia or anti-Semitism is a task for people of all faiths. And the same is true with this struggle for equality.

[26] Conversely, when we see denials and abuses of human rights and fail to act, that sends the message to those deniers and abusers that they won't suffer any consequences for their actions, and so they carry on. But when we do act, we send a powerful moral message. Right here in Geneva, the international community acted this year to strengthen a global consensus around the human rights of LGBT people. At the Human Rights Council in March, 85 countries from all regions supported a statement calling for an end to criminalization and violence against people because of their sexual orientation and gender identity.

[27] At the following session of the Council in June, South Africa took the lead on a resolution about violence against LGBT people. The delegation from South Africa spoke eloquently about their own experience and struggle for human equality and its indivisibility. When the measure passed, it became the first-ever UN resolution recognizing the human rights of gay people worldwide. In the Organization of American States this year, the Inter-American Commission on Human Rights created a unit on the rights of LGBT people, a step toward what we hope will be the creation of a special rapporteur.

[28] Now, we must go further and work here and in every region of the world to galvanize more support for the human

rights of the LGBT community. To the leaders of those countries where people are jailed, beaten, or executed for being gay, I ask you to consider this: Leadership, by definition, means being out in front of your people when it is called for. It means standing up for the dignity of all your citizens and persuading your people to do the same. It also means ensuring that all citizens are treated as equals under your laws, because let me be clear—I am not saying that gay people can't or don't commit crimes. They can and they do, just like straight people. And when they do, they should be held accountable, but it should never be a crime to be gay.

[29] And to people of all nations, I say supporting human rights is your responsibility too. The lives of gay people are shaped not only by laws, but by the treatment they receive every day from their families, from their neighbors. Eleanor Roosevelt, who did so much to advance human rights worldwide, said that these rights begin in the small places close to home—the streets where people live, the schools they attend, the factories, farms, and offices where they work. These places are your domain. The actions you take, the ideals that you advocate, can determine whether human rights flourish where you are.

[Part Four]

[30] And finally, to LGBT men and women worldwide, let me say this: Wherever you live and whatever the circumstances of your life, whether you are connected to a network of support or feel isolated and vulnerable, please know that you are not alone. People around the globe are working hard to support you and to bring an end to the injustices and dangers you face. That is certainly true for my country. And you have an ally in the United States of America and you have millions of friends among the American people.

[31] The Obama Administration defends the human rights of LGBT people as part of our comprehensive human rights policy and as a priority of our foreign policy. In our embassies, our diplomats are raising concerns about specific cases and laws, and working with a range of partners to strengthen human

rights protections for all. In Washington, we have created a task force at the State Department to support and coordinate this work. And in the coming months, we will provide every embassy with a toolkit to help improve their efforts. And we have created a program that offers emergency support to defenders of human rights for LGBT people.

[32] This morning, back in Washington, President Obama put into place the first U.S. Government strategy dedicated to combating human rights abuses against LGBT persons abroad. Building on efforts already underway at the State Department and across the government, the President has directed all U.S. Government agencies engaged overseas to combat the criminalization of LGBT status and conduct, to enhance efforts to protect vulnerable LGBT refugees and asylum seekers, to ensure that our foreign assistance promotes the protection of LGBT rights, to enlist international organizations in the fight against discrimination, and to respond swiftly to abuses against LGBT persons.

[33] I am also pleased to announce that we are launching a new Global Equality Fund that will support the work of civil society organizations working on these issues around the world. This fund will help them record facts so they can target their advocacy, learn how to use the law as a tool, manage their budgets, train their staffs, and forge partnerships with women's organizations and other human rights groups. We have committed more than $3 million to start this fund, and we have hope that others will join us in supporting it.

[34] The women and men who advocate for human rights for the LGBT community in hostile places, some of whom are here today with us, are brave and dedicated, and deserve all the help we can give them. We know the road ahead will not be easy. A great deal of work lies before us. But many of us have seen firsthand how quickly change can come. In our lifetimes, attitudes toward gay people in many places have been transformed. Many people, including myself, have experienced a deepening of our own convictions on this topic over the years, as we have devoted more thought to it, engaged in dia-

logues and debates, and established personal and professional relationships with people who are gay.

[35] This evolution is evident in many places. To highlight one example, the Delhi High Court decriminalized homosexuality in India two years ago, writing, and I quote, "If there is one tenet that can be said to be an underlying theme of the Indian constitution, it is inclusiveness." There is little doubt in my mind that support for LGBT human rights will continue to climb. Because for many young people, this is simple: All people deserve to be treated with dignity and have their human rights respected, no matter who they are or whom they love.

[36] There is a phrase that people in the United States invoke when urging others to support human rights: "Be on the right side of history." The story of the United States is the story of a nation that has repeatedly grappled with intolerance and inequality. We fought a brutal civil war over slavery. People from coast to coast joined in campaigns to recognize the rights of women, indigenous peoples, racial minorities, children, people with disabilities, immigrants, workers, and on and on. And the march toward equality and justice has continued. Those who advocate for expanding the circle of human rights were and are on the right side of history, and history honors them. Those who tried to constrict human rights were wrong, and history reflects that as well.

[37] I know that the thoughts I've shared today involve questions on which opinions are still evolving. As it has happened so many times before, opinion will converge once again with the truth, the immutable truth, that all persons are created free and equal in dignity and rights. We are called once more to make real the words of the Universal Declaration. Let us answer that call. Let us be on the right side of history, for our people, our nations, and future generations, whose lives will be shaped by the work we do today. I come before you with great hope and confidence that no matter how long the road ahead, we will travel it successfully together. Thank you very much. (Applause.)

# Notes

## Introduction

1. Mark Blasius draws on the concept of "same-sex loving" used by some African scholars and activists to reflect ambivalence about conceptualizations of sexuality and homosexuality. See Blasius, "Theorizing the Politics of (Homo) Sexualities across Cultures," in Meredith L. Weiss and Michael J. Bosia, eds., *Global Homophobia: States, Movements, and the Politics of Oppression* (Urbana: University of Illinois Press, 2013), 221. While respecting the range of identities gender and sexual minorities might embrace, Marc Epprecht proposes "gay-ish" in passing as a term that performs similar work. See Epprecht, "Sexual Minorities, Human Rights and Public Health Strategies in Africa," *African Affairs* 111:443 (2012): 242.

2. See, for example, Brooke A. Ackerly, "Girls Rising for Human Rights: Not Magic, Politics," *Journal of International Political Theory* 21:1 (2016): 26–41.

3. Ryan R. Thoreson, *Transnational LGBT Activism: Working for Sexual Rights Worldwide* (Minneapolis: University of Minnesota Press, 2014), 3–4.

4. The concept of moral entrepreneur is drawn from Howard S. Becker, *Outsiders: Studies in the Sociology of Deviance* (New York: Free Press, 1963).

5. *The Economist*, "The War on Gays: Strange Bedfellows," May 4, 2013, http://www.economist.com/news/international/21577043-american-christian-zealots-are-fighting-back-against-gay-rightsabroad-strange-bedfellows (accessed May 7, 2013).

6. Doris Buss and Didi Herman, *Globalizing Family Values: The Christian Right in International Politics* (Minneapolis: University of Minnesota Press, 2003).

7. For the opposition of anthropologists to "the applicability of any Declaration of Human Rights to mankind as a whole," see Ann-Belinda S. Preis, "Human Rights as Cultural Practice: An Anthropological Critique," *Human Rights Quarterly* 18 (1996): 286. For a critique of human rights universality as it applies to transgender rights and identity, see Sally Hines, "A Pathway to Diversity? Human Rights, Citizenship and the Politics of Transgender," *Contemporary Politics* 15:1 (2009): 87–102.

8. The phrase is from Paul R. Gross and Norman Levitt, *Higher Superstition: The Academic Left and Its Quarrels with Science* (Baltimore, MD: Johns Hopkins University Press, 1998), 8. Gross and Levitt take pains to explain and justify their use of "academic left" and "academic leftists" to signal the class of academics whose views they criticize.

9. Questions like these are addressed by many scholars of human rights, but for an example of the integration of these questions into human rights scholarship, see Franke Wilmer, *Human Rights in International Politics: An Introduction* (Boulder, CO: Lynne Rienner, 2015).

10. See Douglas E. Sanders, "377 and the Unnatural Afterlife of British Colonialism in Asia," *Asian Journal of Comparative Law* 4 (2009): 1–49; Richard Phillips, *Sex, Politics and Empire: A Postcolonial Geography* (Manchester: Manchester University Press, 2006).

11. See Jochen von Bernstorff, "The Changing Fortunes of the Universal Declaration of Human Rights: Genesis and Symbolic Dimensions of the Turn to Rights in International Law," *European Journal of International Law* 19:5 (2008): 903–24.

12. See Kelly Kollman and Matthew Waites, "The Global Politics of Lesbian, Gay, Bisexual and Transgender Human Rights: An Introduction," *Contemporary Politics* 15:1 (2009): 8; Carole Pateman, *The Sexual Contract* (Stanford, CA: Stanford University Press, 1988).

13. Wilmer, *Human Rights in International Politics*, 349. For a review of six recent books that take up dignity and/in human rights, see Michael Goodhart, "Recent Works on Dignity and Human Rights: A Road Not Taken," *Perspectives on Politics* 12:4 (2014): 846–56.

14. Karen Zivi, "Dignity at What Cost? Marriage Equality in the United States," in Richard Hiskes, ed., *Human Dignity and the Promise of Human Rights* (New York: Open Society Foundation, 2015), 48–64.

15. See Executive Board of the American Anthropology Association, "Statement on Human Rights," *American Anthropologist* 49:4 (1947): 539–43; Adamantia Pollis and Peter Schwab, "Human Rights: A Western Construct with Limited Applicability," in Adamantia Pollis and Peter Schwab, eds., *Human Rights: Political and Ideological Perspectives* (New York: Praeger, 1979), 13. Here I follow the example of William Easterly and use the term "poor" instead of "developing" nations. A complication of using this term for SOGI human rights–violating states is that not all of these are poor, formerly "third world" nations. Some are former "second world" nations. See William Easterly, *The Tyranny of Experts: Economists, Dictators, and the Forgotten Rights of the Poor* (New York: Basic Books, 2015).

16. See, for example, World Congress of Families, "World Family Declaration," no date, http://worldfamilydeclaration.org/WFD (accessed April 14, 2016).

17. Examples include Ileana Rodríguez, *Liberalism at its Limits: Crime and Terror in the Latin American Cultural Text* (Pittsburgh: University of Pitts-

burgh Press, 2009); Jieh-Yung Lu, "Human Rights Must Be Culturally Relative," in Jacqueline Langwith, ed., *Human Rights: Opposing Viewpoints* (Detroit, MI: Greenhaven Press, 2008).

18. Amartya Sen, "Human Rights and Asian Values," Sixteenth Morganthau Memorial Lecture on Ethics and Foreign Policy, Carnegie Council for Ethics in International Affairs, New York, 1997.

19. Abdullahi A. An-Na'im, "Islam and Human Rights: Beyond the Universality Debate," *Proceedings of the Annual Meeting (American Society of International Law)* 94 (2000): 95–103.

20. Pew Research Center, "The Global Divide on Homosexuality: Greater Acceptance in More Secular and Affluent Countries," June 4, 2013, http://www.pewglobal.org/files/2013/06/Pew-Global-Attitudes-Homosexuality-Report-FINAL-JUNE-4-20131.pdf (accessed June 6, 2013), 1.

21. Jonathan Zimmerman, "A Global Front against Sex Education," *TulsaWorld*, September 13, 2014, http://www.tulsaworld.com/opinion/jonathan-zimmerman-a-global-front-against-sex-education/article_f4abad8d-39d2-59d9-85db-7ff3cb0cc222.html (accessed December 8, 2014).

22. Jack Donnelly, "The Relative Universality of Human Rights," *Human Rights Quarterly* 29 (2007): 281–306.

23. Thomas Hammarberg, Commissioner for Human Rights, "Human Rights and Gender Identity," Council of Europe, 2009, https://wcd.coe.int/ViewDoc.jsp?p=&id=1476365&direct=true# (accessed July 11, 2016).

24. See, for example, Berna Turam, "Islands of Freedom in an Increasingly Authoritarian Regime: The Case of Turkey," presented at the Southern Political Science Association, Puerto Rico, January 8, 2016. Turam analyzes liberal/traditionalist fault lines within Istanbul's Boğaziçi (Bosphorus) University.

25. See arguments such as those in Vincent J. Samar, "Gay-Rights as a Particular Instantiation of Human Rights," *Albany Law Review* 64 (2001): 983–1030.

26. Swedish International Development Cooperation Agency (Sida), no date, http://www.sida.se/english/ (accessed June 29, 2014).

27. Sida, "Human Rights of Lesbian, Gay, Bisexual and Transgender Persons: Conducting a Dialogue," Council for Global Equality, no date, http://www.globalequality.org/storage/documents/pdf/sida%20dialogue%20paper%20on%20development.pdf (accessed June 30, 2014).

28. For the health costs of discrimination, see research by Ellen Riggle, Sharon Rostosky, and colleagues, which is collected at Prism Research, http://prismresearch.org/ (accessed May 1, 2017).

29. The World Bank, News: "The Economic Cost of Homophobia," World Bank, 2014, (accessed June 30, 2014). The author of the research in progress that was the subject of the forum was economist M. V. Lee Badgett.

30. See Mark Blasius and Shane Phelan, eds., *We Are Everywhere: A Historical Sourcebook of Gay and Lesbian Politics* (New York: Routledge, 1997), 133–42.

31. RFSL is still in existence as the Swedish Federation for Lesbian, Gay, Bisexual and Transgender Rights (Riksförbundet för homosexuellas, bisexuellas, transpersoners och queeras rättigheter).

32. Julie Mertus, "The Rejection of Human Rights Framings: The Case of LGBT Advocacy in the US," *Human Rights Quarterly* 29 (2007): 1057.

33. Craig A. Rimmerman, *The Lesbian and Gay Movements: Assimilation or Liberation?*, 2nd ed. (Boulder, CO: Westview Press, 2015), 56.

34. Mertus, "The Rejection of Human Rights Framings," 1050.

35. Mertus, "The Rejection of Human Rights Framings," 1062–64.

36. Astraea Lesbian Foundation for Justice, "What We Do," 2014, http://www.astraeafoundation.org/what-we-do (accessed October 30, 2015).

37. Astraea Lesbian Foundation for Justice, "What We Do: Grantmaking," 2014, http://www.astraeafoundation.org/what-we-do/grantmaking (accessed February 5, 2016).

38. International Lesbian, Gay, Bisexual, Trans, and Intersex Association (ILGA), "ILGA Conferences," 2013, http://ilga.org/ilga-conferences/ (accessed March 2, 2016).

39. North American Man/Boy Love Association, "Who We Are," 2011, http://nambla.org/welcome.html (accessed March 1, 2016).

40. An account of the politics surrounding ILGA's UN status from 1991 to 1995 can be found in Douglas Sanders, "Getting Lesbian and Gay Issues on the International Human Rights Agenda," *Human Rights Quarterly* 18 (1996): 98–103.

41. Wherever the motto originated, variations are used by different organizations, including the UN's Office of the High Commissioner for Human Rights. See United Nations, "Human Rights for Everyone Everywhere," 2008, http://www.ohchr.org/Documents/AboutUs/HumanRightsDay/hrday09_leaflet_en.pdf (accessed June 13, 2017).

42. OutRight Action International, "Why We Changed Our Name," September 28, 2015, https://www.youtube.com/watch?v=1N4o1ro3rHM (accessed March 1, 2016).

43. See http://iglhrc.org/content/about-our-work (accessed June 30, 2014).

44. International Gay and Lesbian Human Rights Commission, "In Their Own Words: Documenting Violence and Discrimination against Lesbians, Bisexual Women, and Transgender People in Asia," November 15, 2013, http://www.youtube.com/watch?v=4tFNLIZaQ5I (January 13, 2014).

45. See Ryan Thoreson's ethnography of IGLHRC for an account of the debate and deliberations over the LGBT organization's consultative status: Thoreson, *Transnational LGBT Activism*, 199–208.

46. Council for Global Equality, "Advancing an American Foreign Policy Inclusive of Sexual Orientation and Gender Identity," 2010, http://www.globalequality.org/ (accessed June 13, 2017).

47. For the role of mainstream human rights nongovernmental organizations as "gatekeepers" of human rights orthodoxy, see Julie Mertus, "Applying the Gatekeeper Model of Human Rights Activism: The U.S.-Based Movement for LGBT Rights," in Clifford Bob, ed., *The International Struggle for New Human Rights* (Philadelphia: University of Pennsylvania Press, 2011).

48. As I note later, Amnesty International was founded in the United Kingdom and has active chapters around the world, including in the United States.

49. Amnesty International, "Who We Are," 2013, http://www.amnestyusa.org/about-us/who-we-are (accessed April 20, 2017).

50. Amnesty International, "LGBT Pride 2012: Lesbian, Gay, Bisexual, and Transgender Rights are Human Rights! Activist Resource Packet," 2012 http://www.amnestyusa.org/pdfs/AIUSA_Pride_Toolkit-2012.pdf (accessed April 24, 2013).

51. Peter R. Baehr, *Human Rights: Universality in Practice* (Houndmills, UK: Palgrave, 2001), 12, 121.

52. Amnesty International United Kingdom, *Breaking the Silence: Human Rights Violations Based on Sexual Orientation* (London: Amnesty, 1997).

53. Human Rights Watch, "Lesbian, Gay, Bisexual, and Transgender Rights," 2014, http://www.hrw.org/topic/lgbt-rights (accessed April 5, 2014).

54. Human Rights First, "Our Mission," no date, http://www.humanrightsfirst.org/about-us/ (accessed July 5, 2013).

55. Michael McClintock, *Everyday Fears: A Survey of Violent Hate Crimes in Europe and North America* (New York: Human Rights First, 2005).

56. Human Rights First, "LGBT Persons," no date, http://www.humanrights-first.org/our-work/fighting-discrimination/lgbt-persons/; Human Rights First, "LGBTI Refugees," no date, http://www.humanrightsfirst.org/our-work/refugee-protection/lgbti-refugees/ (accessed July 5, 2013).

57. Joke Swiebel, "Lesbian, Gay, Bisexual and Transgender Human Rights: The Search for an International Strategy," *Contemporary Politics* 15:1 (2009): 19–35.

58. "The Yogyakarta Principles," no date, http://www.yogyakartaprinciples.org/ (accessed May 31, 2013).

59. "The Yogyakarta Principles: The Application of International Human Rights Law in Relation to Sexual Orientation and Gender Identity," ARC International, 2016, http://www.yogyakartaprinciples.org (accessed March 10, 2015).

60. David Brown, "Making Room for Sexual Orientation and Gender Identity in International Human Rights Law: An Introduction to the Yogyakarta Principles," *Michigan Journal of International Law* 31 (2010): 845–67.

61. Michael O'Flaherty and John Fisher, "Sexual Orientation, Gender Identity and International Human Rights Law: Contextualising the Yogyakarta Principles," *Human Rights Law Review* 8:2 (2008): 236.

62. O'Flaherty and Fisher, "Sexual Orientation, Gender Identity and International Human Rights," 210. See also Roderick Brown, "Corrective Rape in South

Africa: A Continuing Plight Despite an International Human Rights Response," *Annual Survey of International and Comparative Law* 18 (2012): 45–66.

63. Bronwyn Winter, "The 'L' in the LGBTI 'Alphabet Soup': Issues Faced by Lesbian Asylum Seekers and Other Non-Western Lesbian Exiles in France," *Contemporary French Civilization* 40:2 (2015): 179.

64. O'Flaherty and Fisher, "Sexual Orientation, Gender Identity and International Human Rights Law," 228.

65. I'm grateful to Suparna Bhaskaram for bringing *Courage Unfolds* to my attention.

66. *Courage Unfolds*, LeAP! And IGLHRC, 2011, http://vimeo.com/22813403 (accessed May 13, 2015). The film is available in many languages spoken in Asia, and viewers are invited to share it. The last frame reads: "This video is copyrighted. However, it is being made available at no cost for education and advocacy purposes. Please do not edit, change, or in any way alter the contents of this video."

67. David Brown, "Making Room for Sexual Orientation and Gender Identity," 827, 874.

68. Ara Wilson, "Lesbian Visibility and Sexual Rights at Beijing," *Signs* 22 (1996): 214–18.

69. Human Rights Watch, "UN: General Assembly Statement Affirms Rights for All," HRW, December 18, 2008, https://www.hrw.org/news/2008/12/18/un-general-assembly-statement-affirms-rights-all (accessed February 3, 2016).

70. For early efforts and strategies by anti-LGBTQ states, organizations, and advocates, see Doris Buss and Didi Herman, *Globalizing Family Values: The Christian Right in International Politics* (Minneapolis: University of Minnesota Press, 2003).

71. Ban Ki-moon, "Secretary-General's Remarks at Event on Ending Violence and Criminal Sanctions Based on Sexual Orientation and Gender Identity," United Nations, December 10, 2010, http://www.un.org/sg/statements/?nid=4992 (accessed March 1, 2016).

72. Office of the High Commissioner on Human Rights, "Combating Discrimination Based on Sexual Orientation and Gender Identity—Speeches and Statements," United Nations, 2016, http://www.ohchr.org/EN/Issues/Discrimination/Pages/LGBTSpeechesandstatements.aspx (accessed March 1, 2016).

73. United Nations General Assembly, "17/19 Human Rights, Sexual Orientation and Gender Identity," ARC International, July 14, 2011, http://www.arc-international.net/wp-content/uploads/2011/09/HRC-Res-17-19.pdf (accessed July 12, 2013).

74. Human Rights Watch, "Historic Decision at the United Nations," June 17, 2011, http://www.hrw.org/news/2011/06/17/historic-decision-united-nations (accessed April 5, 2014). Recorded as absent from the voting were Kyrgyzstan and Libya.

75. Office of the High Commissioner for Human Rights, "Born Free and Equal: Sexual Orientation and Gender Identity in International Human Rights Law," UN, 2012, 10.

76. See "International Conference on Human Rights, Sexual Orientation and Gender Identity, Oslo 15–16 April 2013: Summary and Toolkit," Republic of South Africa and Norwegian Ministry of Foreign Affairs.

77. Office of the High Commissioner for Human Rights, "Combatting Discrimination Based on Sexual Orientation and Gender Identity," UN, 2015, http://www.ohchr.org/EN/Issues/Discrimination/Pages/LGBT.aspx (accessed May 10, 2015). Emphasis in the original.

78. Special Representative of the Secretary-General for Violence Against Children, "Discrimination and Violence against Individuals Based on Their Sexual Orientation and Gender Identity—Report of the Office of the United Nations High Commissioner for Human Rights," United Nations, May 4, 2015, http://srsg.violenceagainstchildren.org/document/a-hrc-29-23_1359 (accessed January 2, 2016).

79. Phillip M. Ayoub, "With Arms Wide Shut: Threat Perception, Norm Reception, and Mobilized Resistance to LGBT Rights," *Journal of Human Rights* 13 (3): 337.

80. Thomas Risse and Kathryn Sikkink, "The Socialization of International Human Rights Norms into Domestic Practices: Introduction," in Thomas Risse, Stephen C. Ropp, and Kathryn Sikkink, eds., *The Power of Human Rights: International Norms and Domestic Change* (Cambridge: Cambridge University Press, 1999), 3.

81. Between 2013 and 2016 I heard a number of SOGI human rights activists and professionals outside the US government use this phrase to describe the US government's role during the Obama administration.

82. Jeffrey C. Isaac, "Hannah Arendt on Human Rights and the Limits of Exposure, or Why Noam Chomsky Is Wrong about the Meaning of Kosovo," *Social Research* 69 (2): 507.

## Chapter 1

1. See K. A. Cuordileone, *Manhood and American Political Culture in the Cold War* (New York: Routledge, 2004).

2. David K. Johnson, *The Lavender Scare: The Cold War Persecution of Gays and Lesbians in the Federal Government* (Chicago: University of Chicago Press, 2004); see also Craig Loftin, *Masked Voices: Gay Men and Lesbians in Cold War America* (Albany: State University of New York Press, 2012).

3. Gregory B. Lewis, "Barriers to Security Clearances for Gay Men and Lesbians: Fear of Blackmail or Fear of Homosexuals?," *Journal of Public Administration Research and Theory* 11 (2001): 548–50.

4. US General Accounting Office, "Security Clearances: Consideration of Sexual Orientation in the Clearance Process," 1995, cited in Brad Sears, Nan D. Hunter, and Christy Mallory, "Documenting Discrimination on the Basis of Sexual Orientation and Gender Identity in State Employment," Williams Institute, 2009, http://williamsinstitute.law.ucla.edu/research/workplace/documenting-discrimina-tion-on-the-basis-of-sexual-orientation-and-gender-identity-in-state-employment/ (accessed January 27, 2014).

5. Tony Perkins, "LGBT Issues Kerry the Day," Family Research Council, January 9, 2017, http://www.frc.org/get.cfm?i=WA17A14&f=WU17A05 (accessed January 9, 2017).

6. Craig Rimmerman, *The Lesbian and Gay Movements: Assimilation or Liberation?* (Boulder, CO: Westview Press, 2007).

7. GLIFAA, "LGBT + Pride in Foreign Affairs Agencies," no date, https://glifaa.org/ (accessed June 13, 2017).

8. Sara E. Farber, "Presidential Promises and the Uniting American Families Act: Bringing Same-Sex Immigration Rights to the United States," *Boston College Third World Law Journal* 30:2 (2010): 339–40.

9. Dennis Jett, "Why Are There So Few Openly Gay Ambassadors?," *Washington Post*, July 28, 2013, http://www.washingtonpost.com/opinions/why-have-there-been-so-few-openly-gay-ambassadors/2013/07/26/5e7a4694-e8c5-11e2-8f22-de4bd2a2bd39_story.html (accessed July 28, 2013).

10. US Department of State, "The Department of State's Accomplishments Promoting the Human Rights of Lesbian, Gay, Bisexual, and Transgender People," December 6, 2011, http://www.state.gov/r/pa/prs/ps/2011/12/178341.htm (accessed July 1, 2013).

11. US Department of State, "Meet U.S. Ambassador to the OSCE Daniel Baer," YouTube, September 12, 2013, http://www.youtube.com/watch?v=oOLCp3Hx-n4 (accessed December 7, 2013).

12. Michael K. Lavers, "New Group for LGBT Staffers Forms," *Washington Blade*, January 19, 2015, http://www.washingtonblade.com/2015/01/19/new-group-lgbt-embassy-staffers-forms/ (accessed November 20, 2015).

13. Cynthia Burack, field notes, Pride @ State, US Department of State, Washington, DC, June 19, 2013.

14. Stuart Eizenstat, "Statement Before the House Banking Committee, Washington, DC, February 9, 2000," State Department, 2000, http://www.state.gov/1997-2001-NOPDFS/policy_remarks/2000/000209_eizenstat_hbc.html (accessed May 4, 2015).

15. Greg Bradsher, "Turning History into Justice: Holocaust-Era Assets Records, Research, and Restitution March 1996–March 2001," National Archives, April 19, 2001, http://www.archives.gov/research/holocaust/articles-and-papers/turning-history-into-justice.html (accessed April 29, 2015).

16. Philip Staal, *Settling the Account* (Bloomington, IN: iUniverse, 2015), 262–63.

17. US Department of State, "U.S. Department of State Office of the Spokesman Press Statement: Relief for Neediest Holocaust Survivors in Eastern Europe and Former Soviet Union," March 29, 1999, http://www.state.gov/1997-2001-NOPDFS// briefings/statements/1999/ps990329c.html (accessed December 29, 2014).

18. Gay History Projects, "History: The Pink Triangle Coalition," no date, http://kmlink.home.xs4all.nl/07gayhistory/03linkstogayresources/pinktrianglecoalition.htm (accessed June 25, 2013).

19. Pink Triangle Coalition, "*Cy Pres* Allocation Proposal," December 2003,) http://www.swissbankclaims.com/pdfs_eng/PinkTriangleCoalitionEXHIBITS%5BL ambda%5DENG_0076_059.pdf (accessed May 4, 2015).

20. A former academic political scientist, Davis is a scholar of international relations whose academic research focused on Germany and German–Polish relations and the author of *The Art of Economic Persuasion: Positive Incentives and German Economic Diplomacy* (Ann Arbor: University of Michigan Press, 2000). She has served as a US government representative for the human rights of women and other marginalized groups. Before she engaged in international SOGI advocacy, Davis worked on documentation and advocacy of human rights abuses in closed societies such as Russia and post-Soviet nations, as well as in postconflict nations such as Kosovo.

21. Patricia Davis, interview by the author, US State Department, Washington, DC, April 15, 2014.

22. The name of Magnus Hirschfeld's foundation,Institut für Sexualwissenschaft, is also translated as Institute for the Study of Sexuality.

23. Information about this breakdown of funds was documented at one time in a Pink Triangle Coalition "History" web page that no longer exists. Clinton Glenn and Braden Scott relied on this web page in their article, "The Homosexual and State Repression in the Rise of National Socialism: Rupturing the Discursive Framework of Provenance Research," *CUJAH: Concordia Undergraduate Journal of Art History*, http://cujah.org/past-volumes/volume-x/essay-10-volume-10/ (accessed April 28, 2015). The information remains available in affidavits submitted in Holocaust Victims Assets Litigation. See "Affidavit of Julie R. Dorf in support of Joint Objection and Proposal of the Pink Triangle Coalition" and "Proposal for a *Cy Pres* Allocation for the Support and Commemoration of Homosexual Victims of Nazi Persecution, Education and Research on the Fate of Homosexuals in Nazi Germany, and the Prevention of Human Rights Violations on the Basis of Sexual Orientation," December 2003, http://www.swissbankclaims.com/pdfs_eng/PinkTrian gleCoalitionEXHIBITS%5BLambda%5DENG_0076_059.pdf (accessed May 4, 2015).

24. Pink Triangle Coalition, "Proposal for a *Cy Pres* Allocation for Homosexual Victims of the Nazis (Corrected Version)," August 2, 2001, http://www.hirschfeld. in-berlin.de/entschaedigen/cy_pres_11_01.pdf (accessed December 29, 2014).

25. In re Holocaust Victims Assets Litigation: Pink Triangle Coalition, Karl Lange and Pierre Seel, Interested-Party-Appellants, September 9, 2005, https://law. resource.org/pub/us/case/reporter/F3/424/424.F3d.158.html (accessed May 4, 2015).

26. Chris Deliso, "On Ninth Anniversary of Macedonian President Trajkovski's Death, New Details Emerge," Balkanalysis, February 26, 2013, http://www.balkanalysis.com/blog/2013/02/26/on-ninth-anniversary-of-macedonian-president-trajkovskis-death-new-details-emerge/ (accessed November 2, 2015).

27. US Department of State, "Marking Policy," no date, https://www.statebuy.state.gov/fa/Pages/MarkingPolicy.aspx (accessed July 9, 2015).

28. Kerri Houston, "The State Department Works for the American Left in Macedonia," *National Review*, January 6, 2004, http://www.nationalreview.com/article/209033/diplomatic-missteps-kerri-houston (accessed May 24, 2015). The *National Review* article was later reposted to the white supremacist website Stormfront.org.

29. *Advocate*, "U.S. Rebukes Gay Rights Group in Macedonia," January 10, 2004, http://www.advocate.com/news/2004/01/10/us-rebukes-gay-rights-group-macedonia-10944 (accessed November 2, 2015).

30. Deliso, "On Ninth Anniversary of Macedonian President Trajkovski's Death."

31. Ana Petruseva, "Macedonian Gays Come Out From Shadows," Institute for War and Peace Reporting, no date, https://iwpr.net/global-voices/macedonian-gays-come-out-from-shadows (accessed May 25, 2015).

32. US Government, "The United States President's Emergency Plan for AIDS Relief," PEPFAR, no date, http://www.pepfar.gov/ (accessed June 2, 2013).

33. John King and Brianna Keilar, "State Department Official Resigns over 'D.C. Madam,'" CNN, April 28, 2007, http://www.cnn.com/2007/POLITICS/04/27/dc.madam/index.html?eref=onion (accessed June 4, 2016).

34. Mark Dybul, "Lessons Learned from PEPFAR," *Journal of Acquired Immune Deficiency Syndrome* 52:1 (2009): 12–13. A physician, Dybul became Executive Director of the Global Fund to Fight AIDS, Tuberculosis and Malaria in 2013.

35. USA.Gov, "The United States President's Emergency Plan for AIDS Relief: Strategy," PEPFAR, no date, http://www.pepfar.gov/about/strategy/ (accessed November 30, 2015).

36. Scott H. Evertz, "How Ideology Trumped Science: Why PEPFAR Has Failed to Meet its Potential," Center for American Progress, July 2010, https://www.americanprogress.org/issues/healthcare/report/2010/01/13/7214/how-ideology-trumped-science/ (accessed July 12, 2016).

37. On heterosexism, see Gregory M. Herek, "The Context of Anti-Gay Violence: Notes on Cultural and Psychological Heterosexism," *Journal of Interpersonal Violence* 5:3 (1990); Lauren Berlant and Michael Warner, "Sex in Public," *Critical Inquiry* 24 (1998): 548.

38. Sonia Corrêa, Rosalind Petchesky, and Richard Parker, *Sexuality, Health and Human Rights* (New York: Routledge, 2008), 36.

39. Elaine M. Murphy, Margaret E. Greene, Alexandra Mihailovic, and Peter Olupot-Olupot, "Was the ABC Approach (Abstinence, Being Faithful, Using Condoms) Responsible for Uganda's Decline in HIV?," *PLoS* (September 12, 2006),

http://journals.plos.org/plosmedicine/article?id=10.1371/journal.pmed.0030379 (accessed December 1, 2015).

40. Sebastian Krueger, "A Striking Defeat for U.S. Government's Anti-Prostitution Pledge," Open Society Foundations, February 2, 2015, https://www.opensocietyfoundations.org/voices/striking-defeat-us-government-s-anti-prostitution-pledge (accessed November 30, 2015).

41. Dietrich, "The Politics of PEPFAR," 291.

42. Anne Schneider and Helen Ingram, "Social Construction of Target Populations: Implications for Politics and Policy," *American Political Science Review* 87:2 (1993): 334–47.

43. Gregory B. Lewis, Marc A. Rogers, and Kenneth Sherrill, "Lesbian, Gay, and Bisexual Voters in the 2000 U.S. Presidential Election," *Politics and Policy* 39:5 (2011): 655–77.

44. Roper Center for Public Opinion Research, "How Groups Voted in 2000," 2016, http://ropercenter.cornell.edu/polls/us-elections/how-groups-voted/how-groups-voted-2000/ (accessed July 23, 2016).

45. For the 2008 election, see Roper Center for Public Opinion Research, "How Groups Voted in 2008," 2016, http://ropercenter.cornell.edu/polls/us-elections/how-groups-voted/how-groups-voted-2008/ (accessed June 7, 2016). For the 2012 election, see Micah Cohen, "Gay Vote Seen as Crucial in Obama's Victory," *New York Times*, November 15, 2012, http://fivethirtyeight.blogs.nytimes.com/2012/11/15/gay-vote-seen-as-crucial-in-obamas-victory/?_r=0 (accessed June 7, 2016).

46. Dana Milbank, "Vice President Biden's Gay Marriage Gaffe Is Mess for White House," *Washington Post*, May 7, 2012, https://www.washingtonpost.com/opinions/2012/05/07/gIQAOzFw8T_story.html (accessed July 8, 2016).

47. David Axelrod, *Believer: My Forty Years in Politics* (New York: Penguin Press, 2015).

48. Jeremy Diamond and Eric Bradner, "Obama: Axelrod 'Mixing Up' Gay Marriage Stance," CNN, February 11, 2015, http://www.cnn.com/2015/02/10/politics/obama-gay-marriage-axelrod/ (accessed June 18, 2016).

49. Evertz, "How Ideology Trumped Science."

50. Council for Global Equality, "US President's Emergency Plan for AIDS Relief (PEPFAR) Releases MSM Technical Guidance," May 19, 2011, http://globalequality.wordpress.com/2011/05/19/u-s-president%E2%80%99s-emergency-plan-for-aids-relief-pepfar-releases-msm-technical-guidance/ (accessed July 20, 2013), http://www.pepfar.gov/documents/organization/164010.pdf.

51. Office of the Global AIDS Coordinator, "Technical Guidance on Combination HIV Prevention," PEPFAR, May 2011, http://www.pepfar.gov/documents/organization/164010.pdf (accessed July 12, 2016).

52. A statement with links to the "Updated Gender Strategy" and other reports and data is available at US State Department, "PEPFAR: Addressing Gender and HIV/AIDS," PEPFAR, March 7, 2014, http://www.pepfar.gov/press/223084.htm (accessed July 1, 2014).

53. The online title is "Bush AIDS Policies Shadow Obama in Africa," *Washington Post*, June 30, 2013, https://www.washingtonpost.com/world/africa/bush-aids-policies-shadow-obama-in-africa/2013/06/30/0c8e023c-e1ac-11e2-aef3-339619eab080_story.html (accessed June 11, 2016).

54. Albert Ogle, "African Architect of Homophobia Supported by PEPFAR? An Open Letter to U.S. Secretary of State John Kerry," SDGLN, June 7, 2013, http://sdgln.com/social/2013/06/07/rgod2-african-architect-homophobia-supported-pepfar (accessed January 2, 2014).

55. See David F. Schmitz and Vanessa Walker, "Jimmy Carter and the Foreign Policy of Human Rights: The Development of a Post–Cold War Foreign Policy," *Diplomatic History* 28:1 (2004): 113–43. Schmitz and Walker make a case that the Carter administration's integration of human rights into US foreign policy was more successful, and less naive, than critics have usually allowed.

56. The phenomenon is also referred to as "clientism" and "clientelism." Clair Apodaca, *Understanding U.S. Human Rights Policy: A Paradoxical Legacy* (New York: Routledge, 2006), 14; Robert W. Jackman, *Power without Force: The Political Capacity of Nation-States* (Ann Arbor: University of Michigan Press, 1993), 91.

57. Foreign Service Institute, "Protocol for the Modern Diplomat," State Department, 2013, http://www.state.gov/documents/organization/176174.pdf (accessed June 18, 2016).

58. Apodaca, *Understanding U.S. Human Rights Policy*, 29–51.

59. Debra Liang-Fenton, "Conclusion: What Works?," in Debra Liang-Fenton, ed., *Implementing U.S. Human Rights Policy* (Washington, DC: US Institute of Peace Press, 2004), 440.

60. US State Department, *Country Reports on Human Rights Practices, Volume I* (Washington, DC: US Government Printing Office, 2010), 1679.

61. US State Department, *Country Reports on Human Rights Practices, Volume II: Europe and Eurasia, Near East and North Africa* (Washington, DC: US Government Printing Office, 2012), xxiv. Although a hard copy of this volume was printed in 2012, the reports were prepared in 2010 for human rights conditions in 2009.

62. US State Department, *Country Reports on Human Rights Practices, Volume II*, 1223.

63. US State Department, "2009 Human Rights Report: Introduction," March 11, 2010, http://www.state.gov/j/drl/rls/hrrpt/2009/frontmatter/135936.htm (accessed June 7, 2016).

64. Amnesty International United Kingdom, *Breaking the Silence: Human Rights Violations Based on Sexual Orientation* (London: Amnesty, 1997).

65. Edward R. McMahon, "Herding Cats and Sheep: Assessing State and Regional Behavior in the Universal Peer Review Mechanism of the United Nations Human Rights Council," UPR, 2010.

66. A link to a PDF document of the report can be found at Council for Global Equality, "United States Accepts UN Recommendations for Improving LGBT

Rights at Home," March 10, 2011, https://globalequality.wordpress.com/2011/03/10/united-states-accepts-un-recommendations-for-improving-lgbt-rights-at-home/ (accessed February 17, 2016).

67. US State Department, "UPR Recommendations Supported by the U.S. Government," June 2014, http://www.state.gov/j/drl/upr/recommendations/index.htm (accessed July 8, 2016). Emphases and formatting in the original.

68. Brett D. Schaefer and Steven Groves, "U.S. Targeted by Human Rights Abusers at Its Universal Periodic Review," Heritage Foundation, November 5, 2010, http://www.heritage.org/research/reports/2010/11/us-targeted-by-human-rights-abusers-at-its-universal-periodic-review (accessed February 17, 2016).

69. A link to the full statement and a press release can be found at Andrew Park and Adam P. Romero, "Universal Periodic Review of the United States: Subgroup on Civil Rights and Racial and Ethnic Discrimination Issues," Williams Institute, July 8, 2014, http://williamsinstitute.law.ucla.edu/research/international/upr-review-wi-statement-jul-2014/ (accessed July 23, 2016).

70. Andrew Park, "By Foregoing a National Human Rights Institution, the United States is Foregoing an Opportunity to Identify Discrimination against LGBT People," Williams Institute, July 8, 2014, http://williamsinstitute.law.ucla.edu/wp-content/uploads/NHRI.pdf (accessed July 23, 2016).

71. US State Department, "UPR Report of the United States of America," February 6, 2015, http://www.state.gov/j/drl/upr/2015/237250.htm (accessed July 12, 2016)

72. SOGIE is an alternative for SOGI; the final "E" stands for "expression."

73. Flyer, ILGA World UPR Side Event, ILGA World Conference, Bangkok, Thailand, November 29, 2017.

74. Dodo Karsay, Helene Ramos Dos Santos, and Diana Carolina Prado Mosquera, "Sexual Orientation, Gender Identity and Expression, and Sex Characteristics, at the Universal Periodic Review," ARC International, IBHRI, and ILGA World, November 2016.

75. "Freedom House Announces New Program to Help LGBTI People Under Threat," Council for Global Equality, December 17, 2012, https://globalequality.wordpress.com/2012/12/17/freedom-house-announces-new-program-to-help-lgbti-people-under-threat/ (accessed August 10, 2016). The "new program" announced in December 2012 is Dignity for All, a program of the Global Equality Fund. However, CGE refers to Dignity joining Lifeline as a program that supports the human rights of LGBTI people. Most public references to Lifeline after its founding didn't modify the broad designation "human rights defenders" with more specific allusions to threatened identity groups.

76. Patricia Davis, interview by the author, US State Department, Washington, DC, February 29, 2016. Michael Posner was Founding Executive Director and later the President of Human Rights First. Posner is currently the Jerome Kohlberg Professor of Ethics and Finance in New York University's Stern School of Business.

77. US State Department, "Joint Statement on the Fifth Annual Lifeline: Embattled Civil Society Organizations Assistance Fund Donor Steering Committee Meeting," September 28, 2015, http://www.state.gov/r/pa/prs/ps/2015/09/247426. htm (accessed August 1, 2016).

78. Michael Posner, "The Lifeline: Embattled NGOs Assistance Fund," HumanRights.Gov, September 26, 2011, http://www.humanrights.gov/dyn/the-lifeline-embattled-ngos-assistance-fund.html (accessed July 24, 2016).

79. ICSSI Baghdad, "Embattled Civil Society Organizations (CSO) Assistance Fund," April 26, 2015, http://www.iraqicivilsociety.org/archives/4100 (accessed August 1, 2016). An epigraph at the top of the web page quotes a "Pakistani CSO representative" on Lifeline funding for "women's rights and . . . empowerment" in Pakistan.

80. Vanessa K. Burrows, "Executive Orders: Issuance and Revocation," Congressional Research Service, 2010, http://intelligencelaw.com/files/pdf/law_library/crs/RS20846_3-25-2010.pdf (accessed May 17, 2015).

81. Gregory Korte, "Obama Issues 'Executive Orders by Another Name,'" *USA Today*, December 17, 2014, http://www.usatoday.com/story/news/politics/2014/12/16/obama-presidential-memoranda-executive-orders/20191805/ (accessed May 17, 2015).

82. See Jasbir K. Puar, *Terrorist Assemblages: Homonationalism in Queer Times* (Durham, NC: Duke University Press, 2007).

83. See Tom Malinowski, "Stopping the Flow of Corruption," *Washington Post*, December 25, 2014, https://www.washingtonpost.com/opinions/tom-malinowski-stopping-the-flow-of-corruption/2014/12/25/45099118-8a06-11e4-a085-34e9b-9f09a58_story.html (accessed July 20, 2016).

## Chapter 2

1. This title of this section is a variation on two others: first, the Las Vegas tourism slogan that "what happens here, stays here." The second, which plays on the Vegas theme, was delivered by a participant at the Conference to Advance the Human Rights of and Promote Inclusive Development for Lesbian, Gay, Bisexual, and Transgender (LGBT) Persons (US State Department, November 12–14, 2014). The speaker, who noted that "what happens in Geneva, stays in Geneva," was making a point about the relative ineffectiveness of official pronouncements in elite venues on circumstances for vulnerable LGBTQ people on the ground. While this view has merit, I would like to examine more closely the meanings generated by a particular official statement and a range of political and intellectual responses to it within the United States.

2. See Mira Patel, "The Little-Known Origin of 'Gay Rights Are Human Rights,'" *Advocate*, December 8, 2015, http://www.advocate.com/commentary/2015/12/08/little-known-origin-gay-rights-are-human-rights (accessed December 10, 2015).

3. US State Department Virtual Reading Room, "LGBT Speech," December 12, 2011/October 30, 2015, http://foia.state.gov/search/results.aspx (accessed January 27, 2016).

4. Jesse Bernstein, interview by the author, State Department, Washington, DC, October 3, 2016. Bernstein earned an MS from the London School of Economics and Political Science in 2008. Before he became a program officer at the State Department, he interned in Human Rights Watch's LGBT Human Rights Program, served as a protection officer in the UN's Refugee Agency, and was senior associate in the Refugee Protection Program at Human Rights First. He is the author of reports and working papers on migrants and refugees, and he credits his work with LGBT refugees for helping him develop an intersectional approach to human rights advocacy.

5. Jonathan Capehart, "Clinton's Geneva Accord: 'Gay Rights are Human Rights,'" *Washington Post*, December 7, 2011, http://www.washingtonpost.com/blogs/post-partisan/post/clintons-geneva-accord-gay-rights-are-human-rights/2011/03/04/gIQAPUipcO_blog.html (accessed May 24, 2013).

6. US Department of State, "Former Secretary Clinton's Town Halls and Townterviews," no date, http://www.state.gov/secretary/townhalls/ (accessed June 24, 2013).

7. ILGA, "LGBT Activists from Around the World React to Secretary Clinton's Speech," December 9, 2011, http://ilga.org/ilga/en/article/niy2xSu1jX (accessed March 6, 2014).

8. US Department of State, "Meeting with LGBT Activists and Supporters from the Diplomatic Corps," no date, http://www.state.gov/secretary/rm/2011/12/178389.htm (accessed August 18, 2013).

9. Hillary Clinton, "Secretary Clinton's Historic Speech on LGBT Human Rights—Gay Rights are Human Rights" YouTube, December 6, 2011, https://www.youtube.com/watch?v=MudnsExyV78 (accessed November 25, 2014).

10. Sacvan Bercovitch, *The American Jeremiad* (Madison: University of Wisconsin Press, 1978), 16.

11. See David Gutterman, *Prophetic Politics: Christian Social Movements and American Democracy* (Ithaca, NY: Cornell University Press, 2005).

12. Hannah Arendt, *The Human Condition* (Chicago: University of Chicago Press, 1958), 192.

13. I use psychoanalytic thought to perform this particular reading of reparation in the cases of Christian authors and speakers Tony and Peggy Campolo. See Cynthia Burack, *Tough Love: Sexuality, Compassion, and the Christian Right* (Albany: State University of New York Press, 2014), 161–67.

14. Hillary Rodham Clinton, *Living History* (New York: Simon and Schuster, 2003). See also Senator Clinton's remarks on Roosevelt in interview material in Mary Lambert, *14 Women* (Vertical Films, 2007).

15. In the transcript to the remarks, it appears that the words "given bestowed" in paragraph seven represent a choice yet to be made about which

word will be used in the speech. In delivering the remarks, Clinton used both. I add a comma to my version of the transcript for clarity.

16. Dawne Moon, *God, Sex, and Politics: Homosexuality and Everyday Theologies* (Chicago: University of Chicago Press, 2004). See especially chapter 8: "Gay Pain and Politics."

17. Shane Phelan, *Sexual Strangers: Gays, Lesbians, and Dilemmas of Citizenship* (Philadelphia: Temple University Press, 2001), 94. Rebecca Wanzo makes such an argument about the suffering of African American girls and women in *The Suffering Will Not Be Televised: African American Women and Sentimental Political Storytelling* (Albany: State University of New York Press, 2009).

18. Satyam Khanna, "Ahmadinijad Denies Existence of Gays in Iran," Think-Progress, September 24, 2007, http://thinkprogress.org/politics/2007/09/24/16472/ahmadinejad-denies-existence-of-gays-in-iran/ (accessed July 6, 2013).

19. Nazila Fathi, "Despite Denials, Gays Insist They Exist, if Quietly, in Iran," *New York Times*, September 30, 2007, http://www.nytimes.com/2007/09/30/world/middleeast/30gays.html?_r=0 (accessed July 6, 2013).

20. Kathy Lally, "Putin: Gay People Will Be Safe at Olympics if They 'Leave Kids Alone,'" *Washington Post*, January 17, 2014, http://www.washingtonpost.com/world/putin-gays-will-be-safe-at-olympics-if-they-leave-kids-alone/2014/01/17/e6f8c47e-7f7d-11e3-95c6-0a7aa80874bc_story.html (accessed February 7, 2014).

21. Hannah Arendt, *Lectures on Kant's Political Philosophy*, ed. Ronald Beiner (Chicago: University of Chicago Press, 1982); see also Burack, *Tough Love* for discussion of the differences between empathy and representative thinking.

22. Seyla Benhabib, *Dignity in Adversity: Human Rights in Troubled Times* (Cambridge: Polity Press, 2011), 15. Benhabib borrows the concept of jurisgenerativity from Robert Cover.

23. Elizabeth Baisley, "Reaching the Tipping Point?: Emerging International Human Rights Norms Pertaining to Sexual Orientation and Gender Identity," *Human Rights Quarterly* 38:1 (2016): 159.

24. Within a period of three years, the now-defunct organization Exodus International went from counseling same-sex-attracted people that "change is possible" to pointing out that "the opposite of homosexuality isn't heterosexuality—it's holiness." For an exposition of this transformation, see Burack, *Tough Love* chapter 1.

25. Kath Browne and Catherine J. Nash, "Resisting LGBT Rights Where 'We Have Won': Canada and Great Britain," *Journal of Human Rights* 13 (2014): 322–36.

26. Capehart, "Clinton's Geneva Accord."

27. Steven Lee Myers and Helene Cooper, "U.S. to Aid Gay Rights Abroad, Obama and Clinton Say," *New York Times*, December 6, 2011, http://www.nytimes.com/2011/12/07/world/united-states-to-use-aid-to-promote-gay-rights-abroad.html?pagewanted=all&_r=0 (accessed May 24, 2013).

28. Human Rights First, "LGBT Rights Are Human Rights, Clinton Says," December 6, 2011, http://www.humanrightsfirst.org/press-release/lgbt-rights-are-human-rights-clinton-says (accessed May 24, 2013).

29. Amnesty International USA, "A Welcome Step in Respecting and Protecting LGBT Rights Around the World," December 8, 2011, http://www.amnestyusa.org/news/news-item/a-welcome-step-in-respecting-and-protecting-lgbt-rights-around-the-world (accessed May 24, 2013); The Editors, "Clinton to United Nations: 'Gay Rights Are Human Rights,'" Amnesty USA, December 8, 2011. Emphasis in the original.

30. Julie Dorf, "An Unforgettable Night in Geneva," Huffington Post, December 20, 2011, http://www.huffingtonpost.com/julie-dorf/hillary-clinton-gay-rights-speech_b_1161709.html (accessed August 19, 2013).

31. Task Force Blog, "White House Issues Presidential Memorandum and Secretary Clinton Makes Historic Speech on the Human Rights of LGBT People Worldwide," December 6, 2011, http://thetaskforceblog.org/2011/12/06/white-house-issues-presidential-memorandum-and-secretary-clinton-makes-historic-speech-on-the-human-rights-of-lgbt-people-worldwide/ (accessed May 24, 2013).

32. Dani Heffernan, "Obama Administration Addresses Need for Protections and Equality for LGBT People Worldwide," GLAAD, December 7, 2011, https://www.glaad.org/blog/obama-administration-addresses-need-protections-and-equality-lgbt-people-worldwide (accessed May 24, 2013).

33. The Editors, "A Global Gay-Rights Crusade," National Review Online, December 10, 2011, http://www.nationalreview.com/articles/285416/global-gay-rights-crusade-editors (accessed February, 4, 2014).

34. Michael Brown, "Hillary Clinton's 'Gay Rights' Speech and American Hypocrisy," Townhall, December 15, 2011, http://townhall.com/columnists/michael-brown/2011/12/15/hillary_clintons_gay_rights_speech_and_american_hypocrisy/page/full (accessed February 4, 2014).

35. Amanda Winkler, "World Reacts to Clinton's Pro-Gay Speech," Christian Post, December 9, 2011, http://m.christianpost.com/news/world-reacts-to-clintons-pro-gay-rights-speech-64554/ (accessed August 19, 2013).

36. Brian Tashman, "Liberty Counsel, Family Research Council Enraged by Move to Consider Gay Rights in Foreign Aid," People for the American Way, December 6, 2011, http://www.rightwingwatch.org/content/liberty-counsel-enraged-move-consider-gay-rights-foreign-aid (accessed March 3, 2014).

37. See Cynthia Burack, "Christian Right Leader Lauds Homophobic Ugandan Dictator," Salon, December 7, 2012, http://www.salon.com/2012/12/07/christian_right_leader_lauds_homophobic_ugandan_dictator/ (accessed December 7, 2012).

38. Leilani Dowell, "Clinton Says U.S. Will Campaign for Gay Rights," Workers World, December 15, 2011, http://www.workers.org/2011/us/clinton_1222/ (accessed March 5, 2014).

39. Jim Downs, "Hillary Clinton Is Not Helping the Gay Civil Rights Movement," *Huffington Post*, December 7, 2011, http://www.huffingtonpost.com/jim-downs/hillary-clinton-gay-speech_b_1133887.html (accessed February 6, 2014). A direct response to Downs on AMERICAblog clarifies the cleavage between liberal and left-progressive/critical humanist reactions to the speech: John Aravosis, "Leave Hillary Alone: Her UN Speech Was Freaking Great," AMERICAblog, December 7, 2011, http://americablog.com/2011/12/leave-hillary-alone-her-un-speech-was-freaking-great.html (accessed February 6, 2014).

40. Dean Spade, "Under the Cover of Gay Rights," *NYU Review of Law and Social Change* 37 (2013): 87.

41. Jesse Bernstein, interview with the author, US State Department, Washington, DC, October 3, 2016.

42. Jeffrey C. Isaac, "Hannah Arendt on Human Rights and the Limits of Exposure, or Why Noam Chomsky Is Wrong about the Meaning of Kosovo," *Social Research* 69:2 (2002): 519–20.

43. Isaac, "Hannah Arendt on Human Rights and the Limits of Exposure," 519.

44. Thomas F. Pettigrew and Linda R. Tropp, "Allport's Intergroup Contact Hypothesis: Its History and Influence," in John F. Dovidio, Peter Glick, and Laurie A. Budman, eds., *On the Nature of Prejudice: Fifty Years after Allport* (Malden, MA: Blackwell, 2005), 264.

45. Ludwik Fleck, *Genesis and Development of a Scientific Fact* (Chicago: University of Chicago Press, 1979), 39.

46. Randall Balmer, *Thy Kingdom Come: An Evangelical's Lament* (New York: Basic Books, 2006), 8.

47. In fact, some of this research focuses on links between political perspectives, and human biology and evolution. See, for example, John R. Hibbing, Kevin B. Smith, and John R. Alford, *Predisposed: Liberals, Conservatives, and the Biology of Political Differences* (New York: Routledge, 2014); Avi Tuschman, *Our Political Nature: The Evolutionary Origins of What Divides Us* (Amherst, NY: Prometheus, 2013).

48. In research on "the partisan brain," psychologist Drew Westen and his colleagues used brain scans to map neural activity that occurs when political "data clash with desire." Westen's team discovered that "our brains have a remarkable capacity to find their way toward convenient truths—even if they're not all that true" and that education and political sophistication are no protection from "emotion-driven cognitive distortions." Drew Westen, *The Political Brain: The Role of Emotion in Deciding the Fate of the Nation* (New York: PublicAffairs, 2007), xi, 100.

49. Ian Ayres and William Eskridge, "U.S. Hypocrisy over Russia's Anti-Gay Laws," *Washington Post*, February 3, 2014, https://www.washingtonpost.com/opinions/us-hypocrisy-over-russias-anti-gay-laws/2014/01/31/3df0baf0-8548-11e3-

9dd4-e7278db80d86_story.html (accessed February 4, 2014). The title in the newspaper's hard copy was "America's Gay Hypocrisy."

50. Stern refers to the following academic article, which he links to in another essay on Russia: Oleg Kucheryavenko, Kirill Guskov, and Michael Walker, "Cost of Indulgence: Rise in Violence and Suicides among LGBT Youth in Russia," *Health and Human Rights Journal* (December 18, 2013), http://www.hhrjournal. org/2013/12/cost-of-indulgence-rise-in-violence-and-suicides-among-lgbt-youth-in-russia/ (accessed April 23, 2016).

51. Mark Joseph Stern, "Americans Aren't Hypocrites for Criticizing Russia's Homophobia," *Slate*, February 10, 2014, http://www.slate.com/blogs/out-ward/2014/02/10/americans_aren_t_hypocrites_to_criticize_russian_homophobia. html (accessed February 10, 2014).

52. The term "sexual strangers" is from Shane Phelan, *Sexual Strangers: Gays, Lesbians, and Dilemmas of Citizenship* (Philadelphia: Temple University Press, 2001).

53. Meredith L. Weiss and Michael J. Bosia, "Political Homophobia in Comparative Perspective," in *Global Homophobia: States, Movements, and the Politics of Oppression* (Champaign: University of Illinois Press, 2013), 18.

54. Elise Carlson-Rainer and Jacqueline Dufalla, "The Foreign Policy of LGBT Rights: Russia's Reaction and Resistance to US Policy," *Global Studies Journal* 9:4 (2016): 16.

## Chapter 3

1. US Department of State, "Global Equality Fund," no date, http://www. state.gov/globalequality/ (accessed June 17, 2013).

2. US Department of State, "About the Fund," no date, http://www.state. gov/globalequality/about/index.htm (accessed December 3, 2014).

3. The phrase is from Mira Patel, "The Little-Known Origin of 'Gay Rights Are Human Rights,'" *Advocate*, December 8, 2015, http://www.advocate. com/commentary/2015/12/08/little-known-origin-gay-rights-are-human-rights (accessed December 10, 2015). Davis and Bernstein provided other accounts of the formation of the GEF. See Patricia Davis, interview by the author, US State Department, Washington, DC, February 29, 2016; Jesse Bernstein, interview by the author, US State Department, Washington, DC, October 3, 2016.

4. The original designation for Berry's position when it was created in early 2015 was "LGBT Issues." The State Department has added intersex identity to the Special Envoy title and to "LGBT" as a term that references a marginalized population.

5. Jesse Bernstein, interview with the author, October 3, 2016.

6. US Department of State, "Bureau of Democracy, Human Rights and Labor Request for Proposals: Programs for Human Rights Documentation," March 4, 2015, http://www.state.gov/j/drl/p/238602.htm (accessed June 28, 2015).

7. US Department of State, "About the Fund," no date, http://www.state.gov/globalequality/about/index.htm (accessed August 3, 2015).

8. Freedom House, "About Us," https://freedomhouse.org/about-us#.VZA-w0Z9l-w (accessed June 27, 2015).

9. See US Department of State, "Fact Sheet: Global Equality Fund," HumanRights.gov, December 2015, http://www.humanrights.gov/dyn/fact-sheet/global-equality-fund/ (accessed January 2, 2015).

10. Deloitte provided this expertise and produced the GEF Annual Report 2015, published in early 2016. Among other categories, the Annual Report 2015 provides a GEF mission statement, data and graphics about SOGI-related risks and threats, and information about forms of support rendered by the GEF as well as GEF spending, both broken out by global regions. See US Department of State, "Global Equality Fund Annual Report 2015," June 23, 2016, http://www.state.gov/globalequality/releases/259029.htm (accessed July 14, 2016).

11. Patricia Davis, interview by the author, US State Department, Washington, DC, February 29, 2016.

12. US Government, Grants.gov, no date, http://www.grants.gov/ (accessed June 16, 2016).

13. US State Department, "DRLA-DRLAQM-16-074 The Global Equality Fund managed by Bureau of Democracy, Human Rights and Labor (DRL) Notice of Funding Opportunity (NOFO): Advancing Human Rights in the Pacific Islands," Grants.gov, 2016. http://www.grants.gov/web/grants/search-grants.html (accessed May 28, 2016).

14. US Department of State, "The Department of State's Accomplishments Promoting the Human Rights of Lesbian, Gay, Bisexual, and Transgender People," December 6, 2011, http://www.state.gov/r/pa/prs/ps/2011/12/178341.htm (accessed July 1, 2013).

15. The toolkit is not available to the public, and I was not able to acquire a copy.

16. Council for Global Equality, "Accessing U.S. Embassies: A Guide for LGBT Human Rights Defenders," 2012.

17. IGIHE, "U.S. Embassy and Rwanda Artists Celebrate LGBT Pride and Human Rights with Graffiti Show," June 25, 2014, http://en.igihe.com/news/u-s-embassy-and-rwandan-artists-celebrate-lgbt.html (accessed July 23, 2014).

18. Masaki Matsumoto, "Read Before You Write About LGBT Politics in Japan," Gimme A Queer Eye, May 1, 2013, http://gimmeaqueereye.org/entry/173 (accessed March 21, 2016).

19. Embassy of the United States Islamabad, Pakistan, "Embassy Islamabad Hosts GLBT Pride Celebration," June 26, 2011,= http://islamabad.usembassy.gov/pr_062611.html (accessed May 28, 2016).

20. The protests were widely reported; see Patrick Goodenough, "State Dep't Official Warns of Backlash in Promoting LGBT Rights Abroad," *CNS News*, April 17, 2014, http://www.cnsnews.com/news/article/patrick-goodenough/state-dep-t-official-warns-backlash-promoting-lgbt-rights-abroad (accessed May 28, 2016).

21. US State Department, "Gay, Lesbian, Bisexual and Transgender Pride Event Hosted by U.S. Embassy in Islamabad, Pakistan," July 8, 2011, http://www.state.gov/r/pa/prs/ps/2011/07/167864.htm (accessed May 10, 2016).

22. Paul Alster, "Gay Pride Flag Hoisted above US Embassy in Israel," FoxNews.com, June 14, 2014, http://www.foxnews.com/world/2014/06/14/gay-pride-flag-hoisted-above-us-embassy-in-israel.html (accessed June 20, 2014).

23. Todd Starnes, "Check Out What's Flying Over Our Embassy in Israel," FoxNews.com, no date, http://radio.foxnews.com/toddstarnes/top-stories/check-out-whats-flying-over-our-embassy-in-israel.html (accessed March 22, 2016); Steve Berman, "Gay Pride Flag Flies over US Embassy in Tel Aviv: Welcome to Sodom's New Headquarters," RedState, June 11, 2014, http://www.redstate.com/diary/lifeofgrace/2014/06/11/gay-pride-flag-flies-us-embassy-tel-aviv/ (accessed March 22, 2016).

24. Zach Noble, "American Embassy in Israel Does Something with a Flag It Has Never Done Before," *The Blaze*, June 11, 2014, http://www.theblaze.com/stories/2014/06/11/this-embassy-has-never-flown-these-flags-together-before/ (accessed March 22, 2016).

25. BBC News, "Jerusalem Gay Pride: Israel Teenage Stabbing Victim Dies," August 2, 2015, http://www.bbc.com/news/world-middle-east-33752111 (accessed March 22, 2016). I return to the significance of this domestic Israeli disagreement over sexual and gender minorities in chapter 5.

26. NPH stands for "no promotion of homosexuality," or "no promo homo" for short. The phrase often appears in debates over and justifications regarding the perceived propensity of same-sex-attracted people to proselytize their sexuality, especially to children.

27. Cynthia Burack, field notes, SOGI human rights meeting, State Department, Washington, DC, April 14, 2013.

28. Although the Anti-Homosexuality Act was quickly invalidated on a technical issue, many African human rights defenders continued to focus on it and similar pieces of anti-LGBTQ legislation. See Human Rights Awareness and Promotion Forum (HRAPF), "Beyond Quorum: Why the Anti-Homosexuality Act 2014 Was Unconstitutional," *Human Rights Advocate* 2 (March 2015): 1–51.

29. Other organizations that encouraged the administration to recall the ambassador were Health Gap, International HIV/AIDS Alliance, and TransAfrica (a US African American foreign policy organization).

30. Kapya Kaoma, "Warning: U.S. LGBTQ Organizations Falling into Uganda's Anti-Homosexuality Trap," Political Research, February 20, 2014, http://www.politicalresearch.org/2014/02/20/warning-u-s-lgbtq-organizations-falling-into-ugandas-anti-homosexuality-trap/# (accessed February 24, 2014).

31. Sida, "Study on Sida's Work on Human Rights of Lesbian, Gay, Bisexual, Transgender and Intersex Persons" 2014), 15.

32. Amsterdam Network, "The Amsterdam Network Guiding Principles (Version 1.1)," Scribd, February 3, 2016, http://www.scribd.com/doc/297759956/Amsterdam-Network-Guiding-Principles-Version-1-1#scribd (accessed March 18, 2016). A 2013 version of the Guiding Principles was labeled "Version 1.0."

33. Michael K. Lavers, "LGBT Activists Call for More Funding at Berlin Conference," *Washington Blade*, December 6, 2013, http://www.washingtonblade.com/2013/12/06/lgbt-activists-call-global-funding-berlin-conference/ (accessed March 18, 2016).

34. Like Bernstein, Ashforth had a career in human rights advocacy prior to entering government service. Ashforth holds an MS in organizational change management at the Milano School of International Affairs, Management, and Urban Policy at the New School and has been a transgender activist and community organizer. He worked in grants administration for the Arcus Foundation before he was recruited by the State Department for his work with the GEF. He has had a particular interest in securing grants and funding for marginalized communities—such as lesbians and transgender people—within the LGBTI coalition. Kerry Ashforth, interview with the author, US State Department, Washington, DC, July 28, 2016.

35. The Conference Participant Directory listed two other academic participants: Lee Badgett, professor of economics and Director of the Center for Public Policy and Administration at the University of Massachusetts Amherst, and Andrew Park, International Program Director at the Williams Institute, a research think tank for SOGI law and public policy located at the UCLA School of Law. Badgett is a Williams Distinguished Scholar at the institute.

36. Naming the third language in which simultaneous translation was provided might reveal more about the national or regional origins of activist presenters than they would choose to reveal publicly.

37. US State Department, "Key Outcomes from the Annual Conference to Advance the Human Rights of and Promote Inclusive Development for Lesbian, Gay, Bisexual, Transgender and Intersex Persons," November 21, 2014, http://www.state.gov/r/pa/prs/ps/2014/11/234331.htm (accessed November 21, 2014). For an explication of intersex human rights, see Morgan Carpenter, "The Human Rights of Intersex People: Addressing Harmful Practices and Rhetoric of Change," *Reproductive Health Matters* 47:24 (2016): 74–84.

38. Julie Dorf, Council for Global Equality, email to conference participants, December 16, 2014.

39. Representatives of civil society and nongovernmental donors, "Civil Society and Non-State Donor Recommendations from the Conference to Advance the Human Rights of and Promote the Inclusive Development for Lesbian, Gay,

Bisexual, Transgender (and Intersex) Persons," Washington, DC, November, 2014 (December 16, 2014). Emphases in the original.

40. "Equal Rights Coalition: Founding Principles," LGBTI Montevideo, July 13, 2016, http://www.lgbtimontevideo2016.org/admin/files/lgbtimontevideo2016/ upload/files/Equal%20Rights%20Coalition%20-%20Founding%20Principles%20 ENG.pdf; "Equal Rights Coalition: Fact Sheet," Montevideo LGBTI, no date, http://www.lgbtimontevideo2016.org/admin/files/lgbtimontevideo2016/upload/files/ Factsheet%20Equal%20Rights%20Coalition%20ENG.pdf (accessed July 30, 2016).

41. See Louise Diamond and John McDonald, *Multi-track Diplomacy: A Systems Approach to Peace* (West Hartford, CT: Kumarian, 1996).

42. Information in this section is drawn from 2013 conference material, including the conference program; an interview with Patricia Davis conducted by the author on April 15, 2014, US State Department, Washington, DC; and other sources as identified.

43. Benetech, "Martus: The Global Social Justice Monitoring System, Resources: Press Room," Martus, 2013, https://www.martus.org/resources/press_ room.shtml#pr-2010-2 (accessed July 20, 2013).

44. Melissa Hope Ditmore and Dan Allman, "An Analysis of the Implementation of PEPFAR's Anti-Prostitution Pledge and Its Implications for Successful HIV Prevention among Organizations Working with Sex Workers" *Journal of the International AIDS Society* 16:1 (2013): 1–13; Kari Lerum, Kiesha McCurtis, Penelope Saunders, and Stéphanie Wahab, "Using Human Rights to Hold the US Accountable for Its Anti–Sex Trafficking Agenda: The Universal Periodic Review and New Directions for US Policy," *Anti-Trafficking Review* 1 (2012), http://www. antitraffickingreview.org/index.php/atrjournal/article/view/24/42 (accessed May 13, 2017).

45. The 2013 and 2015 conferences were conducted mostly in English, and the 2015 conference featured simultaneous translation for speakers of French, Portuguese, and an indigenous African language. The conference programs for both meetings provided text in English and French.

46. For material in this section I rely on my field notes, ASOGIHRO Conference, Africa, 2015.

47. I was not able to obtain an accurate count of conference registrations, but some attendees estimated attendance at between 200 and 250.

48. US Department of State, "Marking Policy," no date, https://www.statebuy. state.gov/fa/Pages/MarkingPolicy.aspx (accessed July 9, 2015).

49. Gita Sen, Piroska Östlin, and Asha George, "Unequal, Unfair, Ineffective, and Inefficient. Gender Inequity in Health: Why it Exists and How We Can Change It. Final Report to the WHO Commission on Social Determinants of Health," World Health Organization, 2007, http://cdrwww.who.int/social_determinants/resources/csdh_media/wgekn_final_report_07.pdf (accessed May 10, 2016).

50. USAID is an unusual "independent agency" because of its relationship to the State Department, but this appellation is applied to USAID by both agencies. See US State Department, "Department Organization," no date, http://www.state.gov/r/pa/ei/rls/dos/436.htm (accessed July 18, 2016).

51. USAID, "USAID and Department of State Strategic Plan," April 2, 2014, https://www.usaid.gov/documents/1868/usaid-and-department-state-joint-strategic-plan (accessed May 10, 2016); Committee on Evaluation of USAID Democracy Assistance Programs, Development, Security, and Cooperation, Policy and Global Affairs, National Research Council, *Improving Democracy Assistance: Building Knowledge through Evaluations and Research* (Washington, DC: National Academies Press, 2008), 57.

52. Todd Larson holds an MA in international studies and a law degree, and he taught international organizations at Hunter College in New York. He held a number of positions, including at the UN and as cochair of the board of directors of IGLHRC (now OutRight Action International). His work with the UN's Gay, Lesbian, and Bisexual Employees group in the 2000s led to early LGBT-affirming, internal policy initiatives at the UN. Todd Larson, "Moving Forward with USAID's LGBT Vision for Action," White House, July 14, 2014, https://www.whitehouse.gov/blog/2014/07/14/moving-forward-usaids-lgbt-vision-action (accessed July 18, 2016).

53. USAID, "About the U.S. Global Development Lab," May 2, 2016, https://www.usaid.gov/GlobalDevLab/about (accessed May 11, 2016).

54. USAID, "U.S. Global Development Lab," January 20, 2015, https://www.usaid.gov/who-we-are/organization/bureaus/us-global-development-lab (accessed May 11, 2016).

55. USAID, "U.S. Global Development Lab," (no date) https://www.usaid.gov/sites/default/files/documents/2496/CTP_Program_LGBTGlobalPartnership_Targeted%20Outreach_FINAL2.pdf (accessed May 11, 2016).

56. Todd Larson, email to the author, August 9, 2016.

57. Carolyn Lochhead, "U.S. to Begin Aiding LGBT Foreign Rights Groups," SFGate, April 8, 2013, http://blog.sfgate.com/politics/2013/04/08/u-s-to-begin-aiding-foreign-lgbt-groups/ (accessed July 30, 2016).

58. Michael K. Lavers, "US-Backed Indonesian Group Support anti-LGBT Crackdown," *Washington Blade*, August 16, 2016, http://www.washingtonblade.com/2016/08/26/us-backed-indonesian-group-supports-anti-lgbt-crackdown/ (accessed August 18, 2016).

59. Cynthia Burack, field notes, Pride @ State, Department of State, Washington, DC, June 19, 2013.

60. Prior to his appointment, Berry served as the US Consul General in Amsterdam. He was Consul General in Auckland, New Zealand, from 2009 to 2012, and from 2007 to 2009 he served as Deputy Chief of Mission of the US embassy in Kathmandu, Nepal. Berry has also served in Bangladesh, Egypt,

South Africa, and Uganda. He is a graduate of Bethany College and was a Rotary Graduate Scholar at the University of Adelaide, South Australia.

61. The briefing was sponsored by Rep. David Cicilline (D-RI), Rep. Chris Gibson (R-NY), Rep. Richard Hanna (R-NY), and Rep. John F. Tierney (D-MA).

62. Cynthia Burack, field notes, Briefing: The United States' Role in Generating Debate on LGBT Rights, Rayburn House of Representatives Office Building, Washington, DC, July 29, 2014.

63. Congress.gov, "S.302—International Human Rights Defense Act of 2015," no date, https://www.congress.gov/bill/114th-congress/senate-bill/302 (accessed January 20, 2016).

64. Nahal Toosi, "America's New LGBT Envoy," *Politico*, April 26, 2015, http://www.politico.com/story/2015/04/randy-berry-lgbt-envoy-state-department-117347 (accessed March 22, 2016).

65. On this criticism, see Princeton N. Lyman and Robert M. Beecroft, "Using Special Envoys in High-Stakes Conflict Diplomacy," US Institute of Peace, 2015.

66. Adebisi Alimi, "Why I Oppose the United States' Special Envoy for LGBT Human Rights," *Daily Beast*, March 10, 2015, http://www.thedailybeast.com/articles/2015/03/10/why-i-oppose-the-united-states-special-envoy-for-lgbt-human-rights.html (accessed March 11, 2015).

67. Randy Berry, interview by the author, US State Department, Washington, DC, December 22, 2016.

68. Vernon Davidson, "We Came to Listen and Talk, Not to Judge," *Jamaica Observer*, May 27, 2015, http://www.jamaicaobserver.com/news/-We-came-to-listen-and-talk--not-to-judge-_19019331 (accessed August 11, 2016).

69. Michael K. Lavers, "LGBT Advocates from Kyrgyzstan Visit D.C.," *Washington Blade*, March 2, 2016, http://www.washingtonblade.com/2016/03/02/lgbt-advocates-from-kyrgyzstan-visit-d-c/ (accessed June 4, 2016).

70. US Department of State, "Kyrgyz Republic 2015 Human Rights Report," 2015, http://www.state.gov/documents/organization/253179.pdf. (accessed August 11, 2016).

71. US Department of State, "Joint Statement on Australia-United States Dialogue in Support of the Human Rights of LGBTI Persons," October 14, 2016, http://www.state.gov/r/pa/prs/ps/2016/10/263153.htm (accessed October 16, 2016).

72. Angelia R. Wilson and Cynthia Burack, " 'Where Liberty Reigns and God Is Supreme': The Christian Right and the Tea Party Movements," *New Political Science* 34:2 (2012): 172–90.

## Chapter 4

1. Benjamin G. Bishin, Thomas J. Hayes, Matthew B. Incantalupo, and Charles Anthony Smith, "Opinion Backlash and Public Attitudes: Are Political

Advances in Gay Rights Counterproductive?," *American Journal of Political Science* 60:3 (2016): 639.

2. Lydia Bean and Brandon C. Martinez, "Evangelical Ambivalence toward Gays and Lesbians," *Sociology of Religion* 75:3 (2014): 395–417.

3. Scott Lively, "Russia Set to Supplant U.S. as Human-Rights Leader," WorldNetDaily, March 10, 2014, http://www.wnd.com/2014/03/russia-set-to-supplant-u-s-as-human-rights-leader/ (accessed April 6, 2014).

4. Bowers v. Hardwick, 478 U.S. 186 (1986).

5. Doris Buss and Didi Herman, *Globalizing Family Values: The Christian Right in International Politics* (Minneapolis: University of Minnesota Press, 2003), xxxii, xxiv.

6. See Perry L. Glanzer, *The Quest for Russia's Soul: Evangelicals and Moral Education in Post-Soviet Russia* (Waco, TX: Baylor University Press, 2002).

7. Kapya Kaoma, "Globalizing the Culture Wars: U.S. Conservatives, African Churches, and Homophobia," Political Research Associates, December 1, 2009, http://www.politicalresearch.org/2009/12/01/globalizing-the-culture-wars-u-s-conservatives-african-churches-homophobia/#sthash.0nc1RauN.dpbs (accessed January 16, 2013).

8. Didi Herman, *The Antigay Agenda: Orthodox Vision and the Christian Right* (Chicago: University of Chicago Press, 1998), 50.

9. The DC Human Rights Law survives today. In 2010, the law was the basis for the refusal of the Washington, DC, City Council to put same-sex marriage in the district to a popular vote.

10. Jyl J. Josephson, *Rethinking Sexual Citizenship* (Albany: State University of New York Press, 2016), 2. Also on sexual citizenship, see Diane Richardson, "Constructing Sexual Citizenship: Theorizing Sexual Rights," *Critical Social Policy* 20:1 (2000): 105–35.

11. Chris Bull and John Gallagher, *Perfect Enemies: The Religious Right, the Gay Movement, and the Politics of the 1990s* (New York: Crown, 1996).

12. Tina Fetner, *How the Religious Right Shaped Lesbian and Gay Activism* (Minneapolis: University of Minnesota Press, 2008). For an illuminating recent study of how Christian right elites use social labelling, see Brianna A. Smith, Zein Murib, Matthew Motta, Timothy H. Callaghan, and Marissa Theys, " 'Gay' or 'Homosexual'? The Implications of Social Category Labels for the Structure of Mass Attitudes," *American Politics Research*, prepublished May 2, 2017, doi: 10.1177/1532673X17706560.

13. Daniel R. Pinello, *Gay Rights and American Law* (Cambridge: Cambridge University Press, 2003); Scott Barclay, Mary Bernstein, and Anna-Maria Marshall, eds., *Queer Mobilizations: LGBT Activists Confront the Law* (New York: New York University Press, 2009); Carlos A. Ball, *From the Closet to the Courtroom: Five LGBT Rights Lawsuits That Have Changed Our Nation* (Boston: Beacon Press, 2010).

14. For public and hidden transcripts see James C. Scott, *Domination and the Arts of Resistance: Hidden Transcripts* (New Haven, CT: Yale University Press, 1990).

15. For these findings and their implications, see Angelia R. Wilson and Cynthia Burack, " 'Where Liberty Reigns and God Is Supreme': The Christian Right and the Tea Party Movement, *New Political Science* 34:2 (2012): 172–90.

16. See Jill Lepore, *The Whites of Their Eyes: The Tea Party's Revolution and the Battle over American History* (Princeton, NJ: Princeton University Press, 2010).

17. Julie Ingersoll, *Building God's Kingdom: Inside the World of Christian Reconstruction* (Oxford: Oxford University Press, 2015), 9, 64.

18. Thomas A. Birkland, "Focusing Events, Mobilization, and Agenda Setting," *Journal of Public Policy* 18:1 (1998): 53–74.

19. For another perspective, see Joel A. Nichols, "Evangelicals and Human Rights: The Continuing Ambivalence of Evangelical Christians' Support for Human Rights," *Journal of Law and Religion* 24:2 (2017): 629–62. While Nichols conceptualizes diverse views of human rights as "ambivalence," I emphasize the strategic uses of human rights.

20. Mary R. Jackman, *The Velvet Glove: Paternalism and Conflict in Gender, Class, and Race Relations* (Berkeley: University of California Press, 1994), 120.

21. See, respectively, Sarah Posner, *God's Profits: Faith, Fraud, and the Republican Crusade for Values Voters* (San Francisco: Polipoint Press, 2008); Russell H. Conwell, *Acres of Diamonds: A Motivational Classic* (Jersey City, NJ: Start Publishing, 2012); William E. Connolly, *Christianity and Capitalism: American Style* (Durham, NC: Duke University Press, 2008). Popular "historian" David Barton has been a rich source of biblical foundations for contemporary Christian conservative beliefs and policy goals.

22. Heritage Foundation, "Understanding America," 2012, http://site.heritage. org/understandingamerica/ (accessed August 25, 2013).

23. Kim R. Holmes, "How Should Americans Think about Human Rights?," Heritage Foundation, June 13, 2011, http://www.heritage.org/research/ reports/2011/06/how-should-america-think-about-human-rights (accessed June 1, 2016). The booklet is available in PDF and hard-copy versions. Booklets have been distributed free of charge to conferees at recent Values Voter Summits in Washington, DC.

24. Emphasis added.

25. Michael P. Donnelly, "Seeking Refuge in the Land of Liberty: The Romeike's Journey," Home School Legal Defense Association, http://www.hslda. org/courtreport/V26N2/V26N201.asp (accessed June 19, 2013). Emphasis added.

26. Elizabeth Borgwardt, " 'Constitutionalizing' Human Rights: The Rise and Rise of the Nuremberg Principles," in Akira Iriye, Petra Goedde, and William I. Hitchcock, eds., *The Human Rights Revolution: An International History* (Oxford: Oxford University Press, 2012), 79.

27. Maggie Severns, "Dole Battles Home-Schoolers over Disabilities Treaty," *Politico*, July 23, 2014, http://www.politico.com/story/2014/07/bob-dole-home-school-legal-defense-109201.html?hp=l2 (accessed July 23, 2014).

28. Jyl J. Josephson, "The Missing Children: Safe Schools for Some," in Cynthia Burack and Jyl J. Josephson, eds., *Fundamental Differences: Feminists Talk Back to Social Conservatives* (Lanham, MD: Rowman and Littlefield, 2003), 173–87.

29. D.Ø. Endsjø, "Lesbian, Gay, Bisexual, and Transgender Rights and the Religious Relativism of Human Rights," *Human Rights Review* 6:2 (January–March 2005): 102–10.

30. US Government, "The First Annual State Department Report on International Religious Freedom," hearing before the Subcommittee on International Operations and Human Rights of the Committee on International Relations, House of Representatives http://babel.hathitrust.org/cgi/pt?id=pst.000046313645;view=1up;seq=1 (accessed August 24, 2015).

31. Brooke A. Ackerly, *Universal Human Rights in a World of Difference* (Cambridge: Cambridge University Press, 2008).

32. Miranda Blue, "Globalizing Homophobia: Parts 1–4," People for the American Way, October 4, 2013, http://www.rightwingwatch.org/category/topics/globalizing-homophobia (accessed March 9, 2015).

33. Michelle A. Vu, "Rick Warren Launches 'Purpose Driven' Plan in Uganda," *Christian Post*, March 31, 2008, http://www.christianpost.com/news/rick-warren-launches-purpose-driven-plan-in-uganda-31752/ (accessed June 16, 2017).

34. Brian Tashman, "Family Research Institute: 'Capital Punishment Is Warranted' for Homosexuality," People for the American Way, February 5, 2014, http://www.rightwingwatch.org/post/family-research-institute-capital-punishment-is-warranted-for-homosexuality/ (accessed June 16, 2017).

35. Human Rights Campaign, "10 Things You Might Not Know About the American Family Association," no date, http://www.hrc.org/resources/10-things-you-might-not-know-about-the-american-family-association (accessed June 4, 2016).

36. J. P. Duffy, "FRC Statement on H. Res. 1064," Family Research Council, June 4, 2010, http://www.frcblog.com/2010/06/frc-statement-on-h-res-1064/ (accessed September 5, 2010).

37. As an FRC subscriber, I receive daily email alerts that are not archived online by FRC. For this analysis, see Cynthia Burack, "Christian Right Leader Lauds Uganda Dictator as 'Kill the Gays' Bill Is Revived: Tony Perkins Goes Out of His Way to Ensure that the Family Research Council Deserves its Hate-Group Designation," *Salon*, December 7, 2012, http://www.salon.com/2012/12/07/christian_right_leader_lauds_homophobic_ugandan_dictator/ (accessed December 7, 2012).

38. Cynthia Burack, "The Politics of a Praying Nation: The Presidential Prayer Team and Christian Right Sexual Morality," *Religion and Popular Culture* 26:2 (2014): 215–29.

39. John Russell, "Funding the Culture Wars: Philanthropy, Church and State," National Committee for Responsive Philanthropy, 2005, https://ncrp.org/images/stories/Funding_theCultureWars.pdf (accessed April 16, 2015).

40. Richard Meagher, "The 'Vast Right-Wing Conspiracy': Media and Conservative Networks," in Claire Snyder-Hall and Cynthia Burack, eds., *Right-Wing Populism and the Media* (Oxford: Routledge, 2014), 32.

41. See Theda Skocpol and Vanessa Williamson, *The Tea Party and the Remaking of Republican Conservatism* (New York: HarperCollins, 2010), 125. For a recent collection of articles that examine conservative media empirically as well as theoretically, see Snyder-Hall and Burack, eds., *Right-Wing Populism and the Media.*

42. Cynthia Burack, "The Politics of a Praying Nation: The Presidential Prayer Team and Christian Right Sexual Morality," *Religion and Popular Culture* 26:2 (2014): 215–29.

43. Ray Downs, "Obama and Clinton Propose Using Taxpayer Funds to Promote Gay Rights Abroad," *Christian Post*, December 6, 2011, http://www.christianpost.com/news/obama-and-clinton-propose-using-taxpayer-funds-to-promote-gay-rights-abroad-64208/ (accessed June 22, 2013).

44. Carol Mason, *Killing for Life: The Apocalyptic Narrative of Pro-Life Politics* (Ithaca, NY: Cornell University Press, 2002), 139–40.

45. Media Research Center, "Media Research Center: America's Media Watchdog," 2016, http://www.mrc.org/bozells-column (accessed April 17, 2016).

46. CNSNews.com, "About Us," 2013, http://www.cnsnews.com/about-us (accessed June 17, 2013).

47. Originally posted to the CNSNews website, the article was taken down after being posted to other right-wing websites. See Melanie Hunter, "State Department to Spend $450,000 Protecting Transgenders Overseas," *Free Republic*, June 14, 2013, http://www.freerepublic.com/focus/news/3031535/posts (accessed March 23, 2016).

48. The announcement sought proposals from "U.S. non-profit organization[s] meeting the provisions described in Internal Revenue Code section 26 USC 501(c)(3)," "comparable organization[s] headquartered internationally," or "international organization[s]," Grants.gov, "Protecting Transgender Persons from Violence and Combatting Impunity," March 28, 2013, http://www.grants.gov/search/search.do;jsessionid=w2T8R4TL6qHZppLQfNCHXB28Jy2KJ7ZyyTr8hJLDD4QTpndpQF12!641006765?oppId=228453&mode=VIEW (accessed June 20, 2013).

49. For a set of analyses of right-wing populism and media platforms, see Snyder-Hall and Burack, eds., *Right-Wing Populism and the Media.*

50. Patrick Goodenough, "No Gay Diplomats: U.S. and British Promotion of LGBT Rights Abroad Sparks Backlash," *CNSNews*, July 30, 2013, http://www.cnsnews.com/news/article/no-gay-diplomats-us-and-british-promotion-lgbt-rights-abroad-sparks-backlash (accessed November 16, 2013).

51. See Kristen P. Williams, Steven E. Lobell, and Neal G. Jesse, eds., *Beyond Great Powers and Hegemons: Why Secondary States Support, Follow, or Challenge* (Redwood City, CA: Stanford University Press, 2012).

52. Doris Buss and Didi Herman, *Globalizing Family Values: The Christian Right in International Politics* (Minneapolis: University of Minnesota Press, 2003).

53. See links to both reports at Human Rights Campaign, "Exposed: The World Congress of Families: An American Organization Exporting Hate," and "The Export of Hate," 2015, http://www.hrc.org/campaigns/the-world-congress-of-families (accessed May 29, 2016).

54. World Congress of Families, "A Call for Civil Dialogue and Constructive Engagement: The World Congress of Families Responds to the Human Rights Campaign and the Southern Poverty Law Center," 2015, http://wcf9.org/questions-and-answers/ (accessed April 16, 2016). Emphasis in the original.

55. Ghana is a republic with a president and a vice president, and the nation does not have a king. Ghana-born Kingsley Fletcher (also known as Drolor Bosso Adamtey I) is a minister and Christian author who has lived in the United States. According to his bio on the website of Life International, Fletcher has an "accurate prophetic gift" and is an "internationally renowned lecturer." See Life International, "Meet Our Visionary Founders," 2017, http://lifeinternational.us/visionary-founders (accessed June 14, 2017).

56. Catholic News Agency, "Speakers at World Conference of Families Decry Anti-Family 'Cultural Imperialism,'" August 13, 2009, http://www.catholicnewsagency.com/news/speakers_at_world_congress_of_families_decry_antifamily_cultural_imperialism/ (accessed April 17, 2016).

57. Kapya J. Kaoma, "The Marriage of Convenience: The U.S. Christian Right, African Christianity, and Postcolonial Politics of Sexual Identity," in Meredith Weiss and Michael Bosia, eds., *Global Homophobia* (Urbana: University of Illinois Press, 2013), 90.

58. Christopher Stroop, Twitter, May 27, 2017, https://twitter.com/c_stroop/status/868465329281925122 (accessed May 31, 2017).

59. Sharon Slater, dir., "Cultural Imperialism: The Sexual Rights Agenda," (Family Watch International, 2013), https://www.youtube.com/watch?v=YWwRnbv2BOo (accessed May 28, 2016). The film is available on YouTube, and the DVD has been distributed without cost in Christian conservative venues such as the annual Values Voter Summit, where I received a copy.

60. See Rachel Jewkes and Robert Morrell, "Gender and Sexuality: Emerging Perspectives from the Heterosexual Epidemic in South Africa and Implications for HIV Risk and Prevention," *Journal of the International AIDS Society* 13:6 (2010): 1–11.

61. Cynthia Burack, *Sin, Sex, and Democracy: Antigay Rhetoric and the Christian Right* (Albany: State University of New York Press, 2008), 27–30; Cynthia Burack, *Tough Love: Sexuality, Compassion, and the Christian Right* (Albany: State University of New York Press, 2014), 12–15.

62. Family Research Council, "Event Invitation," email, May 27, 2015. Christian conservatives also applied the charge of cultural imperialism. See Robert R. Reilly, "Cultural Imperialism on the March: Obama Promotes Gay Pride Worldwide," *Crisis Magazine*, May 15, 2013, http://www.crisismagazine.com/2013/cultural-imperialism-on-the-march-obama-promotes-gay-pride-worldwide (accessed September 7, 2015).

63. Emphasis in the original.

64. CitizenGO, "Stop Cultural Imperialism: Recall America's LGBT Envoy!," May 26, 2015, http://www.citizengo.org/en/24156-stop-cultural-imperialism-recall-americas-lgbt-envoy (accessed May 27, 2015). "Caribbean" was misspelled in the same way in CitizenGO's online letter template and in the version of the letter I saw that was emailed to officials at the State Department's Bureau of Democracy, Human Rights, and Labor.

65. Cynthia Burack, field notes, Conference to Advance the Human Rights of and Promote Inclusive Development for Lesbian, Gay, Bisexual, and Transgender Persons, US State Department, Washington, DC, November 12, 2014.

66. See, for example, Dana L. Robert, ed., *Converting Colonialisms: Visions and Realities in Mission History, 1706–1914* (Grand Rapids, MI: Eerdmans, 2008); Emily Conroy-Krutz, *Christian Imperialism: Converting the World in the Early American Republic* (Ithaca, NY: Cornell University Press, 2015).

67. Rebecca Sanders, "Norm Proxy War and Resistance through Outsourcing: The Dynamics of Transnational Human Rights Contestation," *Human Rights Review* 17 (2016): 166.

68. Jack Donnelly, *International Human Rights*, 2nd ed. (Boulder, CO: Westview Press, 1998), 33.

69. Jack Donnelly, "The Relative Universality of Human Rights," *Human Rights Quarterly* 29 (2007): 281, 294–95.

70. Roger Ross Williams, dir., *God Loves Uganda* (Full Credit Productions, 2013).

71. Ministry of Foreign Affairs of the Republic of Belarus, "Group of Friends of the Family Launched in the UN," 2015, http://mfa.gov.by/en/press/news_mfa/f8ff663d7481c615.html (accessed May 29, 2016).

72. Peter Montgomery, "Anti-Gay Activism Trumps Religious Freedom at UN 'Family' Event," People for the American Way, May 18, 2016, http://www.rightwingwatch.org/content/anti-gay-activism-trumps-religious-freedom-un-family-event (accessed May 28, 2016).

73. Donnelly, *International Human Rights*, 33.

74. Kaoma, "Globalizing the Culture Wars."

75. For an analysis of the Christian right's internal processes on compassion for same-sex-attracted and postabortive women, see Burack, *Tough Love*.

76. Josh Craddock, "The New Cultural Imperialism," *National Review*, April 28, 2015, http://www.nationalreview.com/article/417556/new-cultural-imperialism-josh-craddock (accessed April 17, 2016).

77. Michael K. Lavers, "Botswana Deports Anti-LGBT U.S. Pastor," *Washington Blade*, September 20, 2016, http://www.washingtonblade.com/2016/09/20/botswana-deports-anti-lgbt-u-s-pastor/ (accessed September 25, 2016).

## Chapter 5

1. Gayatri Chakravorty Spivak, "Use and Abuse of Human Rights," *boundary 2* 32:1 (2005): 145.

2. Alan Johnson, "Interrogating Terror and Liberalism: An Interview with Paul Berman," *Democratiya* 5 (2006): 120, 119.

3. Paisley Currah, "Homonationalism, State Rationalities, and Sex Contradictions," *Theory and Event* 16:1 (2013), http://muse.jhu.edu.proxy.lib.ohio-state.edu/journals/theory_and_event/v016/16.1.currah.html (accessed May 29, 2013).

4. For examples from this subgenre, see Nick Kotz, *Wild Blue Yonder: Money, Politics, and the B-1 Bomber* (New York: Pantheon, 1988); A. Lee Fritschler and Catherine E. Rudder, *Smoking and Politics: Bureaucracy Centered Policymaking* (Upper Saddle River, NJ: Pearson, 2006).

5. Currah, "Homonationalism, State Rationalities, and Sex Contradictions."

6. Judith Butler, *Precarious Life: The Powers of Mourning and Violence* (London: Verso, 2006), 65. Emphasis in original.

7. Robert Jervis, *Perception and Misperception in International Politics* (Princeton, NJ: Princeton University Press, 1976), 284.

8. Paul Maddrell, "Introduction: Achieving Objective, Policy-Relevant Intelligence," in Paul Maddrell, ed., *The Image of the Enemy: Intelligence Analysis of Adversaries since 1945* (Washington, DC: Georgetown University Press, 2015), 6.

9. Cynthia Burack, *Sin, Sex, and Democracy: Antigay Rhetoric and the Christian Right* (Albany: State University of New York Press, 2008). Among those who concurred or offered their own versions of this politics of desert were televangelist D. James Kennedy, popular Christian writer Stormie Omartian, Focus on the Family founder James Dobson, and the conservative Catholic American Society for the Defense of Tradition, Family, and Property.

10. Ward Churchill, " 'Some People Push Back': On the Justice of Roosting Chickens," Denver Channel, December 2, 2013, http://www.thedenverchannel.com/news/-some-people-push-back-on-the-justice-of-roosting-chickens (accessed December 2, 2013). Ellipsis is in the original.

11. Concerned Academics, "An Open Letter from Concerned Academics," Charlotte Laws, March 2, 2005, http://www.charlottelaws.org/open_letter_from_academics_regar.htm (accessed July 16, 2013).

12. Colorado Conference of the American Association of University Professors, "Report on the Termination of Ward Churchill," November 1, 2011, 14.

13. Pat Robertson, *The New World Order* (Nashville, TN: Thomas Nelson, 1991).

14. For an introduction, see Paul Berman, *Terror and Liberalism* (New York: Norton, 2004); Hayat Alvi, "The Diffusion of Intra-Islamic Violence and Terrorism: The Impact of the Proliferation of Salafi/Wahhabi Ideologies," *Middle East Review of International Affairs* 18:2 (2014): 38–50.

15. On homophobia, see George Weinberg, *Society and the Healthy Homosexual: How to Get the Most Out of Being Gay* (New York: St. Martin's Press, 1972). On heterosexism, see Gregory M. Herek, "The Context of Anti-Gay Violence: Notes on Cultural and Psychological Heterosexism," *Journal of Interpersonal Violence* 5:3 (1990); Lauren Berlant and Michael Warner, "Sex in Public," *Critical Inquiry* 24 (1998): 548. On homonormativity, see Lisa Duggan, *The Twilight of Equality: Neoliberalism, Cultural Politics, and the Attack on Democracy* (Boston: Beacon Press, 2003), 50. On homoprotectionism, see Christine (Cricket) Keating, "Conclusion: On the Interplay of State Homophobia and Homoprotectionism," in Meredith L. Weiss and Michael J. Bosia, eds., *Global Homophobia* (Urbana: University of Illinois Press, 2013), 247, 249. On transhomonationalism, see Jasbir Puar, "Bodies with New Organs: Becoming Trans, Becoming Disabled," *Social Text* 33:3 (2015): 46.

16. Patrisse Cullors, Opal Tometi, and Alicia Garza, "A Herstory of the #BlackLivesMatter Movement," Black Lives Matter, no date, http://blacklivesmatter. com/herstory/ (accessed November 2, 2015).

17. Sean Cahill, Juan Battle, and Doug Meyer, "Partnering, Parenting, and Policy: Family Issues Affecting Black Lesbian, Gay, Bisexual, and Transgender (LGBT) people," *Race and Society* 6:2 (2003): 85–98; Sean Cahill, "The Disproportionate Impact of Antigay Family Policies on Black and Latino Same-Sex Households," *Journal of African American Studies* 13:3 (2009): 219–50.

18. Cynthia Burack, field notes, Values Voter Summit, Washington, DC, September 25, 2015.

19. Donald Cohen, "Cry Wolf: Why the Right Was Wrong about the Family Medical Leave Act," Center for Media and Democracy, February 7, 2013, http:// www.prwatch.org/news/2013/02/11973/cry-wolf-why-right-was-wrong-about-family-medical-leave-act (accessed February 20, 2016).

20. For accounts of this process of "centering," see Anna Marie Smith, *New Right Discourse on Race and Sexuality: Britain 1968–1990* (Cambridge: Cambridge University Press, 1994; Anna Marie Smith, "Why Did Armey Apologize? Hegemony, Homophobia, and the Religious Right," in Amy E. Ansell, ed., *Unraveling the Right: The New Conservatism in American Thought and Politics* (Boulder, CO: Westview Press, 2001), 148–72.

21. Sarah Schulman, "Pro-Family Ideology and the Queer Community of Friends," PrettyQueer.com, 2011, http://prettyqueer.com/2013/09/20/pro-family-ideology-and-the-queer-community-of-friends/ (accessed October 2, 2013).

22. See Isabel Kershner, "Deep Rifts among Israeli Jews Are Found in Religion Survey," *New York Times*, March 8, 2016, http://www.nytimes.com/2016/03/09/world/middleeast/study-israel-jews-pew-research.html?_r=0 (accessed March 9, 2016).

23. Terry Goldie, "Queering the Problem," *Reviews in Cultural Theory* 1:2 (2010): 70–75.

24. Jason Ritchie, "Pinkwashing, Homonationalism, and Israel-Palestine: The Conceits of Queer Theory and the Politics of the Ordinary," *Antipode* 47:3 (2015): 616–34.

25. Also interesting are Atonaldomain, "In Response to 'Trending Homonationalism'—or—In Defense of Celebrating the End of DOMA," July 10, 2013, http://atonaldomain.wordpress.com/2013/07/10/in-response-to-trending-homonationalism-or-in-defense-of-celebrating-the-end-of-doma/ (accessed December 12, 2013); Sketchy Thoughts, "Jasbir Puar's Homonationalism Talk: A Real Disappointment," November 6, 2008, http://sketchythoughts.blogspot.com/2008/11/jasbir-puars-homonationalism-talk-real.html (accessed February 1, 2014).

26. Other friendly critiques include Jason Ritchie, "Pinkwashing, Homonationalism, and Israel-Palestine: The Conceits of Queer Theory and the Politics of the Ordinary," *Antipode* 47:3 (2015): 616–34; and C. Heike Schotten, "Homonationalism: From Critique to Diagnosis, or, We Are All Homonational Now," *International Feminist Journal of Politics* 18:3 (2016): 351–370. Schotten is concerned that because homonationalism has lost its edge as a "critique of gay complicity with the state" over time, it is less useful for "radical queer politics" than it once was (352, 366).

27. Cathy J. Cohen, *The Boundaries of Blackness: AIDS and the Breakdown of Black Politics* (Chicago: University of Chicago Press, 1999), 10–11. A similar concept is Goffman's "in-group purification." See Erving Goffman, *Stigma: Notes on the Management of Spoiled Identity* (New York: Touchstone, 1986), 108.

28. Puar cites Cohen as a queer intersectional theorist with citations to Cathy Cohen, "Punks, Bulldaggers, and Welfare Queens: The Radical Potential of Queer Politics," *GLQ: A Journal of Lesbian and Gay Studies* 3:4 (1997): 437–65. See Jasbir K. Puar, *Terrorist Assemblages: Homonationalism in Queer Times* (Durham, NC: Duke University Press, 2007), 23, 221–22.

29. Michael J. Bosia and Meredith L. Weiss, "Political Homophobia in Comparative Perspective," in Meredith L. Weiss and Michael J. Bosia, eds., *Global Homophobia: States, Movements, and the Politics of Opression* (Urbana: University of Illinois Press, 2013): 10–11.

30. Puar, *Terrorist Assemblages*, 128.

31. Angelia R. Wilson, *Why Europe Is Lesbian and Gay Friendly (and Why America Never Will Be)* (Albany: State University of New York Press, 2013).

32. See, for example, Bob Altemeyer, "Changes in Attitudes toward Homosexuals," *Journal of Homosexuality* 42:2 (2001): 63–75; Tina Fetner, *How the*

*Religious Right Shaped Lesbian and Gay Activism* (Minneapolis: University of Minnesota Press, 2008).

33. Puar, *Terrorist Assemblages*, 52, 55, 57, 60.

34. Puar, *Terrorist Assemblages*, 100.

35. As a side note to the "carnival of torture," I am struck by Puar's dismissive tone and language, which is similar at times to Ward Churchill's in his essay "Sometimes People Push Back." For example, buried in a footnote corresponding to her discussion of the September 11 attacks, Puar refers to media coverage of the deaths and their aftermath as the "media jamboree of September 11" as though gleeful prurience stimulated media reporting in the wake of nearly 2,000 deaths in New York City and Washington, DC. Puar, *Terrorist Assemblages*, 270.

36. Puar, *Terrorist Assemblages*, 180.

37. Puar, *Terrorist Assemblages*, 14.

38. See Matthew A. Baum, "The Constituent Foundations of the Rally-Round-the-Flag Phenomenon," *International Studies Quarterly* 46 (2002): 263–98.

39. See Gregory B. Lewis, Marc A. Rogers, and Kenneth Sherrill, "Lesbian, Gay, and Bisexual Voters in the 2000 U.S. Presidential Election," *Politics and Policy* 39:5 (2011): 655–77; Vanessa M. Perez, "Political Participation of LGBT Americans," Project Vote, June, 2014, http://www.projectvote.org/wp-content/uploads/2014/06/RESEARCH-MEMO-LGBT-PARTICIPATION-June-20-2014.pdf. (accessed August 3, 2016).

40. Hannah Fingerhut, "Support Steady for Same-Sex Marriage and Acceptance of Homosexuality," Pew Research Center, May 12, 2016, http://www.pewresearch.org/fact-tank/2016/05/12/support-steady-for-same-sex-marriage-and-acceptance-of-homosexuality/?utm_source=Pew+Research+Center&utm_campaign=1173200409-Weekly_May_12_20165_12_2016&utm_medium=email&utm_term=0_3e953 b9b70-1173200409-399484645 (accessed May 12, 2016).

41. One of Puar's claims relies on widespread knowledge among Americans of the race of the two men arrested having sex in the case that led to the Supreme Court's verdict in *Lawrence v. Texas*. See Donald P. Haider-Markel, Mahalley D. Allen, and Morgen Johansen, "Understanding Variations in Media Coverage of Supreme Court Decisions: Comparing Media Outlets in Their Coverage of *Lawrence v. Texas*," *International Journal of Press/Politics* 11:2 (2006): 64–85.

42. Anna Marie Smith, *New Right Discourse on Race and Sexuality: Britain 1968–1990* (Cambridge: Cambridge University Press, 1994); Anna Marie Smith, "Why Did Armey Apologize? Hegemony, Homophobia, and the Religious Right," in Amy E. Ansell, ed., *Unraveling the Right: The New Conservatism in American Thought and Politics* (Boulder, CO: Westview Press, 2001), 149, 166, 163, 150.

43. See David P. Redlawsk, "Hot Cognition or Cool Consideration? Testing the Effects of Motivated Reasoning on Political Decision Making," *Journal of Politics* 64:4 (2002): 1021–44.

44. Bruno Latour, "Why Has Critique Run Out of Steam? From Matters of Fact to Matters of Concern," *Critical Inquiry* 30 (2004): 227.

45. Michael Bérubé, "The Science Wars Redux," *Democracy: A Journal of Ideas* (2011), http://www.democracyjournal.org/19/6789.php?page=all (accessed November 20, 2015).

46. Latour, "Why Has Critique Run Out of Steam?," 230.

47. Spivak, "Use and Abuse of Human Rights," 133.

48. Joseph Massad, "Re-Orienting Desire: The Gay International and the Arab World," *Public Culture* 14:2 (2002): 372–73, 375.

49. Uma Narayan, "Contesting Cultures: 'Westernization,' Respect for Cultures, and Third-World Feminists," in Linda J. Nicholson, ed., *The Second Wave: A Reader in Feminist Theory* (New York: Routledge, 1997), 396, 397.

50. This sentence closely paraphrases a passage from a paper delivered at a women's studies conference. The paper was written by a graduate student, and I have no interest in singling out a student for criticism. I use the claim for two reasons: first, because it expresses succinctly a view that is taken for granted by many critical humanists; second, because it illustrates that students readily adopt such categorical "facts" from their studies in progressive disciplines such as women's studies.

51. Mary Hawkesworth, *Feminist Inquiry: From Political Conviction to Methodological Innovation* (New Brunswick, NJ: Rutgers University Press, 2006), 33.

52. Ludwik Fleck, *Genesis and Development of a Scientific Fact* (Chicago: University of Chicago Press, 1979). I'm also persuaded by Simon Stow's argument about the distinction that should be recognized between "written" and "unwritten worlds" and the forms of interpretation consistent with these "worlds." See Simon Stow, *Republic of Readers? The Literary Turn in Political Thought and Analysis* (Albany: State University of New York Press, 2008).

53. Aleardo Zanghellini, "Are Gay Rights Islamophobic? A Critique of Some Uses of the Concept of Homonationalism in Activism and Academia," *Social and Legal Studies* 21:3 (2012): 367. Zanghellini borrows the term from Janet Halley, *Split Decisions: How and Why to Take a Break from Feminism* (Princeton, NJ: Princeton University Press, 2008).

54. Ileana Rodríguez, *Liberalism at its Limits: Crime and Terror in the Latin American Cultural Text* (Pittsburgh: University of Pittsburgh Press, 2009), 8.

55. Kim Turcot DiFruscia, "Shapes of Freedom: A Conversation with Elizabeth A. Povinelli," *e-flux*, 2014, http://www.e-flux.com/journal/shapes-of-freedom-a-conversation-with-elizabeth-a-povinelli/ (accessed May 6, 2016).

56. See C. Fred Alford, *Group Psychology and Political Theory* (New Haven, CT: Yale University Press, 1994); Cynthia Burack, *Healing Identities: Black Feminist Thought and the Politics of Groups* (Ithaca, NY: Cornell University Press, 2004).

57. Richard Rorty, *Achieving Our Country* (Cambridge, MA: Harvard University Press, 1998), 98.

58. Rorty, *Achieving Our Country*, 94–97.

59. Michael Goodhart, "Who and How Do Human Rights Persuade?," paper presented at the Annual Meeting of the American Political Science Association, Chicago, IL, August 29–September 1, 2013.

60. Anthony Tirado Chase, "Human Rights Contestations: Sexual Orientation and Gender Identity," *International Journal of Human Rights* 20:6 (2016): 704.

61. Karen Zivi, "Performing the Nation: Contesting Same-Sex Marriage Rights in the United States," *Journal of Human Rights* 13:3 (2014): 301.

62. Phillip M. Ayoub, *When States Come Out: Europe's Sexual Minorities and the Politics of Visibility* (Cambridge: Cambridge University Press, 2016).

63. Margaret E. Keck and Kathryn Sikkink, *Activists beyond Borders: Advocacy Networks in International Politics* (Ithaca, NY: Cornell University Press, 1998), 36.

64. Marc Epprecht, "Sexual Minorities, Human Rights and Public Health Strategies in Africa," *African Affairs* 111:443 (2012): 243.

65. Bosia and Weiss, "Political Homophobia in Comparative Perspective," 22.

66. See also Richmond Blake, "Promoting an LGBT-Inclusive Human Rights Agenda," *Foreign Service Journal*, June 2015, http://www.afsa.org/promoting-lgbt-inclusive-human-rights-agenda (accessed June 24, 2017).

67. Hannah Arendt, " 'What Remains? The Language Remains': A Conversation with Günter Gaus," in Peter Baehr, ed., *The Portable Hannah Arendt* (New York: Penguin, 2000), 16, 19.

## Afterword

1. It's more complicated than this, however. At times critical humanists insist on the immutability of identity, as over 500 did when they signed an open letter in May, 2017 demanding that the journal *Hypatia* apologize for and retract an article on the controversial topic of "transracialism": Rebecca Tuvel, "In Defense of Transracialism," *Hypatia* 32:2 (2017): 263–78.

2. Francis A. Schaeffer, *Plan for Action: An Action Alternative Handbook for Whatever Happened to the Human Race?* (Grand Rapids, MI: Fleming H. Revell, 1980), 68.

3. Carlos A. Ball, "Essentialism and Universalism in Gay Rights Philosophy: Liberalism Meets Queer Theory," *Law and Social Inquiry* 26:1 (2001): 271–93.

4. Examples include Elizabeth Kamarck Minnich, *Transforming Knowledge*, 2nd ed. (Philadelphia: Temple University Press, 2004); Joey Sprague, *Feminist Methodologies for Critical Researchers*, 2nd ed (Lanham, MD: Rowman and Littlefield, 2016).

5. Sami Zeidan, "Navigating International Rights and Local Politics: Sexuality Governance in Postcolonial Settings," in Meredith L. Weiss and Michael J. Bosia, eds., *Global Homophobia* (Urbana: University of Illinois Press, 2013).

6. Amy Gutmann and Dennis Thompson, *Democracy and Disagreement* (Cambridge, MA: Harvard University Press, 1998).

7. See, for example, Heidi Kitrosser, *Reclaiming Accountability: Transparency, Executive Power, and the U.S. Constitution* (Chicago: University of Chicago Press, 2015).

8. The European Union has been a prolific site of scholarship and political debate about barriers to transparency and accountability. See Daniel Naurin, *Deliberation behind Closed Doors: Transparency and Lobbying in the European Union* (Essex, UK: European Consortium for Political Research Press, 2007).

9. Michael Petrelis, "State Dept's $7.5M Global Equality Fund—Transparency Now!," February 1, 2014, http://mpetrelis.blogspot.com/2014/02/state-departments-7.html (accessed June 30, 2015).

10. Marc Epprecht, "Sexual Minorities, Human Rights and Public Health Strategies in Africa," *African Affairs* 111:443 (2012): 229.

11. The survey is not available to the public, and I wasn't able to obtain a copy.

12. Global Philanthropy Project, "Expanding Philanthropic Support for the Global LGBTI Community," Astraea Lesbian Foundation for Justice, 2015, http://globalphilanthropyproject.org/ (accessed February 16, 2016).

13. Naa Hammond, Lyle Matthew Kan, and Ben Francisco Maulbeck, "2013–2014 Global Resources Report: Government and Philanthropic Support for Lesbian, Gay, Bisexual, Transgender, and Intersex Communities," Funders for LGBTQ Issues, June 20, 2016, http://www.lgbtfunders.org/resources/pub.cfm?pubID=87 (accessed July 26, 2016). According to the GPP report, in 2013–14 the US government spent $11,137,208 that is not included in country contributions to the GEF. On behalf of GEF member nations, the United States disbursed $11,384,884 during this time period.

14. Kelly Kollman and Matthew Waites express this concern in their introduction to the special issue of *Contemporary Politics* on "The Global Politics of LGBT Human Rights": Kollman and Waites, "The Global Politics of Lesbian, Gay, Bisexual and Transgender Human Rights: An Introduction," *Contemporary Politics* 15:1 (2009): 13.

15. Jack Donnelly, "The Relative Universality of Human Rights," *Human Rights Quarterly* 29 (2007): 288.

16. For an extensive survey of critiques, see Marwan M. Kraidy, "Hybridity in Cultural Globalization," *Communication Theory* 12:3 (2002): 316–39, doi: 10.1111/j.1468-2885.2002.tb00272.x.

17. See, for example, Gloria Anzaldúa, *Borderlands/La Frontera: The New Mestiza* (San Francisco: Aunt Lute, 1987).

18. Meredith L. Weiss, "Prejudice before Pride: Rise of an Anticipatory Countermovement," in Meredith L. Weiss and Michael J. Bosia, eds., *Global Homophobia: States, Movements, and the Politics of Oppression* (Urbana: University of Illinois Press, 2013), 159.

19. Michael J. Bosia and Meredith L. Weiss, "Political Homophobia in Comparative Perspective," in Meredith L. Weiss and Michael J. Bosia, eds., *Global Homophobia: States, Movements, and the Politics of Oppression* (Urbana: University of Illinois Press, 2013), 16.

20. Hannah Arendt, "On Humanity in Dark Times: Thoughts about Lessing," in *Men in Dark Times* (New York: Harcourt, Brace and World, 1968), 18.

21. Hannah Arendt, *The Portable Hannah Arendt* (New York: Penguin Books, 2000), 12.

22. "Interview with Wanja Muguongo-ED," UHAI EASHRI, 2012, http://www.uhai-eashri.org/FRE/16-blog/13-interview-with-our-ed (accessed March 19, 2014).

23. For a statement of this concern see Christine (Cricket) Keating and Cynthia Burack, "SOGI Human Rights," in Michael Goodhart, ed., *Human Rights: Politics and Practice*, 3rd ed. (Oxford: Oxford University Press, 2016), 182–97. For LGBTQ advocacy that's specifically related to immigration policy, see Immigration Equality, "The Nation's Leading LGBTQ Immigrant Rights Organization," 2015, http://www.immigrationequality.org/ (accessed July 3, 2016).

24. As examples of this phenomenon of different culturally inflected configurations of sexual and gendered identification, see, for example, Suparna Bhaskaran, *Made in India: Decolonizations, Queer Sexualities, Trans/National Projects* (New York: Palgrave Macmillan, 2004); Ara Wilson, *The Intimate Economies of Bangkok: Tomboys, Tycoons, and Avon Ladies in the Global City* (Berkeley: University of California Press, 2004). Some culturally specific terms for minority gender/sexual identity may even be playful, including the Cambodian "sim pi"—"literally, 'two sim cards' "—for bisexual. See Caitlin MacQuarrie, "When We Talk about LGBTQI+: A Brief Exploration of the Queer Lexicon," *Q: Pride Issue* 10 (2017): 15.

25. The addition of "I," added to LGBT to denote intersex identity, was occasionally used at the 2015 ASOGIHRO meeting. However, I didn't hear any discussion at the meeting of human rights struggles specifically related to intersex conditions or identification.

26. Sami Zeidan, "Navigating International Rights and Local Politics: Sexuality Governance in Postcolonial Settings," in Meredith L. Weiss and Michael J. Bosia, eds., *Global Homophobia: States, Movements, and the Politics of Oppression* (Urbana: University of Illinois Press, 2013), 213.

27. Cynthia Burack, field notes, ASOGIHRO Conference, Africa, 2015.

28. All three letters are reprinted in Colin Stewart, "N.Y. Times under Continued Attack for Anti-LGBTI Article," 76 Crimes, December 29, 2015, https://76crimes.com/2015/12/29/n-y-times-under-continued-attack-for-anti-lgbti-article/ (accessed February 16, 2016).

29. Ludmilla Alexeeva, "In Russia, Human Rights Groups Need Western Aid More than Ever," *Washington Post*, February 24, 2016, https://www.washington-post.com/opinions/in-russia-human-rights-groups-need-western-aid-more-than-

ever/2016/02/24/b8e934d2-d1c0-11e5-b2bc-988409ee911b_story.html (accessed February 24, 2016).

30. Physicians for Human Rights, "Securing Afghanistan's Past: Human Identification Needs Assessment and Gap Analysis," 2013, 3–4.

31. See Marla Brettschneider, Susan Burgess, and Cricket Keating, eds., *LGBTQ Politics: A Critical Reader* (New York: New York University Press, 2017).

32. This concern is expressed, for example, in Christine (Cricket) Keating and Cynthia Burack, "Sexual Orientation, Gender Identity, and Human Rights," in Michael Goodhart, ed., *Human Rights: Politics and Practice*, 3rd ed. (Oxford: Oxford University Press, 2016), 192.

33. Dean Spade and Craig Willse, "Sex, Gender, and War in an Age of Multicultural Imperialism," *QED: A Journal in GLBTQ Worldmaking* 1:1 (2014): 7, 9.

34. Craig and Willse, "Sex, Gender, and War in an Age of Multicultural Imperialism," 16, 22. Emphasis added.

35. The controversy has continued. See Stuart G. Erdheim, "Could the Allies Have Bombed Auschwitz-Birkenau?," *Holocaust and Genocide Studies* 11:2 (1997): 129–70; Richard H. Levy, *The Bombing of Auschwitz Revisited: A Critical Analysis* (New York: St. Martins Press, 2000).

36. Joseph S. Nye, *The Future of Power* (Philadelphia: Public Affairs, 2011).

37. The Telegraph, "Widows in Belarus Accuse Regime of Assassination," *Telegraph*, September 2, 2001, http://www.telegraph.co.uk/news/worldnews/europe/belarus/1339258/Widows-in-Belarus-accus e-regime-of-assassination.html (accessed June 24, 2013).

# Index

ABC ("abstinence, be faithful, use a condom") approach to sex education, 45
abstinence-only sex education, 45, 130
academic left, 2–4, 178, 228n8. *See also* critical humanists
ACT UP (AIDS Coalition to Unleash Power), 13
activism
　backlash to. *See* backlash; blowback
　citizen, 206
Afghanistan, 203
Africa, 186
African Sexual Orientation and Gender Identity Human Rights Organization (ASOGIHRO). *See* indigenous SOGI advocacy
Ahmadinejad, Mahmoud, 74
AIDS, 150. *See also* PEPFAR
AIDS Coalition to Unleash Power (ACT UP), 13
AIDS relief, president's emergency plan for, 44–46
Albania, 53
Alexeeva, Ludmilla, 202–3
Alford, C. Fred, 262n52
Alimi, Adebisi, 123
Amnesty International, 54
　as first mainstream human rights organization supporting LGBTQ rights, 17

Amnesty International USA (AIUSA), 81
An-Na'im, Abdullahi A., 9
Anti-Homosexuality Act. *See* Uganda Anti-Homosexuality Act
anti-LGBTQ bias, 34, 72–73, 92–94, 107. *See also specific topics*
anti-LGBTQ civil rights politics, US, 130–33
anti-LGBTQ discourses
　identity categories embraced in response to, 198–99
　"no human right to sodomy," 128
anti-LGBTQ ministries, 157. *See also* Christian right/Christian conservatism
anti-LGBTQ movements, 198–99. *See also* backlash; blowback; CitizenGO; cultural imperialism; homophobia; SOGI human rights: the "external" critique of; Uganda Anti-Homosexuality Act; *specific topics*
　SOGI vs. religion in human rights, 139–47
　Western sexual binary imposed by, 199
"anticipatory anti-imperialism," 199
"anticipatory homophobia," 198–99
Apodaca, Clair, 52
apology, public, 34, 175

267

Cohen, Cathy J., 172–73, 260nn27–28
Conference to Advance the Human
     Rights of and Promote Inclusive
     Development for Lesbian, Gay,
     Bisexual and Intersex Persons,
     108–9, 114, 119, 152, 240n1
confirmation bias, 172
Conscience Protection Act (Arkansas
     HB 1228), 143
conspiracy theories, 166, 178
constitutional rights claims, 14
Cooper, Helene, 80
Cooper, Kurtis, 42–43
corrective rape, 71, 83, 124
     nature of, 21
Council for Global Equality (CGE),
     16, 48, 55–56, 67, 82, 101
Country Reports on Human Rights
     Practices, 51–59, 124
Courage Unfolds (film), 21–22,
     232nn65–66
credentialing by pain, 72–73
criminalization of LGBT status or
     conduct, combating, 212
critical humanism, 184. See also
     humanist critics
   critique running out of steam,
     177–79
   defined, 4
   when critique goes bad, 163–68
critical humanist academic left, 3–4.
     See also academic left
critical humanists, 62, 159, 178–81,
     187, 190, 192
   blaming America first, 187, 188
   on blowback, 164
   Christian right compared with, 32,
     186–87, 189–90
   Christian right contrasted with,
     190–91
   Clinton's speech and, 85–91, 88t

defined, 4
democracy and, 201
identity(ies) and, 189, 191, 362n1
imperialism and, 188, 191, 198,
     199, 204
liberalism and, 182, 184
pinkwashing and, 87, 170
on same-sex marriage, 173
simplistic conceptualization of the
     state, 160–63
thought style, 182
on US hypocrisy, 54–55
critical modes of argument, 178
critical/radical/progressive/humanist
     scholarship, 4. See also specific
     topics
cultural hybridity, 198
cultural imperialism, 187, 195
   Christian right and, 29, 85, 130,
     148–52, 155, 157
   and imposition of forms of identity,
     197, 198
   Jim Downs on, 86
   Obama and, 85, 150–51
   the travels of, 147–53
Cultural Imperialism: The Sexual Rights
     Agenda (film), 150
"Cultural Imperialism and the Obama
     Administration" (Eastman),
     150–51
cultural left, 184. See also critical
     humanism
cultural relativism, 92
   Christian conservatism as, 153–
     56
   projective, 154–56
   versions of, 154–56
"cultural terrorism," promotion of
     LGBT rights as, 103
cultural values, 219
Currah, Paisley, 161–63

9 781438 470146